Verbivoracious Press

Festschrift Volume Five

RAYMOND

FEDERMAN

Verbivoracious Press

Festschrift Volume Five

edited by G. N. Forester and M. J. Nicholls

RAYMOND

FEDERMAN

"And so, for me, the only fiction that still means something today is the kind of fiction that tries to explore the possibilities of fiction beyond its own limitations; the kind of fiction that challenges the tradition that governs it; the kind of fiction that constantly renews our faith in man's intelligence and imagination rather than man's distorted view of reality; the kind of fiction that reveals man's playful irrationality rather than his righteous rationality."

Verbivoracious Press

Glentrees, 13 Mt Sinai Lane, Singapore

First published in Great Britain and Singapore

by Verbivoracious Press

www.verbivoraciouspress.org

ISBN: 978-981-09-9346-7

Printed and bound in Great Britain and Singapore

CONTENTS

Introduction

EDITORS

Raymond Federman—tireless innovator in fiction and poetry, renowned Beckett scholar, relentless self-mythologiser, impish postmodern theorist, riotous humorist, playful pedagogue, friend and father—we adore you. This festschrift celebrates his considerable influence with a range of memoir, essays, and the odd fiction. We also present several unpublished works from the Federman files, material that was intended for an abandoned volume known as *Abandoned Fictions* (the annotated [abandoned] preface to which is included here). Our thanks to Simone Federman, whose co-operation and input in assembling this volume was generous and essential, and to the contributors who took the time to fête Federman in style.

Raymond Federman and His Cohort

JEROME KLINKOWITZ

"Hey, you guys!" This invocation repeated so many times in Raymond Federman's fiction deserves an explanation now, just as it will merit a footnote years hence when its origins in American popular culture of the twentieth century are more distant. It references Federman to that culture in ways that characterize his fiction and indicate as well the milieu in which he thrived.

Classically American in its vernacular tone, this phrase was the hallmark of an innovative children's television show that began in the early 1970s, when Federman himself was helping raise his beloved daughter, Simone. Produced for PBS, the public broadcasting system that had evolved from what was originally educational TV, "The Electric Company" and its companion program "Sesame Street" broke from tradition by incorporating metafictive techniques and orientations that were characteristic of the innovative fiction being pioneered at the same time. It was called out at the beginning of each show by actress Rita Moreno, famous for her brassy urban style on Broadway and in films. Before, hosts of children's programming had been gently benevolent. Now, Ms. Moreno was sounding the call in accents redolent of New York City's mean streets. Indeed, the show's main set was a shabby alley in which at least one puppet character called a garbage can home. How different from the winsomeness of "Mr. Rogers' Neighborhood" and other programs that soothed kids' emotions and quieted their fears. On this new show, youngsters were summonded to action not by proper cultural references dating back to *Alice in Wonderland* and *The Wizard of Oz*, but by street-smart plays and games that made learning the alphabet and adding numbers as familiar as dealing with the realities of life, grouches and players and operators and all. Book spin-offs from the program often read like the innovative novels Federman and his friends were writing; consider *The Monster at the End of This Book*, in which the title character is shown tying down, bricking up, and otherwise trying to halt the turning of pages, until at the end he discovers that the "monster" is none other than his own loveable self.

"Sesame Street" and "The Electric Company" featured a repertory of remarkable characters, styled outrageously so as to emphasize their artificiality, their cartoon-like self-referentiality to their own condition of being fabricated. No viewer was asked to suspend disbelief. Instead, what was being shown was a fabulative exercise in playing up the emotions that things in real life had roused. As self-apparent creations, located in puppet-like characters whose imaginative status was the very reason for their existence, they invited young viewers to play along on the same level of creativity. In the process much was learned, from numbers and the alphabet to emotional adjustments for dealing with daily life. The gang within these programs acted much like Federman and his friends, not simply rejecting conventions but cavorting with them in ways that highlighted their condition of being made.

Double or Nothing, Federman's first novel, emerged (at almost precisely the same time) from the world that had created "Sesame Street" and was showing its nature in music, film, and art as well. Printed as a photographic offset of the author's typewritten manuscript, it speaks for its own reality on every page. This technique reflects the novel's theme, which is the task of holing up with a year's supply of food and other necessities in order to write the great novel of one's life. That quest, of course, is an outright sham, for people everywhere have that one book in them. *Double or Nothing*'s originality is making the silliness of that sham its own subject. Just like the story of the monster at the end of its own book,

Federman's narrative consists not of the achievement but its retardation, which is wound up in calculating the amount of supplies. These calculations are endless, literally to an infinity beyond the book itself, because the initial terms are found to be incorrect, mandating a total restart with a different set of provisions.

Was all this just a self-serving game? No more so than were the shenanigans of "Sesame Street" and "The Electric Company." On television, the shows' young audiences were being educated and counselled, while in *Double or Nothing* the author was devising elaborate games to show just how impossible was his project, which was to articulate the absent center of his life, the erasure (noted as X-X-X-X) of his four immediate family members in the Holocaust.

With *Double or Nothing* in print; Federman was quickly linked with a number of slightly younger writers who had recently published similarly innovative works. Ronald Sukenick's novel *Up* shared an almost identical premise: the task of writing a novel during which any number of obstacles, both in action and on the page, would interfere. Steve Katz's *The Exagggerations* [sic] *of Peter Prince* put a similar emphasis on the act of creation, the novel taking on a life of its own as the materiality of its production became its subject. Sukenick's *The Death of the Novel and Other Stories* presented pieces of short fiction as similar exercises, as did Katz's *Creamy and Delicious: Or, Eat My Words (In Other Words)*. For Federman, Sukenick, and Katz, the methodology was much the same. The difference was in motivation: for the younger writers, there was no X-X-X-X to wrestle with, at least not yet.

Despite this difference, initially less apparent because of the oblique view Federman had taken of his loss, these writers quickly began working as a group. Such alliances had never been popular in the United States, but Federman brought a European flavor to the mix and helped guide it toward cooperation, all the time acting more American than any of the others. Who else could boast of serving in the U. S. Army paratroop force, or playing jazz with Charlie Parker, or driving his shiny, chrome-laden Buick Special on roadtrips as fabulous as Jack Kerouac's? As happens so often in revolutionary groups, anthropologists tell us, there was a visibly active figure, an organizer, and an adhering group—three functions that were performed in turn by Federman, Sukenick, and (among others) Katz. Federman was the great performer, his readings being hilariously comic affairs, mocking the conventions of literature even as his deliberately overdone French accent and Continental manners made the presentation almost vaudeville in nature. The organizer was Sukenick, taking control of the Coordinating Council of Literary Magazines (for grants to innovators), founding *The American Book Review* (to report on these innovations), and transforming the Master of Fine Arts program in Creative Writing at the University of Colorado into a place where innovation not only happened but provided employment for any number of innovative fictionists, beginning with Steve Katz. Swelling the numbers of innovation's adherent group were the writers who published in another organization of which Federman, Sukenick, and Katz were among the principal organizers, The Fiction Collective. By the mid to late 1970s, Raymond Federman and his cohort were dominating critical discussion and scholarly research. This was a remarkable period in American literary history, standing between the previous celebration of realism as manners and morals (John Updike, Philip Roth, and Saul Bellow in the 1960s) and the yet-to-come reinvention of realism known as Minimalism (Raymond Carver, Ann Beattie, and Bobbie Ann Mason—in the early 1980s).

Adherents inside and out of The Fiction Collective began their careers with self-conscious experiments at home with both *Double or Nothing* and *The Monster at the End of This Book*—think of Clarence Major's *Reflex and Bone Structure* and Walter Abish's *Alphabetical Africa*. Equally innovative yet supportive only from a distance (because of their commercial success) were Robert Coover (*The Universal Baseball Association*) and Donald Barthelme (*Unnatural Practices, Unnatural Acts*). Internationally, Christopher Bixby's discovery that the Treaty of Rome provided abundant funds for international conferences on contemporary fiction spawned a group of scholars known as the Tri-Laterals. Bixby and Malcolm Bradbury in the U. K., Marc Chénetier and Régis Durand in France, and Heidi Ziegler and Alfred Hornung in Germany brought so much attention to American innovations that soon a young student, Peter Torberg, could translate Federman's novels and place them with the prestigious firm of Suhrkamp. Other writers from Federman's group received good treatment from other translators and publishers, and at the Sorbonne (Université de Paris-III) André Le Vot established a center for research on contemporary American literature that brought the writers and critics in Federman's gang into the orbit of the Tri-Laterals. As a result, no other single period of fiction in the twentieth century's second half was studied so thoroughly, at its inception, in the U. S. and abroad.

As indicated, the innovations so rampant in the 1970s lost their charm, for both critics and readers, in the 1980s. The innovators themselves saw it coming: as early as 1972 Sukenick could see imminent change when he announced it as "The New Cultural Conservativism" for a special issue of *Partisan Review*. Hence fiction that he and others wrote with the age of Ronald Reagan looming began taking on a somewhat different cast. There was an increasing attention to content (over technique), and an occasional sense of the apocalyptic. In the cohort, however, was one author who'd reckoned with the challenges of subject matter early on, and who as a child had faced his own apocalypse. Thus Raymond Federman could take his place as the cohort's true leader.

The most dramatic example of Federman's influence on Sukenick is in the latter's novel *98.6*, published by The Fiction Collective in 1975. This work shares much with Sukenick's previous fiction, its first section ("Frankenstein") looking back to the disruptions of *Up* and its second ("The Children of Frankenstein") exploiting the sociogeographical transformation achieved in *Out*. It is the third section, titled "Palestine," that shows Federman's mark, because now for the first time Sukenick engages his Jewish American heritage. Here a fictive visit to "the State of Israel" is defined as an exploration of consciousness, as in "state of mind." The doings, like much of his earlier work, are hilarious, but the utopia this part of the narrative projects is in fact a tribute to Federman, who for the past several years had been the most influential writer in Sukenick's life. That this influence continued is made clear by what would be the author's last two novels, *Mosaic Man* (which used the Old Testament to refashion the Jewish American literary experience for the twenty-first century), and *Last Fall* (where the America of Sukenick's revitalized imagination is tested by the attacks of September 11, 2001).

Parallel to Sukenick's new developments were ones undertaken by other members of the cohort. In *How German Is It* Walter Abish put the methods of realism to their most severe test by writing about a Germany he had never visited, having fled his native Austria (for China) at the outset of the Nazi Anschluss. Meanwhile Steve Katz turned back to his childhood in New York City's ethnically diverse northern regions in *Florry of Washington Heights*. With *Such Was the Season* Clarence Major revisited the rural Georgia of his past, examining matters of race for the first time. And so forth for any number of innovators, who were now using their interrogations of realism in order to serve a social as well as artistic purpose.

And what of Raymond Federman? At first edging closer to the experience of losing his family in the Holocaust, he finally began confronting it directly. In novels such as *Aunt Rachel's Fur* and *Return to Manure* he dealt with this period of his life directly, yet without abandoning his scorn for suspending disblief. His ultimate success with this method came with his last novel, *Shhh: The Story of a Childhood*. Here the novel itself posed questions to its author, challenging as if with a "Hey you, guy!" That the other guys in his gang had been doing much the same was surely satisfying.

Traitor to the Cause

RAYMOND FEDERMAN

I lost both my mother and my mother country at a very young age. I left France an orphan, with nothing. No education. No family. No money to my name.

I left France in summertime, practically naked. My luggage: shorts a size too small, a worn shirt, and ragged sandals. I was nineteen.

But I did carry with me a very precious gift: the French language. All this time, it has remained with me and in me. Sometimes it lay somewhat buried, as if stuck between parentheses. At other times, when it seemed too diminished, too corrupted by English, it suddenly resurfaced. It would rise in revolt, and for stretches of time, English would become parenthetical. It was during one of these periods of revolt that I wrote *Amer Eldorado*, first published in 1974. *Amer Eldorado 2001* was written during a more recent revolution.

But there may be another reason to explain why my mother tongue regained its voice. My first novel, *Double or Nothing*, which had been written in English, fell by chance into the hands of a major French publisher, which refused to publish the book in translation because they considered a Frenchman writing in another language to be a traitor. That's exactly what the rejection letter said—plus the fact that, and I quote, "it's very expensive to translate books." It's true that this major publisher was above all interested in selling books. They could easily have been shoe salesmen who believed that Frenchmen who bought Italian shoes were traitors to the cause.

But I'm not exactly sure which cause I had betrayed. The cause of French nationalism? French culture? French heritage? Perhaps it was simply the cause of the French language.

Yes, it must have been the language. My French had become foreign to me: a foreign language. And in France, foreigners are not always well-perceived or well-received, as I know well. My father was a foreigner who spoke seven languages, including French, which is why I speak French. My French was France's gift. And now I want to return what France has given me: the language that I brought with me to America, the language that permeates my books.

Which is why I formally bequeath all my books to France, in the spirit of François Villon. I give them freely. All that I ask of France in return is to mount a small plaque somewhere that would say: "Federman lived here. A traitor to the cause."

Federman's Stories

JEFFREY R. DI LEO

For friends of Raymond Federman, swapping stories about him is like a sport. Like fish stories, the tales only grow in exaggeration.

Poet and critic Charles Bernstein recently visited my campus to give a reading for the *American Book Review* Reading Series. Bernstein, who wrote the preface to *Federman's Fictions: Innovation, Theory, and the Holocaust*, a book that I edited in 2011, was Federman's colleague at SUNY Buffalo. Very soon the Federman stories started to dominate our conversations.

One of Bernstein's stories in particular surprised me.

Federman was the ultimate anti-establishment writer. He published all of his fiction with small presses, refused to footnote any of his citations, and never wanted quotations checked for accuracy. He celebrated plagiarism and was upset when others tried to edit his work. He railed against corporate publishing and broke every rule he could find in the literary and scholarly canon.

But, according to Bernstein, Federman loved to play golf with the president of SUNY Buffalo, the man in charge of preserving and enforcing establishment rules.

Years earlier, Federman had come to my campus to participate in the *American Book Review* Reading Series. His on-campus presentation was a direct attack on the literary establishment and the publishing industry.

Later in the evening, a patron of the reading series hosted a reception for him in her home. Federman was asked to read a short selection from his work to the well-heeled crowd assembled that evening.

At the appointed time, Federman eyed up the room, smiled at me, and with a glimmer in his eye, began to read.

"Susan was rich," started Federman, "that's her name, but American women who have money you cannot imagine how stingy they can be, and Susan she was loaded, she had inherited a million dollars, yes one million from an old aunt in Boston, can you believe that, I'm not exaggerating, one fucking million bucks, I was dumbfounded when she told me, I would have married her immediately if she'd let me, with all that dough we could have been so happy Susan and I . . ."

The patrons were now very quiet. A nervous unease spread through the room.

Federman, with a wide smile on his face, continued.

"Ah Susan, that's really her name, but me I always called her Sucette, you know Sucette, like a lollipop, because she always gave me fantastic blow jobs, I don't know where she learned, but I tell you, for a rich puritan American, a Wasp from Boston, Sucette when it came to sucking, wow . . ."

The tension in the room mounted as he read on.

"I was so fed up with America, the great American dream, more like a nightmare, a nightmare of misery, violence, loneliness, bigotry, racism, greed, and everywhere, everywhere failures who still believe in the American dream, drunks, winos, jobless homeless bums who sleep on the sidewalk in cardboard boxes or wrapped in newspapers, bag ladies who push their little buggies from one garbage can to another, dope addicts with eyes like oysters, and everywhere cowards, assholes, religious fanatics, crooked politicians, hillbillies who speak the language as if they had marmalade in their mouth, and what's more, car salesmen, ah yeah the car salesmen, thousands, millions of car salesmen who sweet talk you while trying to put one over on you, they all look the same, they all dress the same, they're like clones of each other, have you ever tried to buy a car in America, it's a total rip-off, pure unadulterated swindling, those miserable car salesmen what a bunch of crooks, and that's not all, that's not all . . ."

He was at his anti-establishment best as he turned into a few pages about "how capitalism uses merchandise" like toothpaste "to deceive you, to make you suffer, to torture you."

The more uncomfortable his audience became, the more Federman relished the moment. He was having precisely the effect on his audience that he was describing as the effect of merchandise under the influence of capitalism: making them suffer and torturing them the way that capitalism tortures its consumers.

It was brilliant and he knew it.

"They say America is a melting-pot," concluded Federman that evening, "where anyone can become whatever he wants to be, bullshit, me, I'll tell you what it is, not a melting-pot, but a stewing pot, a huge marmite in which the exploited, the oppressed, the dispossessed, the displaced are slowly being cooked for the benefit of those who exploit, oppress, dispossess, displace them, the second third and fourth class citizens, the Afros, the Chicanos, the Red Skins, the Good-for-Nothings, the Underpriviledged, The Rabble . . ."

The book that Federman read was from near the end of his career—and I think one his best. I've taught *Aunt Rachel's Fur* to my students and they love it. When Federman visited my Chicago classroom years earlier, he read just about the same passage as he did that evening in Victoria, Texas.

Where the students laughed uproariously, the audience at the reception heard the cutting criticism behind the humor. The folks that night could not help but hear Federman dismantle the American dream. While they did not laugh, they were engaged. He knew the effect it would have on them: the joke that enrages, the comedy of discomfort.

Raymond read that night with impish delight. Applause was hesitant and scattered as he finished the last words, but many came up to introduce themselves. This was when Raymond won them over—in individual encounters where he could ask questions and lay on the charm.

After his visit to Texas, I wanted to put together a serious collection of essays on his work in honor of his upcoming eightieth birthday, a scholarly volume that looked at some of his contributions to innovative fiction, translation, Beckett studies, Holocaust studies, trauma studies, philosophy of language, postmodern theory, body criticism, narrative theory, and so on. I saw his work as traversing philosophy, comparative literature, foreign languages, history, linguistics, sociology in addition to English, the standard province of Federman scholarship in the United States.

Federman's Fictions came out two years after his death. Though he knew that I was editing a scholarly book on him, he never saw the contents and knew some but not all of the contributors.

I think he would have liked it.

The idea of the volume was to direct conversations about his work in a more academic direction. To spark increased interest in studying his fiction as a singularly unique contribution to the American canon that traversed more than just conversations about innovation in fiction but included his substantial contributions to literary theory and Holocaust studies.

The plan was for him to be around to revel in the increased attention to his work, something it deserved. Unfortunately, his untimely death turned it into a memorial volume.

The life and thought of Raymond Federman is one of the more remarkable chapters of the twentieth century. It is my hope that we continue to study and unpack his complex writing and complicated personality. There is a lot to be learned from both.

Raymond Federman was always "on," always poking, provoking, questioning, engaging, laughing, and playing.

Establishment figures didn't fare well in his fiction or in conversation. Like his car salesman in *Aunt Rachel's Fur*, "they all look the same, they all dress the same, they're like clones of each other."

Perhaps this is why I found it surprising that Federman would play golf with the president of his university.

But then I think about his visit to Texas, when my eldest son was only 6 years old. Raymond passed the football around in the backyard and played Pokemon cards at the kitchen table. He gave his full attention to the moment, the child, the game, and his humanity cut through the jokes and tall tales.

There was a playfulness to Raymond Federman, an eagerness to engage. Maybe it really is not that surprising to learn that he played golf regularly with the president of his university. After all, whether 9 holes of golf with a senior administrator or Pokemon with a six-year-old, play is play.

Surfiction: Four Propositions

RAYMOND FEDERMAN

Now some people might say that this situation is not very encouraging but one must reply that it is not meant to encourage those who say that!

RAYMOND FEDERMAN
DOUBLE OR NOTHING

Rather than serving as a mirror or redoubling on itself, fiction adds itself to the world, creating a meaningful "reality" that did not previously exist. Fiction is artifice but not artificial. It seems as pointless to call the creative powers of the mind "fraudulent" as it would to call the procreative powers of the body such. What we bring into the world is per se beyond language, and at that point language is of course left behind—but it is the function of creative language to be left behind, to leave itself behind, in just that way. The word is unnecessary once it is spoken, but it has to be spoken. Meaning does not pre-exist creation, and afterward it may be superfluous.

RONALD SUKENICK
a letter (1972)

Writing about fiction today, one could begin with the usual clichés— that the novel is dead; that fiction is no longer possible because real fiction happens, everyday, in the streets of our cities, in the spectacular hijacking of planes, on the Moon, in Vietnam, in China (when Nixon stands on the Great Wall of China), and of course on television (during the news broadcasts); that fiction has become useless and irrelevant because life has become much more interesting, much more incredible, much more dramatic than what the moribund novel can possibly offer. And one could go on saying that fiction is now impossible (as so many theoreticians and practitioners of fiction have demonstrated) because all the possibilities of fiction have been used up, exhausted, abused, and therefore, all that is left, to the one who still insists on writing fiction, is to repeat (page after page, *ad nauseam*) that there is nothing to write about, nothing with which to write, and thus simply write that there is nothing to write (for instance, the so-called New French Novel of the last 15 years or so).

And indeed, such works as *In Cold Blood*, *The Day Kennedy Was Shot*, *Armies of the Night* and other Mailer books, and all those autobiographies written by people who have supposedly experienced real life in the streets of our cities, in the ghettos, in the jails, in the political arena, are possibly better fictions than those foolish stories (love stories, spy stories, businessman stories, cowboy stories, sexual deviate stories, and so on) the novel is still trying to peddle, and make us believe. Indeed, one could start this way, and simply give up on fiction. For, as Samuel Beckett once said: "It's easy to talk about being unable, whereas in reality nothing is more difficult."

Well, I propose that the novel is far from being dead (and I mean now the traditional novel—that moribund novel which became moribund the day it was conceived, some 400 years ago with *Don Quixote*); that, in fact, this type of novel is very healthy today (and very *wealthy* too—I know many novelists who can brag that their latest book has brought them 200,000, 300,000, half a million dollars, or more—*Love Story* is but one of those phenomena). But if we are to talk seriously about fiction, this is not the kind of fiction I am interested in. The kind of fiction I am interested in is that fiction which the leaders of the literary establishment (publishers, editors, agents, and reviewers alike) brush aside because it does not conform to *their* notions of what fiction should be; that fiction which supposedly has no value (commercial understood) for the common reader. And the easiest way for these people to brush aside that kind of fiction is to label it, quickly and bluntly, as *experimental fiction*. Everything that does not fall into the category of *successful fiction* (commercially that is), or what Jean-Paul Sartre once called "nutritious literature," everything that is found "unreadable for our readers" (that's the publishers and editors speaking—but who the hell gave them the right to decide what is *readable* or *valuable* for their readers?) is immediately relegated to the domain of experimentation—a safe and useless place.

Personally, I do not believe that a fiction writer with the least amount of self-respect, and belief in what he is doing, ever says to himself: "I am now going to experiment with fiction; I am now writing an experimental piece of fiction." Others say that about his fiction. The middle-man of literature is the one who gives the label EXPERIMENTAL to what is difficult, strange, provocative, and even original. But in fact, true experiments (as in science) never reach, or at least should never reach, the printed page. Fiction is called experimental out of despair. Beckett's novels are not experimental—no!—it is the only way Beckett can write; Borges' stories are not experimental; Joyce's fiction is not experimental (even though it was called that for some 30 or 40 years). All these are successful finished works. And so, for me, the only fiction that still means something today is that kind of fiction that tries to explore the possibilities of fiction; the kind of fiction that challenges the tradition that governs it; the kind of fiction that constantly renews our faith in man's imagination and not in man's distorted vision of reality—that reveals man's irrationality rather than man's rationality. This I call SURFICTION. However, not because it imitates reality, but because it exposes the fictionality of reality. Just as the Surrealists called that level of man's experience that functions in the subconscious SURREALITY, I call that level of man's activity that reveals life as a fiction SURFICTION. Therefore, there is some truth in that cliché which says that "life is fiction," but not because it happens in the streets, but because reality as such does not exist, or rather exists only in its fictionalized version. The experience of life gains meaning only in its recounted form, in its verbalized version, or, as Céline said, some years ago, in answer to those who claimed that his novels were merely autobiographical: "Life, also, is fiction . . . and a biography is something one invents afterwards."

But in what sense is life fiction? Fiction is made of understanding, which for most of us means primarily words—and only words (spoken or written). Therefore, if one admits from the start (at least to oneself) that no meaning pre-exists language, but that language creates meaning as it goes along, that is to say as it is used (spoken or written), as it progresses, then writing (fiction especially) will be a mere process of letting language do its tricks. To write, then, is to *produce* meaning, and not *reproduce* a pre-existing meaning. To write is to *progress*, and not *remain* subjected (by habit or reflexes) to the meaning that supposedly precedes the words. As such, fiction can no longer be reality, or a representation of reality, or an imitation, or even a recreation of reality; it can only be A REALITY—an autonomous reality whose only relation with the real world is to improve that world. To create fiction is, in fact, a way to abolish reality, and especially to abolish the notion that reality is truth.

In the fiction of the future, all distinctions between the real and the imaginary, between the conscious and the subconscious, between the past and the present, between truth and untruth will be abolished. All forms of duplicity will disappear. And above all, all forms of duality will be negated —especially duality: that double-headed monster which, for centuries now, has subjected us to a system of values, an ethical and aesthetical system based on the principles of good and bad, true and false, beautiful and ugly. Thus, the primary purpose of fiction will be to unmask its own fictionality, to expose the metaphor of its own fraudulence, and not pretend any longer to pass for reality, for truth, or for beauty. Consequently, fiction will no longer be regarded as a mirror of life, as a pseudorealistic document that informs us about life, nor will it be judged on the basis of its social, moral, psychological, metaphysical, commercial value, or whatever, but on the basis of what it is and what it does as an autonomous art form in its own right.

* * * *

These preliminary remarks serve as an introduction to four propositions I would like to make now for the future of fiction. My propositions, of course, are but an arbitrary starting point for the possibilities of a new fiction. Each essay, in its own way, represents another position towards fiction. But these positions often overlap, or complement, each other. And that is how it should be.

PROPOSITION ONE — *The Reading of Fiction:*
The very act of reading a book, starting at the top of the first page, and moving from left to right, top to bottom, page after page to the end in a consecutive prearranged manner has become *boring* and *restrictive.* Indeed, any intelligent reader should feel frustrated and restricted within that preordained system of reading. Therefore, the whole traditional, conventional, fixed, and boring method of reading a book must be questioned, challenged, demolished. And it is the writer (and not modern printing technology) who must, through innovations in the writing itself —in the typography and topology of his writing—renew our system of reading.

All the rules and principles of printing and bookmaking must be forced to change as a result of the changes in the writing (or the telling) of a story in order to give the reader a sense of free participation in the writing/reading process, in order to give the reader an element of choice (active choice) in the ordering of the discourse and the discovery of its meaning.

Thus, the very concept of syntax must be transformed—the word, the sentence, the paragraph, the chapter, the punctuation need to be rethought and rewritten so that new ways (multiple and simultaneous ways) of reading a book can be created. And the space itself in which writing takes place must be changed. That space, the page (and the book made of pages), must acquire new dimensions, new shapes, new relations in order to accommodate the new writing. And it is within this transformed topography of writing, from this new paginal (rather than grammatical) syntax that the reader will discover his freedom in relation to the process of reading a book, in relation to language and fiction.

In all other art forms, there are three essential elements at play: the creator, the medium through which the work of art is transmitted from the creator, and the receiver (listener or viewer) to whom the work of art is transmitted. In the writing of fiction, we have only the first and third elements: the writer and the reader. Me and you. And the medium (language), because it is neither auditory nor visual (as in music, painting, and sometimes poetry), merely serves as a means of transportation from me to you, from my meaning to your understanding of that meaning. If we are to make of the novel an art form, we must raise the printed word as the medium, and therefore *where* and *how* it is placed on the printed page makes a difference in what the novel is saying. Thus, not only the writer creates fiction, but all those involved in the ordering of that fiction; the typist, the recorder, the printer, the proofreader, and the reader partake of the fiction, and the real medium becomes the printed word as it is presented on the page, as it is perceived, heard, read, visualized (not only abstractly but concretely) by the receiver.

PROPOSITION TWO — *The Shape of Fiction:*

If life and fiction are no longer distinguishable one from the other, nor complementary to one another, and if we agree that life is never linear, that, in fact, life is chaos because it is never experienced in a straight, chronological line, then, similarly, linear and orderly narration is no longer possible. The pseudo-realistic novel sought to give a semblance of order to the chaos of life, and did so by relying on the well-made-plot (the story line) which, as we now realize, has become quite inessential to fiction. The plot having disappeared, it is no longer necessary to have the events of fiction follow a logical, sequential pattern (in time and in space).

Therefore, the elements of the new fictitious discourse (words, phrases, sequences, scenes, spaces, etc.) must become digressive from one another—digressive from the element that precedes and the element that follows. In fact, these elements will now occur simultaneously and offer multiple possibilities of rearrangement in the process of reading. The fictitious discourse, no longer progressing from left to right, top to bottom, in a straight line, and along the design of an imposed plot, will follow the contours of the writing itself as it takes shape (unpredictable shape) within the space of the page. It will circle around itself, create new and unexpected movements and figures in the unfolding of the narration, repeating itself, projecting itself backward and forward along the curves of the writing—(much here can be learned from the cinema—that of Jean-Luc Godard in particular). And consequently, the events related in the narration will also move along this distorted curve. The shape and order of fiction will not result from an imitation of the shape and order of life, but rather from the formal circumvolutions of language as it wells up from the unconscious. No longer a mirror being dragged along reality, fiction will not reproduce the effects of the mirror acting upon itself. It will no longer be a representation of something exterior to it, but self-representation. That is to say, rather than being the stable image of daily life, fiction will be in a perpetual state of redoubling upon itself. It is from itself, from its own substance that the fictitious discourse will proliferate —imitating, repeating, parodying, retracing what it says. Thus fiction will become the metaphor of its own narrative progress, and will establish itself as it writes itself. This does not mean, however, that the future novel will be only "a novel of the novel," but rather it will create a kind of writing, a kind of discourse whose shape will be an interrogation, an endless interrogation of what it is doing while doing it, an endless denunciation of its fraudulence, of what it really is: an illusion (a fiction), just as life is an illusion (a fiction).

PROPOSITION THREE — *The Material of Fiction*:

If the experiences of any man (in this case the writer) exist only as fiction, as they are recalled or recounted, afterwards, and always in a distorted, glorified, sublimated manner, then these experiences are inventions. And if most fiction is (more or less) based on the experiences of the one who writes (experiences which are not anterior to, but simultaneous with, the writing process), there cannot be any truth nor any reality exterior to fiction. In other words, if the material of fiction is invention (lies, simulation, distortions, or illusions), then writing fiction will be a process of inventing, on the spot, the material of fiction.

The writer simply materializes (renders concrete) fiction into words. And as such, there are no limits to the material of fiction—no limits beyond the writer's power of imagination, and beyond the possibilities of language. Everything can be said, and must be said, in any possible way. While pretending to be telling the story of his life, or the story of any life, the fiction writer can at the same time tell the story of the story he is telling, the story of the language he is manipulating, the story of the methods he is using, the story of the pencil or the typewriter he is using to write his story, the story of the fiction he is inventing, and even the story of the anguish (or joy, or disgust, or exhilaration) he is feeling while telling his story. And since writing means now filling a space (the pages), in those spaces where there is nothing to write, the fiction writer can, at any time, introduce material (quotations, pictures, diagrams, charts, designs, pieces of other discourses, doodles, etc.) totally unrelated to the story he is in the process of telling; or else, he can simply leave those spaces blank, because fiction is as much what is said as what is not said, since what is said is not necessarily true, and since what is said can always be said another way.

As a result, the people of fiction, the fictitious beings, will also no longer be well-made-characters who carry with them a fixed identity, a stable set of social and psychological attributes—a name, a situation, a profession, a condition, etc. The creatures of the new fiction will be as changeable, as unstable, as illusory, as nameless, as unnamable, as fraudulent, as unpredictable as the discourse that makes them. This does not mean, however, that they will be mere puppets. On the contrary, their being will be more genuine, more complex, more true-to-life in fact, because they will not appear to be simply what they are; they will be what they are: word-beings.

What will replace the well-made-personage who carried with him the burden of a name, a social role, a nationality, parental ties, and sometimes an age and a physical appearance, will be a fictitious creature who will function outside any predetermined condition. That creature will be, in a sense, present to his own making, present to his own absence. Totally free, totally uncommitted to the affairs of the outside world, to the same extent as the fiction in which he will exist (perform that is), he will participate in the fiction only as a grammatical being (sometimes not even as a pronominal being). Made of fragments, disassociated fragments of himself, this new fictitious creature will be irrational, irresponsible, irrepressive, amoral, and unconcerned with the real world, but entirely committed to the fiction in which he finds himself, aware, in fact, only of his role as fictitious being. Moreover, not only the creator but the characters (and the narrator, if any) as well will participate (in the same degree as the reader) in the creation of the fiction. All of them will be part of the fiction, all of them will be responsible for it—the creator (as fictitious as his creation) being only the point of junction (the source and the recipient) of all the elements of the fiction.

PROPOSITION FOUR — *The Meaning of Fiction:*

It is obvious from the preceding propositions that the most striking aspects of the new fiction will be its semblance of disorder and its deliberate incoherency. Since, as stated earlier, no meaning pre-exists language, but meaning is produced in the process of writing (and reading), the new fiction will not attempt to be meaningful, truthful, or realistic; nor will it attempt to serve as the vehicle of a ready-made meaning. On the contrary, it will be seemingly devoid of any meaning, it will be deliberately illogical, irrational, unrealistic, non sequitur, and incoherent. And only through the joint efforts of the reader and creator (as well as that of the characters and narrators) will a meaning possibly be extracted from the fictitious discourse.

The new fiction will not create a semblance of order, it will offer itself for order and ordering. Thus the reader of this fiction will not be able to identify with its people and its material, nor will he be able to purify or purge himself in relation to the actions of the people in the story. In other words, no longer being manipulated by an authorial point of view, the reader will be the one who extracts, invents, creates a meaning and an order for the people in the fiction. And it is this total participation in the creation which will give the reader a sense of having created a meaning and not having simply received, passively, a neatly prearranged meaning.

The writer will no longer be considered a prophet, a philosopher, or even a sociologist who predicts, teaches, or reveals absolute truths, nor will he be looked upon (admiringly and romantically) as the omnipresent, omniscient, and omnipotent creator, but he will stand on equal footing with the reader in their efforts to *make sense* out of the language common to both of them, *to give sense* to the fiction of life. In other words, as it has been said of poetry, fiction, also, will not only mean, but it will be!

* * * *

One should, I suppose, in conclusion to such a presentation, attempt to justify, or at least illustrate with examples, the propositions I just made for the future of fiction. But justifications and illustrations are readily available, and to a great extent most of the writers discussed in the following list have already forged the way into this new type of fiction. For, I must confess, I am not alone in these wild imaginings. Many contemporary writers, each in his own personal "mad" way, have already successfully created the kind of fiction I tried to define in the preceding pages: Samuel Beckett, of course, in French and in English, Jorge Luis Borges and Julio Cortazar in Spanish, Italo Calvino in Italian, Robert Pinget, Claude Simon, Philippe Sollers, Jean Ricardou, J.M.G. Le Clezio, and many others, in France, and in their own individual manner, a number of American writers such as John Barth, John Hawkes, Ronald Sukenick, William Burroughs, Donald Barthelme, Richard Kostelanetz, Jerzy Kosinski. None of them, however, would pretend to have solved, singlehandedly, the problems of fiction, nor to have presented the only possible way for future fiction. I, like them, only know that this is the path I, as a fiction writer, want to explore in order, perhaps, not to succeed (commercially, socially, or otherwise), but in order to give fiction another chance, or, as one of the greatest fiction writers alive, Samuel Beckett, once said, in order "to make of failure a howling success."

OCT 1958

The Missed Generosity of the Circle Jerk

JACOB PAUL

We ought to begin by allowing the 4th person a kind of interlocutor a referee for the intramural activities of the other three persons implied acknowledged even but not exactly spoken to speak this 4th person would naturally invoke a 5th person a 6th 7th and 8th person and so on a sequence relatively unremarkable amongst the various infinities but for its insinuation that a Derridean trace would prove little but the banality of ghosts of course I am only accessing this 4th person through a 23-year-old memory of an 18-year-old who arrived in Buffalo by train from NYC which he had previously arrived at by bus from the Catskills where he had worked at an Orthodox Jewish Camp Camp Mishkon a camp for profoundly retarded men the bus from the camp had left him in Brooklyn from whence the bus to the camp had departed really the 18-year-old had been 17 years old when he arrived (and left) Brooklyn that prior summer he had arrived from Rochester also by train where he had attended a black-hat orthodox yeshiva a boarding school the kind of place where one studied Talmud all day instead of secular studies except of course a few secular studies all of them called English classes in the afternoon though to the extent that there was an emphasis – there wasn't – that emphasis was on science and math the Talmudic Institute of Upstate New York being decidedly NOT a college preparatory school but one where students stayed post high school for bait midrash (seminary) though frequently only after spending a year learning at bait midrash in

Israel and then post-nuptials kolel (also seminary just not living in the dorms) the 41-year-old would like to interject here that finally as a 39-year-old he came to recognize that European poststructuralists totally missed the point and origin of Derrida Derrida the 39-year-old realized is a Talmudist a mystic applying his people's primary mode of discourse to a Kabbalistic fascination with an ecstatic center necessarily ineffable and therefore effing unable to speak dictate mandate or create OK back to TIUNY despite this lack of emphasis on anything other than Talmud (and a bissel Torah Mishnah Navi and Halachah) the 17-year-old then 16 years old had met his first French Jewish mentor a physics teacher except that this physics teacher was only sort of French having fled to London with his family as an adolescent from Shanghai when the Japanese invaded and after the war as a 14-year-old moved to Paris by himself in an act of rebellion that necessitated his stringing of electrical wires across alleyways to undim his small chamber a service he provided his neighbors too which led to a fascination with physics a graduate degree a trip across the Atlantic and finally amongst other things a part-time gig teaching yeshiva students physics the 16-year-old had self-studied under this mentor for the AP exam on which he did well also the 16-year-old's father was a physicist (the 4th person 41-year-old's father is too) also also the yeshiva was the kind of place that didn't allow its denizens to see movies lest there be exposed female skin nor watch TV lest there by exposed female skin nor talk to girls lest there be etc . . . but it didn't put any energy into preventing the 16-year-old and his best friend Chaim from brewing beer in the basement in what had once been the morgue emergency shower (the building had once been a hospital) which led the 16-year-old to use his free time to read organic chemistry books to better understand enzymatic starch conversions in malted grain and fermentation processes also they hid the beer once bottled in the morgue elevator an unused and unusable accordion-doored lift designed to deliver corpses to the parking lot which the school shared with the Park Bench a bar next door whose patrons overdrank every weekend which led to the 17-year-old's first sight of a vagina that didn't belong to a sibling which happened when two very intoxicated young women yelled up to his dorm window one late Friday night which is to say early Saturday morning for toilet paper because they were peeing behind the hedges against the school wall their pants down their butts beautiful and exposed and tilted and revealing when they called up (yes of course he threw down a roll) all of which led the 17-year-old to declare physics his major (not the two women they had nothing to do with it except that if he hadn't brewed beer he wouldn't have been awake at 2 am Saturday morning drinking homemade beer) and also math a choice that halfway through his first semester he readily understood would not lead to the reading of books so sometime shortly after turning 18 the 18-year-old registered for a fiction-writing class for the spring semester of his freshman year this class being taught by his second influential French Jewish mentor Raymond Federman who derided the class' students' inadequately imaginative attempts at play (amongst other things like say wanting to change the world by writing or say not having read all of Shakespeare whose books Federman didn't believe had changed the world that notoriety being reserved for three texts The Bible Capital and Origin of the Species and especially for say not using proper grammar though one might also say that he most hated their compunction to use punctuation at least he would say not for the first page) Federman defined play as loosening using the classroom door to demonstrate and so the 18-year-old who owned a manual typewriter (as does the 41-year-old though now he doesn't use it for papers and homework let alone the composition of his fictions) took advantage of the opportunity to explore concrete prose's exploration of the typewriter as medium and wrote a series of things some of which "Generation" magazine was willing to publish such as a piece entitled "The Party" which was a series of lines of disconnected dialogue splayed in all directions over a single page that led his friends to comment that they liked it and that they didn't really get it but they liked it the same response he's gotten to every piece he's published since except for when they don't like it but sure the apex of his indoctrination adulation and emulation into and of all things Raymond

Federman took the form of the piece below submitted for class shortly after the 18-year-old turned 19 halfway through fall semester 1993 during which the 19-year-old was enrolled in his second Federman class also a fiction writing class but if he remembers correctly the level below the fiction writing class he took in spring semester 1993 apotheosis though it may be the story that follows never made it between the covers of anything (nor beneath them though their submission to class led to the moment when Federman finally told the 19-year-old that he would never get anything published but that obviously he wasn't going to stop writing ever either and that at least is mostly true truly I had yet to figure out that it's all a joke and that the joke IS the point of . . . . well if I went further it wouldn't be a joke anymore) (also I know that you're wondering who was the third French Jewish mentor the third French Jewish mentor was Francois Camoin but this isn't a feldshrift submission about the 4ᵗʰ person's MFA or PhD so that's all you get) OK the story written in 1993 by a 19-year-old for Federman's fiction writing class:

```
AND IT WAS UNDERSTOOD THAT
SOMETHING WAS WRONG SOMETHING
TERRIBLY WRONG AND THEY SOON SAW
THAT IT WAS NOT GOOD AND THEY
REALIZED THAT THE MUSHROOMING CLOUD
OF HOSE PIPES KNIVES GUNS RUBBER
BULLETS OF ROTTING GUTTER
VEGETABLES GREENER THAN BEFORE WITH
MOLD AND DISEASE WAS NOT AND THEY
UNDERSTOOD THAT SOMETHING HAD GONE
SO WRONG AND THEY DID NOT
UNDERSTAND WHY OR WHAT IT WAS THAT
HAD GONE WRONG ONLY THAT IT WAS SO

        it has always been us you see who get
        lost in this chaotic diarrhea of words
        who find ourselves trapped it is also us
        who have burned candles out of our own
```

flesh it is even us who sit here wishing
the was was more open so much more of
the time so that we could at last say
here are my troubles so that we could
surrender and allow fate out of our
hands

away knowledge it blinding like sapphires it
cut skin like glass

The third column has always seemed
the best one to allow the author to
write in though the argument could of
course be made that as the authors
only job is to explain the voices
being recorded why not write in the
first column That's just what I
always did intend but the voices jump
out and squash me back I am in
control but only if I keep it that
way of course the voices are going
the conversations are flowing
continuously when I address the
reader it's the same as hitting the
pause button on a tape player or VCR
or cd player though I firmly believe
that nothing I write is coherent
enough to compare with digital sound

things are becoming so
strange all of the time that
it is relatively hard to see
beyond the blocks these
quiet corners of repose that
are as easy to hide inside
of as they are to skim
without reading maybe that's
what's going wrong we're
scared getting in the shower
and crouching down in that
one little corner where the

water rarely splashes and
spending ten minutes trying
not to get wet

    AND THEY SAW THAT THE SUBSEQUENT
    CONVERSATIONS WERE OFTEN IDIOTIC AND
    ALMOST DESPOTIC AND THEY HAD NO IDEA
    HOW IT WAS MEANT THAT THEY SHOULD
    CONVEY WHAT THEY SAW AS INHERENT TO
    THAT WHICH WAS TERRIBLY WRONG THAT
    WHICH THEY FELT THEY MUST DISCUSS TO
    SEE THE WHY AND THEY SAW THAT IT WAS
    NOT GOOD

keeping me under wear away orange hair and
broken teeth all

You must understand of course that the search
for shape inside of form had become a sailing
ship of nonsense and we felt ourselves
seemingly abandoned in a sea of consonants and
vowels randomly juxtapositioned into mindless
depthless stuff nonsense without exclamation
points to hide behind quotation marks to
capture within without even the simple joys of
periods and commas to pause and hurdle it was
stranded here in strings of monologue to no one
ending and stating within the page's own
genesis and raison d'etre
    On the fourteenth day of our sojourn the
native suggestions approached us with offerings
of moderate usage of perhaps far more moderate
devices it's absolutely shocking at the
uncivilized archaic esoteric manner in which
they brutalize the members of our written
language not belonging to the alphabet
discrimination as such can only leave the
explorer aghast
    We have decided that separate but equal is
as petrifying an idea as together but unequal
an infusion of punctuation into this text seems

only fair in fact it has been so long since
they held their sway that as Maimonidies once
iterated to straighten a bent page one must
bend it back in the other direction this will
be our approach to these we extend them a
gargantuous

```
  !       !   " " " " " "   ?          ####        ;        .            .   ((((((
  !   !   !   "             ?          #          ;   ;       .  .       . .   (
   !   !   !   " " " " " "   ?          #          ;        ;    .     .      .   ((((((
    !! !!       "             ?          #          ;     ;       .             .   (
   !      !    " " " " " "   ?????   ####         ;       .             .   ((((((
```

Perhaps we have now solved our problem
perhaps things aren't so wrong after all if
that ain't integration then what is but of
course it seems that this still is unpunctuated
well there are cures to this also we will act
like the natives and marry into punctuation in
the next grouping of words

Asking my friend for his opinion, "So Bob,
what do you think of our dilemma?" He replied
(rather fitfully I might add)"Well, I reckon
your dilemma's a mighty poor one to get your
arse all stuffed up over!" Shocking language;
pouring forth like that I felt I had no choice
bet to respond. "But Bob," I said, "Didn't
someone else once say, 'Procession without
dilemma and poor language has been called and I
quote,"Blasphemers Blasphemers run hither from
an angry god!!"'" I continued. "For Heavens
sake man as the old saying goes! "Git you a
grip,"and progresses to, "on yourself man!"
listen #23 @ a new conjunction (we all hope-
that is to say ,"We pray;-)"

Of course we saw that our friends
punctuation had ended in a smiley face and as
such felt no fear, no none at all, when it came
to using our newly found punctuation in any
manner we see fit. For instance, we no longer
feel that punctuation has been placed in it's

proper form by these uncivilized tribes around us and in our next battery of words we shall use them how they should be in hopes of it becoming the norm or ala mode so to speak as we debark off this sailing ship of woe and descend onto a hostile shore in need of cultivation where the fields of our truth lay ripe to be sown in forest-land dark foreboding

AND THEY HAD SEEN THAT SOMETHING WAS TERRIBLY WRONG AND THEY UNDERSTOOD THAT THIS WAS AN UNDEFINABLE THING AND THEY SAW THE EVILS OF THOSE TO WHOM THEY HAD RUN IN DESPERATION AND THEY REALIZED THAT THE EXCLAMAITON POINT WAS MERELY A BARRIER WITH A PEEPHOLE AND THE COLON WAS A CORRAL UPON WHICH WORDS BECOME SQUASHED AND BACKED UP AND THEY SAW THAT PERIODS WERE SPEED BUMPS CAPABLE OF THROWING ALIGNMENT AND THEY SAW THAT SHAPE WAS AMBIGUITY AND THEY RAN OBEYED THIS AND IT WAS GOOD and it no long-er was us who found our-selves hem-med in by words on every side caught in this back-wash of sil-age be-yond our con-trol and washed to and fro and fin-al-y it is us who ap-proach ci-vi-li-za-tion and in-te-gra-tion in a new place we have dis-cov-er-ed and it is here that things fall into sy-la-ables where the

quo-ta-tion mark is only a
word's tears eas-il-y re-
placed by the portions
available to all parts of
speach But it is fitting
that the author should have
discovered this and that he
now prepares to infuse it
into the voyager in his
final and parting moments
with Bob Isn't it sad" to
see us. go. Oh I suppose it
is but I'll just hide
behind this here! and stick
my? out into the clear
streams here and git me a
fish to put in the# for my
old lady to cook] Bob I
can't hear(you talk louder
you're all damned in[what's
that I'm just fishing I
can't hear you where are
all the fish] I think the
gravedigger beat you to it
Bob there are no commas
we've left the
hieroglyphics behind
[W'h'e're' a're' my'f'ish
man w'h'r"e"s my ? to catch
them with))]] no more
running no more hiding only
fighting by god the
problems aren't in the
shower no more hiding out
of the rain no more not
using soap we're going to
be clean damn it we'll
fight Webster's till the
very end we'll smash down
the MLAwe'renotgonnatakeany
morelosts shampoowerealclea
nwerealcorrectwef:::::::::

Reflections on Ways to Say Where I Live

RAYMOND FEDERMAN

If I walk with a visitor from out of town in front of the house where I live, I can say: *I live here.*

Or, more specifically: *I live in this house, the one with the fenced yard.*

Or, I can simply say, pointing to my house: *this is my home.*

But if I wish to give a more administrative touch to this assertion, I can say: *I live in this modern house, the one with the French car parked in front of it. My wife's car.*

If I am entering the street where I live, again with a stranger, or this time with a foreign visitor [a poet in search of a center for his circle], I can point and say: *I live over there — number 46 — the house with the ivory tower.* Or I can simply state: *I live at 46 on this street.*

But I could also say: *I live down this street — the third house from the corner.*

Or: *I live down this street — next to the ugly green house with the broken down porch.*

Or: *I live three houses down from that two-story pseudo-Greek structure with the big columns and the black shutters.*

If someone in Buffalo [the city where I live] inquires where I reside, I have the choice of a good two dozens possible ways of answering. However, I can only say: *I live on Four Seasons Street,* to someone who I am sure knows where Four Seasons Street is, otherwise I have to specify the geographic location of that street.

For instance, I have to say: *I live on Four Seasons, off Saratoga Avenue, not far from the V.A. Hospital* [a landmark known to all the taxi drivers and all the war veterans].

Or else I can explain: *I live on Four Seasons Street in Eggertsville, a suburb of Buffalo,* even though I always write Buffalo as my return address on the letters I mail — doesn't make any difference, and it simplifies things because people don't have to ask: *Where is Eggertsville?*

I have on occasions said: *I live on Four Seasons Street, about five minutes on foot from the State University.*

But I have also said: *I live just a few blocks from the Zoo.*

Or: *I live across the street from the President of M & T Bank — my bank.*

Or: *I live around the corner from the Jewish Synagogue,* even though this has nothing to do with my religion, or my lack of religious belief.

In some exceptional circumstances, I could even be brought to say: *I live in Erie County.* Probably when being questioned about my taxes.

Or else: *I live in Western New York State.* Or: *I live on Lake Erie, near the Canadian border.* Or: *I live in the snow-belt.*

I doubt I will ever say: *I live in the postal zip code zone 14226.*

Almost anywhere in the U.S. [if not specifically in Buffalo or in Greater Buffalo], I think I can be almost certain to make myself understood when I say: *I live in Buffalo,* or *Buffalo is where I live,* or *Buffalo is my home,* or *I have been living in Buffalo for the past thirty years,* or *I moved to Buffalo in 1964.* There is a difference between these various ways of saying where one lives, but I don't exactly know what that difference is.

What I know for sure, is that I don't want to die in Buffalo. Anywhere but Buffalo, though I suppose dying in Peoria Illinois might be worse.

I could say, if the request called for it: *I live in the second largest city in New York State.* I don't think I have ever said that, but I could.

Though I did once say ironically to a friend from Texas: *I live in The Armpit of America.* I said this to him after the Buffalo Bills defeated the Oakland Raiders 51 to 7 [that was before the Raiders moved to Los Angeles], when after the game one of the Raiders' dejected coaches referred to Buffalo as *The Armpit of America.*

Nothing prevents me to imagine that I could say, since it is true: *I live not far from Niagara falls.* Or: *I live twenty minutes by car from Niagara Falls.*

Or: *I live in what is known as The City of Friendly Neighbors.*

Or: *I live in The Queen City,* but that sounds too much like the beginning of a bad novel than the indication of an address.

If I am on vacation on an island — say, off the coast of New England — and I am asked where I normally live, I can answer: *On the mainland.*

However, if I am traveling in England and someone asks me where I come from because my English does not sound quite proper, quite British, I must explain: *I come from the continent,* though in my case I would have to specify which continent.

I will undoubtedly not be understood, or receive a rather puzzled stare, if I say something like: *I live at 42°—‹ of latitude north, and 73°—‹ of longitude east.*

Would anyone give a damn if I say: *I live 2834 miles from San Diego; 1048 Miles from Topeka, Kansas; only 612 miles from Peoria, Illinois; 6156 miles from Jerusalem; 12397 miles from Melbourne, Australia.*

Would anyone really know where I live if I say: *I live north of the Tropic of Cancer,* or *I live south of the North Pole.*

If I lived in California — Northern California — I could casually say: *I live in the Bay Area.* Or if I lived in Southern California, I could snobbishly say: *I live in Beverly Hills.* However, since I live in Buffalo, or rather in the suburb of Buffalo known as Eggertsville, I cannot say, either casually or snobbishly or any other stupid way: *I live in California.* No, I cannot say that, because in fact I am stuck in Buffalo.

Also I cannot really see in which cases I could be in a position to have to say: *I live east of the Mississippi,* or *north of the Rio Grande.*

I live in America, or *I live in the United States of America.* I may have to give this information if I find myself in a place outside the boundaries of our country.

I live in North America. This type of information may be of interest to a European — let's say a French businessman — with whom I am having a conversation at a reception in the Japanese Embassy in Abidjan [Republic of Ivory Coast].

Ah! vous habitez en Amérique du Nord, he would say in French, and I would no doubt be led to specify [also in French to show that I have understood what he said]: *mais oui, je vis aux Etats-Unis. Je suis ici en affaires pour quelques jours, quelques semaines . . .*

I live on the Planet Earth. Will I ever have the occasion of saying this to someone? To another living creature from some other planet. If it is to an

Alien [especially of the 3rd kind] descended on Earth from a remote corner of the Universe, he would probably already know that. Aliens of the 3rd kind are much smarter than we Earthlings.

And if it is me who finds myself somewhere around Arcturus, let's say, in the beautiful constellation Bootes, or near Alpha KX2809°—‹, it would certainly be necessary for me to specify: *I live on the third planet [the only one which bears life] of the Solar System in order of increasing distance from the Sun.*

Or: *I live on one of the planets of one of the younger smaller yellow stars situated on the edge of a galaxy of rather mediocre importance in the Universe designated quite arbitrarily as the Milky Way.*

There is approximately one chance in hundred thousand million of billions [that is to say only 10 to the power of 20] that my alien interlocutor will answer: *Oh yeah, I know, you mean Earth!*

Returning to the Closet

DOUGLAS MESSERLI

On Tuesday, October 6, 2009, Raymond Federman died in his San Diego home at the age of 81.

I published—or more correctly, I *republished*—two books by Ray, *The Twofold Vibration* in 2000, a fiction first published in 1982 by Indiana University Press, and, six years earlier on Sun & Moon, *Smiles of Washington Square*, first published by Thunder's Mouth Press in 1985.

I seem to have known Ray (who preferred to be called Raymond, but who I knew as Ray) forever. Long before I met him, I had read his criticism, *Surfiction: Fiction Now and Tomorrow*, and referred to it extensively in my PhD dissertation of 1979. Ray seemed to me one of the few critics of the time who had attempted to do what I myself was trying to accomplish, to define the differences between modernist and non-modernist (narrowly referred as postmodern) fiction. Like Ray, I saw its roots from the beginning of the 20th century, from Gertrude Stein on, and I wanted to create a kind of handbook which would help people see its different approaches to voice, character, place, theme, and, most of all, form.

I think I must have first met him in the flesh—and the words "in the flesh" are important when describing Ray because he is so very much larger than life—in the early 1980s, when I began distributing Fiction Collective and other small presses along with my own Sun & Moon Press. I had found a small band of independent sales representatives to sell these and my own books across the country, and each season I would meet with them, describing the new titles, in New York.

Ray, whose important fiction *Take It or Leave It* was published by the Fiction Collective, was a member of that group, and he and others wanted to meet with my representatives to sell their own titles. The art of describing new works to sales people who have hundreds of books to represent each season is a difficult one, which I felt I had mastered. Accordingly, I tried to dissuade the Fiction Collective authors from coming to speak with my representatives, but they were insistent. Ray, along with Russell Banks and Jonathan Baumbach (yes, the father of Noah Baumbach played by Jeff Daniels in the film *The Squid and the Whale*)—all sublime egoists, each capable of dominating any conversation—showed up late to the meeting and took so much time describing their three new titles that my reps insisted that they would never see them again! I was, accordingly, put in the difficult position of scolding the three, but two of them, at least, Ray and Russell remained lifetime friends.

That is not to say that I wasn't a bit taken back by Ray's dynamic personality. Indeed, in his unpredictable enthusiasms, directed mostly toward his own writing projects and, later, his understandable delight with the French and German attention to his writing, along with his winking sexual innuendos about women, sometimes irritated me and even, on occasion, scared me a little. I liked him enormously, but on occasion he was not where you thought he was. As one of his own characters describes "the old man" in *The Twofold Vibration* (clearly a mirror image of the narrator, Federman):

> yes, that's how our old man was, so
> unpredictable, so changeable, and so careless
> with his own life, despondent one day, hopeful
> the next, always more interested in the process
> than finalities . . . . not an easy man to deal with

And then there was his voice, with a French accent, of course, but seemingly also from another time and place. As French fiction writer Jean

Frémon once told me, "When I met Raymond Federman I could not believe what I was hearing. It was a voice from another time. Only a small neighborhood in Paris spoke French that way, the way Maurice Chevalier had spoken and sung, and it has long disappeared. I asked him, my God, where did you get that accent? He told me his story, how as young boy he was hidden away from the Nazis in a closet. And when he finally came out, that was the way he would remain the rest of his life, since by the end of the War he had escaped to the US, joining the Army."

Federman's family, his mother, father and, sisters were sent to Auschwitz, where they died.

When I visited SUNY-Buffalo several years later, on tour with fellow poet Rae Armantrout, we dined with Susan Howe, Charles Bernstein, and the Federmans, Ray and his wife Erica, at a very pleasant Italian restaurant. On our way home, after having left the Federmans and Susan, the two of us chuckled to ourselves about Ray's grandiose manner, I adding my reservations about the man. Charles quickly interrupted, "How else might you expect him to be, given the life he has led, his childhood, the condition of creating several new beings? He had no choice but to become a series of alternating voices."

I was embarrassed, and realized the truth of what Charles had said. To be fair, moreover, Ray has never denied the forcefulness and energy of his own being. In fact, he celebrates it, just as he celebrates a world in which all the action is placed on something in process without ever coming to fruition. He writes what he calls "pre-texts," texts that exist before any happening; and, in that respect, his work is about potentiality more than plotted events, the writing existing as a potential for changes not only in the future but the past.

Smiles on Washington Square, for example, is the story of a chance meeting between a poor, immigrant American Moinous (one of Federman's regular stand-ins for himself) and a New England born, slightly order sophisticate, Sucette (who shares some of Erica's qualities). The two meet, but say nothing, only smiling at one another. The rest of the tale is a series of possibilities for their future encounter(s) and relationship, all of which entail a great deal of patient waiting and outright frustration for Moinous. Their relationship, in this non-existent reality (which is, at its heart, what all fiction is about), is a touching, even romantic tale, as these two opposites gradually reveal themselves before the inevitable breakup.

This work is perhaps Federman's closest in tone to his friend Samuel Beckett. For here, the major character, like many of Beckett's tragic clowns, is an insecure, lonely, and despairing figure who bluffs his way through life. Like Federman, he has lived in the protective closet before sneaking out to enter—barefoot, armored only by an outsized overcoat—a world of excitement and danger, a tyrannical innocent ("A typical bull with his feet on the ground and his head in the clouds who struggles constantly to conquer vanity and indolence") in a world he can never completely comprehend.

In Federman's futurist fiction, *The Twofold Vibration*, his friends Moinous and Namredef (Federman spelled backwards) attempt to uncover what "the old man" has done to be sent to the space colonies along with other undesirables on the eve of the new Millennium. To Federman, the writer, they tell the story of their friendship and as much as they know about "the old man's life," but have no clue, in this comic Kafkaesque tale, what his criminal acts have consisted of.

Like Ray, "the old man" has been hidden in a closet, and to this part of his own story, he adds other tales, how he was later arrested and sent to the camps, escaping from his railway car at the stop to eat potatoes in another train car that had paused alongside them. More stories emerge, a brief involvement in radical politics, a short affair with a Jane Fonda-like movie star, and travels across the US and Europe, including a visit to a concentration camp, encompassing excesses and suffering, boisterous outbursts of philosophical thoughts and deep retreats into fear and doubt. His famed *The Voice in the Closet* screed was to have been at the center of this work, but was rejected by Indiana University Press' editors.

Through it all, Federman is represented to his reading audience as outsized, a being at once affable and slightly embarrassing. Yet his friends

—and that might include any sympathetic reader—can find nothing in his past so terrible that it might result in his being sent into outer space for what, most believe, is certain death.

The search for his unknown crime is played out almost like a mystery tale, but, as usual in Federman's works, no ending seems appropriate. As the thousands of soon-to-be expelled individuals are gathered in a large room, Moinous and Namredef are there to see their friend off. "The old man" appears reposed, even resigned, finally ready for his fate. One by one the names are called, the prisoners taken on board and their families sent off, until only "the old man" remains. The shuttle is about to be sent into space without him! What has happened? his colleagues wonder. "BUT WHAT ABOUT ME, WHAT ABOUT ME," the old man cries out, striking his chest with his hand. He has been put back into the closet a second time. The snake has swallowed its own tail; the past has become the future, a twofold vibration. The survivor without a clue how to survive is left to start his struggle all over again.

Now, finally, Ray has been removed from that closet, that coffin-like precursor of death, forever. He has joined the dead by giving up his voice. For us still here, still trapped in each of our personal closets, so to speak, we can only, like "the old man," become lonely and forlorn. We miss that larger than life wise fool so very desperately. And, gathering today, we need to speak of our great emptiness, to share it with others. As Ray himself wrote some time before his death, however, in the humorous and profound short essay, "Reflections on Ways to Improve Death":

> The fact that Federman cannot say I am dead.
> The fact of being unable to speak one's death is
> the supreme category which abolishes all the
> others. It is the ultimate category, the category
> of the unspeakability of death. Whether one dies
> in bed, dies in one's books, dies with one's boots
> on, dies on the vine, dies in harness, dies
> prematurely or in one's sleep, dies in a gas

chamber, dies while making love to one's lover, when all is done and said, that is the category of death that has reached total improvement because it can no longer be spoken.

Language vanishes into death, and death vanishes into silence. Or is it, death vanishes into language, and language into silence?

Abandoned Preface to Abandoned Fictions

LARRY McCAFFERY & RAYMOND FEDERMAN

Calibri: Larry McCaffery

[Gentium Book Basic: Raymond Federman]

Yo, Federman, listen: I need your help constructing my preface to your *Abandoned Fictions* collection—you know, the one I've decided to develop in the form of a list of reasons why *Abandoned Fictions* needs to be read immediately?

[The best reason is that *AF* may be Federman's last book. I mean book in the old way. Federman doesn't write books any more. You know books that look like little boxes that you open and inside you find neatly arranged pages with words lined up on them. Federman now writes language that floats freely in space. That is why his *AF* should be published. As a last concrete record of Federman's oeuvre. And besides Federman needs the money.]

The problem I'm having is that there's TOO MANY reasons for me to list— I've already come up with several hundred and need you to help me pare things back to something more manageable (10 reasons should be enough, don't you think?)

[One will suffice. As stated above. Federman needs the dough. But you could also explore the fact that Federman has never been able to finish anything. His books are always left unfinished. And so are his sentences. This brings up an interesting paradox concerning the AF. Perhaps what Federman calls abandoned fiction may in fact not be abandoned but simply be unfinished fiction. And as such finished fiction since Federman's fiction is always unfinished.]

[Larry I would prefer if you would not have to tell me when I can come into this mess. I want to be free to float in it. To insert myself anywhere I want. I'm trying to help you. But if you're going to act like you own the place. Then I'm out of here.]

Anyway, here's where we stand right now. Don't forget to look over my footnotes. [I can't believe you still use footnotes. How cacademic of you. Maybe soon you'll regress into quotation marks and semi-colons.] Of course, I will forever be in your debt now (even deeper in debt than I already am, due to our annual bet on the Cowboys [and Chargers — as of today you owe me 60 bucks.]

Prefatory Remarks on Federman's (Temporarily) Abandoned Fictions (An Endless Story): A Listatory Gesture [Nicely said Larry. I like the temporary. It suggests that perhaps one day Federman will rescue the AF and finish them. Imagine that. It will be an historical day. Federman finishing a fiction.]

This is not the beginning: BRIEF DIGRESSION

1:

I'm wondering: can a digression be presented before any other narrative or textual material (i.e., is digression possible if there is not first some other story or melody that the digression "departs" from?)

ON LISTS.

List: a series of names, words, numbers, etc. *set forth in order*, used in writing catalogues: to reckon, count up.

Webster's Third Abridged Dictionary. Italics, mine.

Numbered Lists

2:

For my purposes, a "list" implies a *numbered* sequence of related items, whereas the items appearing in a "catalogue" are not numbered and hence unfold somewhat chaotically, more democratically. Of course, there are many famous examples of authors who are well known for their catalogues: Rabelais, Whitman, Proust, Elkin, Gass, Coover, Stein, and many others. But Raymond Federman is among the far fewer number of authors who have employed *the list* on a regular basis. Incidentally, I happen to know for a fact that these lists don't just show up by accident — in his so-called "real life" Federman himself is a fanatical list-maker. I've always assumed these lists were just another indication of the constant battle between waged inside Federman between the rational, orderly, anal-retentive side of Federman (we might also refer to this as his right brain, or Apollolinian aspect) and side associated with chaos, disorder, irrationality, emotion (the left brain, the Dionysian side, etc.). Federman's lists, then, are a textual indication of his right brain desperately struggling to bring order to situations that ultimately can't be ordered — hence the poignancy and humor of these lists.

Lists are many things — memory aids, containers of information, a means of organizing materials, efforts to prioritize, gestures meant to bring order out of the flux of existence. Lists are also one of many peculiar rhetorical devices that pop up regularly in Raymond Federman's work. Indeed, beginning with the numerous lists that play such an important structural function in his first novel, *DON* (1971), lists have played *such* a prominent role in Federman's work that one can easily imagine that a critic writing a

preface to Federman's latest book of fiction could decide to cast his introductory remarks in the form of a list that might well read something like the following: [Good try Larry. But it won't work. We are beyond the era of lists with AF. We are in a totally new zone. Perhaps what you should try to define is in what genre *AF* falls. Or does *AF* create a new genre. Remember Beckett's *From an Abandoned Work.* And what about Joyce's *Work in Progress.*]

10 Reasons for Reading Raymond Federman's *Abandoned Fictions* — A Prefatory List [Well if you insist. We'll go with your list.]

1. Because *AF* is the first collection of short [oh how I hate the word short when talking about a work of fiction. How does one determine the length of] fiction published in English by Raymond Federman, a Jewish-American author [I don't see the relevance here to have to point to Federman's Jewish ethnicity — some readers might read a touch of anti-Semitism in the way you publicize it] whose wildly innovative early novels — *DN* (1971), *TIOLI* (1976) and *VIC* (1979) — [this makes it sound as though Federman stopped innovating in 1979 — what about the other books — a little publicity never hurts] collectively represent a kind of "high watermark" [Oh my god! I'm going to faint. Quotation marks in an introduction about Federman. Sacrilege!] of the sort of radical experimentalism that appeared in the 70s when the first wave of postmodern experimentalism was cresting; [not only a dumb reason Larry. But a semi-colon at the end. You really want to kill me. And kill this book. Can't you just say Another masterpiece from Federman and leave it at that.]

2. Because of the status of these "abandoned fictions" as "conditional fictions" (BRIEF DIGRESSION ON WHAT THE TERM "ABANDONED FICTIONS" IMPLIES. That is, since Federman began each of these fictions assuming that they would eventually evolve into book-length works; he continued working on them — for periods ranging from about a week ("Ramona" and "Into the Foxhole"), to several months ("In Search of Mona"), to several years (as with

the excerpt from his first, unpublished novel, *And I Followed My Shadow*) —
before abandoning them. [I am not going to say anything any more about
the quotation marks and the semi-colons. You decide how you want to be
perceived as the introductor of Federman's *AF*.] Moreover, these were all
works that RF initially believed would be novels (or what other people might
designate as novels — long, book-length texts), but which for various
reasons, he eventually stopped working on — they can all be read not only
for what they "are" but for what they MIGHT HAVE BEEN had they not been
abandoned. However, it should also be noted [I thought expression like it
should be noted went out of business in the 20th century] that as far as I
can tell Federman has never *actually* "abandoned" anything he has ever
written — [exactly what I said above] there is always a later recuperation
process in which EVERYTHING, or ANYTHING that has been set down (on
paper or the screen) and transformed into the blood ink of language will be
reprocessed, rewritten, reincorporated into later works. (Incidentally, this
applies not just to texts Federman himself has "authored," but to ANY TEXTS
— personal correspondence, novels, literary criticism, poetry, whether these
be published or unpublished, are all "fair game" for Federman.) A couple of
examples should clarify what I mean. *Double or Nothing* included numerous
appropriations from earlier texts that Federman had abandoned (most
notably his unpublished first *And I Followed My Shadow*) . [Makes sense to
me since it's obvious that Federman has no idea what a novel is. His books
are not novels. But nobody. Not even you Larry. Has been able to explain
what they are.]

Thus, [Larry I cannot believe you still use Thus after having spent so much
time in Federman's workshop] while all the texts included in *AF* were
indeed begun and then abandoned, they should more accurately be
described as being only TEMPORARILY abandoned, still "alive" but living in a
kind of suspended animation — [I like that Larry — yes still alive —
Stirrings Still — as Sam put it in his final work] a kind of conditional or
virtual life from which they will inevitably be reawakened, reanimated by

RF's memory (itself a remarkable entity capable of near-photographic reconstructions, with its own remarkable power now considerably expanded by technological devices such a hard drives, zip drives, computer discs, CD ROMs, and the like). [Now you're rolling Larry. More stuff like that to excite the potential readers of *AF*.]

3. Because irrespective of the terminology we employ, or their origins (i.e., each text was originally begun as a novel), [I think I made it clear that I have no idea what a novel is — or does anybody? So perhaps you should try to use another word] or current status as "failures" [Oh yeah. Failures. That's good. *Fizzles* Sam called his.] (after working on them for various periods, RF eventually abandoned them) — and despite Federman's own repeated, almost gleeful claims that his books are "unreadable" — these fictions are all *great reads*. [Thanks Larry for saying this.] Thus, while these fictions display the obsessive self-reflexiveness and foregrounding of artifice, the exuberant word play, the philosophical, aphoristic asides, and wildly digressive narratives, and all the other peculiar features that we have come to expect from any Federman text, they also display an aspect of RF's work that has rarely been emphasized sufficiently — his great gifts as a storyteller. [Finally you said it — that's why the potential readers should buy this book. Because of the great stories in it.] And several of the stories readers will encounter here are as vivid and hilarious, and poignant, and memorable as any of his earlier accounts — stories such as (in the excerpt from "AIFMS") the story of a young orphan riding on a ride who chooses to escape from the destiny this train ride is taking him towards by following the example of one of his companions, who jumped off the train. This episode is included in the excerpt from Federman's first extended effort to tell his story — the unpublished novel ms. AIFMS which he began while still an undergraduate student at Columbia during the mid-50s and continued working on for several years until he abandoned the book as being too . . . [This is not clear. You have to rephrase this or nobody is going to understand what the fuck is going on in that scene.]

("Into the Foxhole") The behind-the-scenes story of Federman's love-at-first-sight meeting with Erica, the woman he would be married to for 40 years, [44 now] meeting on an elevator results in love-and-first-sight and a marriage that is still going strong forty years later, [repetitious here] but not before a harrowing episode involving Federman arriving back at Erica's home following a round of golf, where he seats himself comfortably in deep leather arm chair, when Erica's current (but estranged) husband suddenly arrives, words are exchanged, fisticuffs ensue, the husband finds a huge carving knife in the kitchen, and Federman is forced to flee unceremoniously through the front door. [Do you have to give all these sordid details. Let the potential reader find out for himself].

("In Search of Mona") The "spontaneous love story invented on the spot" about why Federman decided to abandon his attempt to relocate himself in Paris in 1958 and return to America in 1958; the reasons behind this crucial decision unfold as part of a story about his alter ego Moinous's encounter with a mysterious woman at an airport in France while he's waiting for a plane that will take him back to America. [good]

["Out of the Foxhole"] The story of how Federman was nearly killed and also smoked his first cigarette during one miserably cold night that he spent with a kid from New Jersey in a foxhole during the Korean War. [I like the brevity of this statement]

("Jazz and Tubes") The story of Federman's arrival back in Paris in 1945 hitched a ride back to Paris on an American tank, and how he managed to survive the postwar devastation by getting a job in a toothpaste factory, and how he of his first encounters with jazz soon after his arrival back in Paris after the War riding on an American tank and how spending first heard jazz. [You could have pointed out the symbolic aspect of the tubes in relation to jazz instruments].

The "prehistoric chronicle" of the circumstances leading up to the moment when the earliest human beings first arose "from a four-legged posture to a biped posture and screaming with pain into the wildness launched us to our present state of confused erection." A work that yokes Kubrick's "Dawn of Man" sequence from *2001* and Calvino's marvelous, whimsical fables about the origins of color, language, love, and other early inventions (in *Cosmicomics*), "Chouchou" is an excerpt from one of Federman's best-known abandoned projects — a collaboration that he worked during the early 1980s with his close friends and fellow Fiction Collective authors George Chambers, Ronald Sukenick, and Steve Katz. [No comment]

5. Because these fictions help fill in several crucial gaps in Raymond Federman's ongoing life-story. Although this fictionalized autobiography has unfolded over the years in discrete publications in different forms (including nine novels, several volumes of poetry, books of criticism, as well as in numerous unpublished collaborations), But for all the variety in length, genre, subject matter, and poetry or prose, RF's writing has always been so obsessively concerned with exploring a single topic — his own life-story as the sole surviving member of a French Jewish family whose other members were erased by the Nazis in the concentration camps — that, as is true of Proust, Burroughs, Miller, Céline, and other authors of similarly compulsive-obsessive instincts, all of Federman's writing really amount to a single continuous book, one long stream of words and stories that all seek to give voice to the unspeakable reality what took place to his family. [Very true. But then if *AF* is part of this big book then how can these fictions be called abandoned. The entire big book then is an abandoned fiction. Or something like that.]

But while each Federman text can be said to have been initially generated by the closet episode, it is also clear that each novel has also explored a variety of key events been set in particular places and times that were especially significant:

DN: (1947-9) Period of RF's arrival in the U.S., and his life on the margins RF's departure from France, his arrival in America, the early years of

TIOLI and *AE* (early 50s, including his move from Detroit to NY, and his years he spent in the Army); Federman no longer living on the margins of America but taking the plunge

VIC (specifically his closet episode)

TTV. Set ostensibly in on the eve of the new Millennium, TTV moves backwards and forwards in time, focusing on the tumultuous 60s, when Federman was a highly radicalized faculty member at SUNY-Buffalo, and also Federman's first recounting of another primal scene that had up until this time been too painful to explore: the shower scene in Auschwitz where his father lost his life (transformed from Auschwitz to Dachau)

SMILES. Mid 50s. McCarthy era when Federman was a poor student.

TWIMC. Inspired by the year Federman spent in Israel on a Fulbright Fellowship, also explores the period Federman spent in Paris after the War with his cousin

ARF—two crucial periods, one in 1958 when Federman returned to Paris only to discover he no [missing]

RTM. Period RF spent on a farm in southern France following the loss of his family in the closet episode.

[Very good Larry. Very useful. But try now to organize these piece of the big book according to their order in Federman's life and the order of their publication. And you will realize that there is an important moment/piece missing. Tokyo.]

6. Because *Abandoned Fictions* includes the longest excerpt yet published

from Federman's very first novel, *And I Followed My Shadow*, a manuscript he began while still a student at Columbia and then continued working on for several years while he was working on his Ph.D, in Comparative Literature at Columbia University. Federman would later allude to, and appropriate sections of *AIFMS* which gradually has assumed an almost mythic status as one of contemporary American literature's best-known unpublished novels. And as Federman's first (failed) attempt to fictionalize the traumatic experiences he endured during the war, AIFMS provides a fascinating glimpse down the road not taken — a more realistic direction that Federman might have chosen to tell his life-story might have. [That alone should attract the rich and curious bibliophiles — we could make a fortune with this book.]

7. Because AF includes "Ramona" — Federman's most vivid and extended portrait of his father, which I regard to be the finest short story he has ever written. [Thank you Larry!]

8. Because the variety and extremity of the various kinds of formal experiments employed throughout *AF* provides further confirmation that Federman is postmodern American fiction's most radically innovative and deeply obsessive fiction writer. [Maybe you should leave out the word postmodern. Postmodern died on November 22, 1989] [Oh! How do you reconcile innovative with obsessive?]

9. Because several of the most recent of these abandoned projects ("In Search of Mona," demonstrate the ways that Federman has begun to take advantage of the opportunities made available by the Internet (and email) for creating new sorts of playgiarized, collaboratively developed texts. [Can you prove it?]

10. Finally, by foregrounding [oh do I detest the word foregrounding. Sounds like a word you use to bury somebody. Larry you're a retired professor now. Abandon cacademic jargon.] Federman's skills as a story-

teller, *AF* demonstrates why Federman has recently become increasingly recognized as having created the most original body of "Holocaust" writing (or "anti-Holocaust" writing) of all [something wrong here in the syntax] impossibility of being the most original fiction has recently begun to attract so much attention outside the United States. This new anthology of previously uncollected fictions by Raymond Federman confirms the obvious — i.e., that Federman's remarkable, unclassifiable work is now being published in greater quantity, and with more fanfare and critical acclaim, than ever before. During the past two years alone, Federman has published several new book-length works, in English and French, and had dozens of translations of his work have also appeared in Germany, Poland, France and even in China (where *TIOLI* ... [you didn't finish your sentence.]

LARRY THIS IS PERFECT THIS WAY — I MEAN IT — 10 REASONS ARE ENOUGH — ESPECIALLY SINCE THEY ARE SUCH POWERFUL REASONS.

SHIT I DIDN'T REALIZE THERE WERE SO MANY TYPOS — THEY SHOULD BE CORRECTED — MAYBE BEFORE THE BOOK GOES TO THE PRINTER

OR MAYBE WE SHOULD LEAVE THE LIST AS YOU HAVE IT. AFTER ALL THESE FICTIONS WERE ABANDONED WITH THEIR DEFECTS. EXCELLENT IDEA. THE LIST OF TYPOS STAYS. AND ALL THE REST.

Writers are Egomaniacs

JULIA FREY

The above photo is not typical, because Ray is not in the foreground, but it identifies the guilty parties. My late husband, novelist Ron Sukenick, considered Ray to be one of his best friends. In memory of their friendship, though memory is notoriously unreliable, I conjure up a few memories of Ray the man. I am only a biographer. I leave commentary on his writing to others. Except to say that I loved it — particularly in French, and especially *La Fourrure de ma tante Rachel.*

My two memories, one from the beginning and one from the end of our long friendship, reveal something of the time, of Ray's personality, and maybe of the ways of writers in general.

The first time I met Ray, in 1980, Ron and I had just begun living together. I was nervous about meeting my lover's friend, particularly since, although they were separated, Ron was still married to his first wife, Lynn. Ray had been married to Erica for many years. They were both back in Paris from a writers' conference I forget where in Germany. Rumor had it that Ron had been treating a cold with whiskey and was drunk and disorderly all weekend. Later Ron told me that Erica didn't like Ray to hang out with him, because she thought Ron was a bad influence. Or maybe it was the other way around, and Lynn didn't like Ron to hang out with Ray for the same reason. Anyway, the consensus was that they egged each other on to sleep around, drink too much and generally misbehave. It was as if they believed partying, collecting groupies and getting into trouble together was part of their ethos as the bad boys of *autofiction*.

Ron was sober by the time he got home, and had set up a date that hot summer evening for us to meet Ray at the Paris apartment of a small dark-haired writer named Yvonne Caroutch. Ray had translated one of her books into English in 1965. When we walked into her place on the Montagne Sainte-Genevieve in the Latin quarter, she and Ray were passionately entangled on the couch. She looked enamored. After they untangled, we all went out to dinner on a restaurant terrace in the Place du Pantheon. Maybe after that he straightened out, or at least was more discreet, because every other time I saw Ray over some 35 years, Erica was with him, or if he was alone, he seemed totally engaged with book business. When we were all in Paris, we habitually went out together to the Carrefour de l'Odeon near our apartment, for *choucroute* at an Alsatian restaurant sadly now replaced by a chic café. It had delicious Gewürztraminer, and the new café watered their wine.

The overwhelming impression of Ray that I got from our many meetings over the years was that having miraculously escaped from the Nazis (the story he could not stop writing) he felt as if the rest of his life was gravy. He was fearless, a risk-taker. Parachuting out of bombers in the US army in WW2 hadn't bothered him. He knew he was a protected man. Or at least that you never had much control over when luck might end. He always fell asleep on takeoff.

He believed in living hard and fast, and enjoying every minute. He took laughing very seriously — it was the only way to get by. Erica had the same philosophy. They played and lived high whenever they could afford it: golfing and gambling and traveling — moving to La Jolla California as soon as he could retire from his teaching job in freezing Buffalo ('Farbelow' we called it).

Ron loved Ray. Me too. His energy and enthusiasm were contagious. But he also exhibited a frustrating mixture of generosity and egomania. He was wonderful about sharing his contacts. He pushed Ron to get together with people he would not otherwise meet, introducing him to European scholars, critics and publishers who might want to translate his work. He was instrumental in getting Ron a Fulbright to teach creative writing in Israel in the 1980s. In a peculiarly French tradition, Ray was always trying to get Ron to create a 'movement' with him to get vanguard writers to band together, to write a manifesto which would change the way the world perceived the word. They often collaborated on new literary ventures and projects, but Ron was only vaguely receptive to the idea of manifestos and clans. American writers are typically too eccentric to join a club.

Perhaps there was also something about wanting to head up a *mouvement littéraire* that seemed like an ego-trip on Ray's part. He was strangely innocent, for example, about how others might react to his frequent emails enumerating his successes and accomplishments. I think it simply never occurred to him that everyone wouldn't be thrilled to learn that he was doing better than they were. I know in the beginning Ron laughed off the constant bragging, saying "that's just Ray. He can't believe his own good luck."

But after 1992, when Ron was diagnosed with an incurable orphan disease, inclusion body myositis, Ray's self-felicitation began to wear thin. Ron would get depressed hearing about how his friend was speeding ahead while he himself was shopping for wheelchairs. They stayed close of course. Ray came to see us whenever he was in town, particularly after September 11, 2001. That day had left Ron, now profoundly disabled, stuck in an apartment overlooking the smoking ruins of New York's World Trade Center.

In April 2004, Ray's egotism finally got to me, too. Ron, who was dictating short stories about his approaching death to his word processor using speech recognition software, got one of the habitual bragging emails from Ray. It looked like a personal email except that there was nothing personal in it. Ray never even asked how Ron was doing. Ron fell apart. "Ray is hopeless," he said, staring down at his paralyzed hands. "He is so self-involved he didn't even bother to ask himself how I would feel about getting an ebullient email about all his glory when I'm on my way out."

I never messed with their friendship, but Ray's grandiosity when Ron was so sick made me furious. I called him up in California and told him how hurt Ron was. Ray was stunned and contrite. He explained that it was a mass mailing and he hadn't even thought about Ron being on his mailing list. I told him if he wanted to see Ron again, he'd better come to NY soon, because Ron couldn't live more than a few months. Once he tuned in, Ray was full of good will. He and Erica got on a plane and came to NY. They hung out with Ron and talked about old times. They told him goodbye. Ron died in July.

Ray was a fine writer, a tireless and generous man. He was charming, cheerful, funny — very lovable. He was never petty, stingy or intentionally mean. But unless someone made him stop to think how what he did was affecting others, it was all about him. Then again, writing is a solitary, anguishing activity where you lay your soul on the line. Maybe to survive being so vulnerable, any writer has to be an egomaniac.

Pictures:
1. Left to right, Ronald Sukenick, Julia Frey and Raymond Federman at dinner in Paris, for the engagement of Ray's sister's son. 1980.
2. Left: Ronald Sukenick, center: Raymond Federman, right: Robert Coover, in a panel discussion at a German literary conference, possibly June 30, 1980.
3. Same characters, same day, photo 2
4. Raymond Federman on a visit to Ron Sukenick and Julia Frey in Boulder CO. ca. (1990).
5. Erica and Raymond Federman at Borrego Springs CA, (visiting Larry McCaffery during the year of the comet, late 1990s.)

What is to love

RAYMOND FEDERMAN

what an immense question
to love what's that
to say I love you
three little words
to which one could answer
with three letters
j~~~~~~t~~~~~~m
but love is more than that
it's so many unspeakable things
things one says and things one does not say
to love cannot be summed up with words
all the I love you one whispers
are not necessarily thought
they are often simply felt
so many people who say
I love you to anyone anywhere
without knowing what it means
one says I love you
when all the other words
have been exhausted
to express what one feels
I love you expresses the muteness of love
to love is what one does excessively
everyday with the loved one

to love is to become more than one
it's to share two bodies and two minds
it's to give all while dividing oneself
to love is to give out e-mot-ions
to love is to exchange blissful words
to love sometimes is to say nothing
silence is love too
to love is to let oneself go
to the extravagance of pure madness
to see nothing else but the loved one
to love it to look at oneself in the mirror
and see the reflection of the loved one
to love is to speak in a vacuum
knowing the loved one is listening
to love is to speak delirious words endlessly
and hear the voice of the loved one as an echo
to love is to see blue butterflies like angels
or to look at a photo and whisper I love you
to love is to forget the difficult moments
and remember only the sublime moments
to love is to laugh with tears in one's eyes
or to cry with laughter in one's throat
to love is to suffer and smile and die
to love is to make oneself immortal
so that one can love even more
to love is to say that time does not exist
and in so saying render time permanent
to love is to invent a kingdom in the sky
where to escape and indulge in jouissance
to love is to dream inside the dream in technicolor
to love is to be patient until the next time
but to be impatient for the next time
to love is to want to possess everything
the loved one has and give everything one has
to love is to want to give and receive recklessly

to love is to know how to vanish without being forgotten
to love is to close one's eyes to see the loved one better
to love is to touch hear smell see taste the loved one
to love is to breathe the loved one

Federman and the Nightingale: A Playgiarism of Hans Christian Andersen's Nattergalen

GEOFFREY GATZA

Hidden among the lush spice forests, Raymond Federman sat comfortably in a rather large rattan lounging chair looking out onto the rolling green foothills from the veranda on the southern side of his extremely large and fashionable house.

Just north of the cinnamon groves his home appeared to grow right out of the white hawthorn and the wild nutmeg bushes.

Federman's home was more of a palace than a house, as so many guests had said on more than one occasion. No matter what you called it, it was truly a wonder of the world. This house let anyone and everyone who happened to ponder how much money Federman had, know exactly how wealthy Federman was. Which is to say, Federman was loaded. Federman did not make his money by being foolish; he was great at business. So when he saw opportunity he was sure to take it.

Federman was entertaining several friends for the weekend and after a fine dinner they moved onto the porch for banana flummery and cake served by his pastry chef. He relaxed in his chair and enjoyed the pungent, peppery scents of allspice wafting through the air while drinking a short cup of strong coffee waiting for his dessert.

All the guests looked out on his magnificent gardens. They were populated with the most beautiful flowers, the most ornate plants and of course his collection of rare spice trees.

The gardens went on for what seemed to be miles and miles, displaying the precision and artistry of the best gardeners money could afford to employ. Federman never did things in halves. He would go out of his way to purchase the very best of whatever his garden needed.

He hung silver bells on his favorite plants so that as you would pass by, the bells would sound and draw your attention towards them. And when the wind picked up, the garden was a chorus of chimes, setting off tones and harmonies in symphonies composed by nature itself.

All things in the garden were organized according to Federman's design, though how far and wide it extended, not even the gardeners knew.

If you walked far enough you would come upon a secret forest where the tall trees almost would touch the skies. These trees protected very deep blue lakes; and beside of one of the crystal blue lakes, in a plum tree, nested a very special nightingale.

The common nightingale is a small brown bird with touches of red in its tail feathers. They are not particularly pretty birds; they are not the most colorful of birds.

That said; they are well known to sing exquisitely charming songs and long lamenting refrains. In spontaneous bursts, the nightingale can sing the most moving of songs that can bring those listening to them to tears.

Many people would come to the nightingale's forest just to hear him sing.

Sometimes the nightingale would fly around Federman's gardens singing his wondrous sounds and inspire poets to write their poetry, dancers to dance, painters to paint and sculptors to sculpt.

Musicians would go into the forest to search for the nightingale, making a journey with their minds as well as with their feet. They hoped to become inspired by the nightingale and compose new pieces of music.

As Federman drank his coffee on his veranda, a guest played one of his new musical compositions on a grand piano; the music was based upon the nightingale's song he heard that afternoon.

Surprising as it may sound, this was the first Federman had ever heard of the nightingale. He knew of many fine bird species that lived on his estates, but never did he hear of the nightingale or it's celebrated singing.

'*Incredible,*' the musician cried out, 'to have so much at your command and yet not know of the most wonderful of all birds lives on your estate; it's too much to comprehend!'

It was too much to comprehend, thought Federman. 'In the morning, will you take me to where the nightingale lives?' he asked the musician who readily agreed.

It seems that everyone knew about the nightingale but him, probably assuming that *of course* Federman must know about the bird; it was his home, his estate and thus, his bird. But no, unfortunately the bird had never revealed himself or his music to Federman.

They set up an early morning expedition into the spice forest to find the nightingale. Federman wanted to meet this famous bird and to hear for himself the melodious songs so many people had already heard.

As they traveled for miles and miles across the forests, they heard many different kinds of wildlife. Federman would hold his breath and listen very carefully. He would ask, 'Was that it? Is that the nightingale?'

And each time the musician would say, no, 'That was a goose,' or 'No, that was a rhinoceros,' or 'No, that was a flamingo,' or 'No, that was a giraffe,' or 'No, that was a frog, but if we are patient I think we shall hear him soon.'

By the late afternoon, Federman was getting discouraged when out of a small clearing the nightingale, sitting in his plum tree, began to sing his provincial songs.

The musician pointed to the small bird seated in the country green and told Federman to look and listen.

They listened for a very long while, mesmerized by the bird's beautiful melodies. To Federman the bird song sounded like happiness, like glass bells chiming. He was astounded that he had never heard this before.

As he listened he heard such majesty in the bird songs, such longing and spontaneity. The song moved around a varying theme, sung for this moment in time and for no other, like warming sunlight enjoyed only for an afternoon's mirth.

Federman was surprised by how unassuming the bird appeared. It was a pale brown, not the glorious bird he had dreamed up in his mind. He thought it would be a striking blue, like a peacock or dazzling red like a cardinal.

But no, the nightingale was a very common looking bird with an uncommon voice filled with truth.

The nightingale sang and sang his sweet, blushful songs. Tears welled up into Federman's eyes and rolled down his cheeks. Then the nightingale sang another sweet song and Federman's heart dissolved into the dim forests.

And there he sat, a weepy mess, listening with joy to the sounds that this dull colored bird could sing while wiping his eyes with his silken handkerchief.

Federman was so enthused that in gratitude, he removed his golden necklace and hung it around the nightingale's tiny, feathered neck.

'Thank you, but no. I could not possibly take such a beautiful object,' the nightingale said politely to Federman. 'I have already been abundantly compensated by your wonderful presence here. I have seen tears in your eyes. I could feel the tensions that so harmed and hampered you slowly unwind. This is an usually powerful response to my music, one I will always draw on for strength in my future, lonelier days.' And then he sang again, gloriously.

Federman invited him to stay at his house in the spice forest and entertain his guests. He promised him that he would have several assistants to help him, cook for him and take care of his daily needs.

The nightingale considered this for a long while and once he was assured that he would not be Federman's pet, but rather a free bird that could come and go as it pleased, the nightingale agreed.

A music room was built for the nightingale and the musician to perform. And a beautiful bird's nest was built in the nearby nutmeg bushes by a famed professor of ornithology from Oxford, to ensure that the nightingale would be comfortable in Federman's home.

Sometimes, he would stay with Federman for weeks at a time. He would perform nightly for the many famous guests Federman would entertain. And when he was not performing for an audience, he would sing accompaniment with the musician as he wrote his new compositions.

During these times with the musician, the nightingale learned a great many things about music. The nightingale was never trained as a musician, but rather as a poet he tried to intone what he felt at that moment.

Federman was so pleased with the nightingale he asked it to perform several times a day. He would listen to his anthems with an open heart. Federman adored the wonderful songs and tears would run down his cheeks, proclaiming his utmost joy.

When the nightingale missed his home, he would pick up and fly past the near meadows, over the still streams and over the rare spice trees, through the majestic gardens and find his way back to his plum tree. He would relax in the comfort in his own nest among his own things and simply be among his family.

On one of the nightingale's trips home, Federman received a large package labeled *The Nightingale*. It was sent to him from his friend, Denby.

Thinking it was yet another portrait of his now famous nightingale; Federman opened the box halfheartedly. However much to his delight, he found a stunning gift inside.

It was a replica of the nightingale cast in gold and encrusted with diamonds, rubies and sapphires. But instead of a lifeless sculpture, this was a golden windup animatronic. It was made of gears, motors and gyros, and when the clockwork bird was wound up with a small cut-glass key, it could sing one of the nightingale's songs.

As it would sing, the bird's head would look around the room. And at times it would waggle its glittering golden tail.

Federman owned many fine things and displayed them around his luxurious home, but he was quite surprised to hold such a treasure in his hands.

Around the artificial nightingale was wrapped a golden ribbon that read, 'Merry Christmas, from your dear friend Denby.'

Denby was always one to try to outdo his friends, and Federman always looked on him with suspicion, however, this gift was a heartening delight to Federman's eyes.

He wound up the bejeweled clockwork nightingale and it played its song. 'It sounds like my nightingale,' cried Federman.

Even though it was unlike the wonderful living nightingale that would sing whatever came to its mind, this clockwork nightingale played the same song over and over again.

Federman fell in love with his new nightingale very quickly. When it wound down he would wind it back up again.

He would take the clockwork bird with him around his house. He would bring it to him during his meetings with clients and friends. He would bring it to his meals. He would even bring the golden bird with him when he exercised.

It was not uncommon to see him carry the bird with him throughout the whole day from the moment he awoke to the moment his head touched the pillows for sleep.

The clockwork bird would sing the same song to Federman; and Federman was very happy.

When the nightingale returned to Federman's house in the spice forests, he was just in time to witness a performance. The clockwork nightingale was to sing with the musician for a large group of Federman's friends.

Federman was very happy to show the nightingale his new nightingale. 'Aren't you impressed?' Federman asked enthusiastically.

The nightingale was impressed, 'What a lovely thing you have here.' He bowed to the clockwork nightingale and took a seat next to Federman. The musician began to play a black grand piano and slowly the clockwork nightingale began to sing.

As the artificial bird sang, the musician played soft sweeping background sonatas. Their timing was perfect and the breath-taken audience was visibly moved. When they finished their concert everyone rose to their feet to applaud their brilliant music.

Federman was filled with joy and looked meaningfully down towards his friend, the real nightingale who was equally overjoyed by the music. 'So tell me what did you think?' asked Federman.

'I thought it was sublime,' said the nightingale. 'I cannot enjoy my own songs in the same way that one does when they are listening to me sing. I can only hear them as emotions that come to my mind that I sing. So this was a rare treat indeed. I dearly thank you Federman.'

The musician called out to the real nightingale, 'Would you join us on stage for a duet?' The audience thought this was a fine idea and began to applaud. Embarrassed, the nightingale joined the clockwork nightingale on top of the shining piano. They both bowed to the musician and then bowed towards the audience.

The musician played slowly in sweeping background sonatas. The clockwork nightingale sang its song again. As soon as the real nightingale found his footing within the song he joined in, singing a beautiful solo that fit the song perfectly, taking the music into a new direction with a new feeling.

This took everyone by surprise. The audience started to shift in their seats, some started to shuffle and feel uncomfortable. And others began to whisper to their neighbors. Others talked outright, saying to anyone who might listen that they were not enjoying the real nightingale as much as the artificial one.

They had expected to hear the same song that they had just heard and were not sure that they liked what they were listening to. It was too new, too pretentious, and they had expected to re-experience the same feeling that they had just felt.

When the musician finished playing, their song over, he applauded the clockwork nightingale, much to the approval of the audience. He shook the wing of the real nightingale and politely said, 'Next time we shall practice a bit more before I put you on the spot like this again.'

The nightingale said thank you and looked out to the audience. They were all glaring at him as if he had done something very wrong. Even

Federman did not look pleased.

The nightingale bowed to the musician, he bowed to the golden, jewel-encrusted nightingale, and then he flew into the right hand of Federman and bowed to him. He then flitted up into the air and flew off over the nutmeg bushes and then faded off into the west.

Federman was saddened to see his friend leave so quickly. The audience began to murmur. They began to talk badly about the nightingale. They were glad it had left.

Some began to say how plain and unbecoming the bird was, and not nearly as fine as the golden bird that was still here seated politely on the piano.

The musician spoke to the audience, 'Ladies and gentlemen, no one ever really knows what to expect from a real nightingale. But with this artificial bird everything goes according to plan. If we had to have one bird, I think we are better off with this mechanical bird. We can always be sure that nothing is left to chance, that there is no spontaneity with our fine clockwork nightingale.'

Federman readily agreed with the musician and asked on behalf of the audience, 'Would you play your song once again, if you please?'

The clockwork nightingale remained with Federman and sat on a cushion near his desk. When Federman would need to hear the song again, he would wind it up and let it play.

Some days Federman would let it play all day long. And it was not unusual to hear the golden bird sing its song one hundred and forty four times.

Federman was very pleased that so many people enjoyed listening to his clockwork bird. It made him feel very special, even more special than even his wealth made him feel.

Somehow this song made him seem complete, even though it was a lesser feeling than what he enjoyed when in the company of the real nightingale.

But with a groan he realized that with his artificial nightingale he felt almost happy, almost nearly complete.

And one night when Federman was feeling almost nearly complete, a strange clicking sound came from his clockwork nightingale. It sprung, sputtered and clicked. It gave a loud *Clack* and then it stopped singing altogether.

With quiet breath the clockwork bird was broken. Federman was in a forlorn panic; he never imagined that it could breakdown.

He called in an expert to have a look at the inoperative nightingale, but the expert was not encouraged from his findings. The expert concluded that its clockwork mechanism had worn down from over-use, wear and tear, and lack of regular maintenance.

There was nothing that could be done to fix the bird, as there was no real way to replace the pieces that it needed without causing further damage. It was a one-of-a-kind object and being one-of-a-kind, it could not be easily repaired.

The expert even warned that if they tried to repair it, there would be no guarantee that it would be able to play the song it had always sung in the same way that it did before.

The expert fixed the golden nightingale just enough that Federman could play it once a year. Federman decided that he would choose that day to be Christmas.

Each Christmas, Federman invited his friends to come and listen to the clockwork bird sing its song once and only once. Then it was whisked away and placed behind a glass window, on its silken cushion displayed in Federman's bedroom. There, he could enjoy looking at the bird even though it could no longer sing.

For five years this ritual took place, and each year when the clockwork bird would sing, rather than making Federman happy it made him feel very, very sad.

His sadness would fill the room making it heavy and wearisome on his guests. Over the years, fewer and fewer people accepted his Christmas invitation, and this year only the musician decided to come.

The musician wrote a very popular song from the clockwork nightingale's melody. It was a bestselling album around the world and soon the whole planet was singing the nightingale's song, so he always felt indebted to Federman.

When the musician arrived at night to Federman's home in the spice forests, Federman's assistant told the musician that the Christmas celebration would not be held. Federman was very ill and was near death.

The musician was very upset to hear this and demanded to see him.

Federman lay cold and pale on his magnificent bed. Moonlight shone on Federman and his artificial bird. When the musician saw him laid out, he thought Federman was dead.

Federman was not dead but very sad to see the musician. He could hardly breathe, feeling as if a great weight was sitting on his chest.

When Federman looked properly, he saw that it was Death sitting right on him, right on his chest, poking at his heart with a bony finger.

Federman saw the blackness that overshadowed him in Death's limpid eyes.

From his death cloak, Death drew out a magical flute from a hidden pocket. It played a cankerous sound from its cacophony flute. And magically, a set of ghostly velvet curtains emerged from beyond.

From behind the curtain materialized hundreds of mournful faces of people from Federman's past.

Some were horrifying and frightening, while others were gentle, caring and compassionate. Death sat on Federman's heart and laughed.

These faces made him recall his past deeds and how well or poorly, he treated the people in his life.

'Do you remember me?' the ghostly faces would ask Federman, as other faces would simply stare through him in a state of pure serenity. Other faces would lean into Federman and tell him phantasms that made cold sweat run down his forehead.

'Sing, sing to me,' Federman cried out to the broken nightingale. But the broken bird could not sing. It only looked at him with its starry ruby eyes, motionless.

'Please sing, please just a little bit of music!' Federman called out. But the musician stood silent not knowing what he should do. Through his great hollow eyes, Death looked out into infinity and it was quiet, deathly quiet.

Suddenly, a sweet burst of sound filled Federman's bedroom. Sitting on the branches of an allspice tree, the little live nightingale from Federman's past began to sing.

In the nighttime the brown bird appeared to be jet black and Federman feared it was another ghost asking him to revisit his troubling memories.

Federman had always felt horrible at how the nightingale left his home. He wanted the nightingale to feel admiration in the same way that he admired the nightingale.

The musician spoke, 'Please little bird, come and sing for poor Federman. He has never needed your comfort more than at this moment.'

As he sang, the phantasms grew pallid and slowly began to fade. The colors of life began to come back to Federman's face and slowly he sat upright.

Death perilously listened to the beautiful song being sung by the nightingale. And when the nightingale caught Death's hallow eyes, Death was entertained. 'Please little nightingale continue with your delightful song!'

The little nightingale agreed, 'Only if you promise to release Federman. He is my friend and this is not his time to go. You know this as well as I do, and we should like to spend a bit more time with him on this Christmas day.'

As an ornamental vision, Death stood up and unseated his pale, ghastly form from Federman's chest and moved to a silken cushion where he sat down with crossed legs.

The nightingale sang a song of a lovely white garden where white roses grow among nutmeg bushes. He sang of green grasses and lush trees filled with plums. He sang of friends long since passed on whom we still miss to this day. And finally he sang of the hopeful, silver days still in front of us in which we can do anything, change anything and make good the mistakes that we are obligated to mend.

The nightingale continued to sing and sing, charming Death with faded anthems to make it long for its home; and in a cold gray mist Death apperated into the hereafter of neverwhere.

When it was clear that Death had gone away Federman was ecstatic in his appreciation. 'Thank you, thank you, thank you!' Federman cried out while the musician stood in the far corner and applauded the most amazing piece of music he ever heard.

'Little nightingale, you came back to me in my hour of need. I treated you so badly and yet you have magically sent Death gleefully away from my heart. How can I ever repay you for such a wonderful gift?' asked Federman.

'You need not repay me anything, my dear Federman,' said the nightingale. 'We have always been close, ever since you wept in the secret forest. This is more wonderful to me than any amount of gold could ever be. Now lie back and rest yourself while I sing you back to proper health.'

He sang until Federman fell into a sound, inspirational sleep. In the morning, the nightingale was still singing and Federman woke up a new man.

'Please my friend, would you stay with me always,' asked Federman. 'Sing to me only when you wish, come and go as you would like. I will even break the clockwork bird into a thousand pieces if it would please you. Just please stay.'

'Oh, no please that would be terrible waste. The clockwork bird did its best; keep it near you as a memory of today. I will stay in my forest and come and visit you often. I will come to your window and sing to you. I will sing songs of life, songs of the poor, and I will sing songs of those who need help more than you just received. I will sing to you of farmers and fishermen and factory workers. I will sing of bankers and lawyers, and I will sing to you of the sick and the brave doctors who attend to them. I make sure that you will never be without song again. I promise you this. For I love your heart more than I do your wealth, which may be a silly thing to say. But I am a bird and birds care little for things they cannot eat or what they cannot sing about. Never fear, I will come and sing to you if you will promise me one little thing.'

'All that I have is yours,' cried Federman, who stood up from his bed and bowed a deep bow to the nightingale. The nightingale bowed back to him and said, 'tell no one about my visits,' and he flew away.

A Useful List

RAYMOND FEDERMAN

In language, "fuck" falls into many grammatical categories.

It can be used as a verb, both transitive: "John fucked Mary"

and intransitive: "Mary was fucked by John"

It can be an action verb: "John really gives a fuck"

a passive verb: "Mary really doesn't give a fuck"

an adverb: "Mary is fucking interested in John"

or as a noun: "Mary is a terrific fuck"

It can also be used as an adjective: "Mary is fucking beautiful"

or an interjection: "Fuck! I'm late for my date with Mary"

It can even be used as a conjunction: "Mary is easy, fuck she's also stupid"

As you can see, there are very few words with the overall versatility of the word "fuck".

Aside from its sexual connotations, this incredible word can be used to describe many situations :

1. Greetings: "How the fuck are ya?"

2. Fraud: "I got fucked by the car dealer."

3. Resignation: "Oh, fuck it!"

4. Trouble: "I guess I'm fucked now."

5. Aggression: "FUCK YOU!"

6. Disgust: "Fuck me."

7. Confusion:"What the fuck . . . ?"

8. Difficulty: "I don't understand this fucking business!"

9. Despair: "Fucked again . . ."

10. Pleasure: "I fucking couldn't be happier."

11. Displeasure: "What the fuck is going on here?"

12. Lost: "Where the fuck are we."

13. Disbelief: "UNFUCKINGBELIEVABLE!"

14. Retaliation: "Up your fucking ass!"

15. Denial: "I didn't fucking do it."

16. Perplexity: "I know fuck all about it."

17. Apathy: "Who really gives a fuck, anyhow?"

18. Suspicion: "Who the fuck are you?"

19. Panic: "Let's get the fuck out of here."

20. Directions: "Fuck off."

21. Disbelief: "How the fuck did you do that?"

It can be used . . .

in an anatomical description — "He's a fucking asshole."

to tell time —"It's five fucking thirty."

in business — "How did I wind up with this fucking job?"

maternal — "Motherfucker."

political —"Fuck George W. Bush!"

It has also been used by many notable people throughout history:

Mayor of Hiroshima —"What the fuck was that?"

General Custer — "Where did all these fucking Indians come from?"

Captain of the Titanic —"Where the fuck is all this water coming from?"

John Lennon —"That's not a real fucking gun."

Richard Nixon — "Who's gonna fucking find out?"

Anne Boleyn — "Heads are going to fucking roll."

Willard Scott — "It's someone's 100th fucking birthday today!"

Albert Einstein — "Any fucking idiot could understand that."

Picasso — "It does so fucking look like her!"

Pythagoras —"How the fuck did you work that out?"

Michael Angelo —"You want what on the fucking ceiling?"

Walt Disney — "Fuck a duck."

Edmund Hilary — "Why? Because its fucking there!"

Joan of Arc —"I don't suppose its gonna fucking rain?"

Donald Trump — "She wants how much fucking money?!?!?"

Orville Reddenbacher — "Look! Almost every fucking kernel popped!"

Raymond Federman — "Oh! Look a fucking flying saucer!"

An "Intense Concentration of Self":
Publishing Raymond Federman

TED PELTON

I met Raymond Federman as a student at State University of New York at Buffalo in 1983. In years to come, I would publish four of his books with the nonprofit small press I founded and directed, Starcherone Books: *The Voice in the Closet* (2001), *My Body in Nine Parts* (2005), *Twilight of the Bums* (2008), and *Shhh: The Story of a Childhood* (2010), Raymond's final novel. Despite being a micropublisher with no paid staff, rarely ordering first runs of more than 1,000 copies, Starcherone became one of the two publishers (the other being FC2/University of Alabama Press) mainly responsible for printing and disseminating Federman's work in the US during the first decade of the new millennium. I am very proud of this. I group my reflections about the life and art of one of the most remarkable authors of our time around three of these books, for what they say about Raymond's importance as a literary figure and for what he and his books meant to me personally, although about both of these subjects there is much more to say than I've been able to manage here.

The Voice in the Closet (2001)

In 1983, in the first undergraduate fiction workshop class I ever had with Raymond, I won the end-of-semester class vote for what Raymond called, in typically charming megalomaniac fashion, "The Federman Prize," and he awarded me a signed copy of the initial edition of *The Voice in the*

Closet / La voix dans les cabinet de débarras, produced by Coda Press in Madison, Wisconsin, in 1979. This edition was roughly eight inches square, printed in dos à dos (from the French for "back-to-back"), the book split in half between French and English versions, and in the center a text by Maurice Roche, *Echoes*. Roughly twenty years later, in 2001, Raymond asked me to do the reprint edition. The book had long been out of print, but it had attracted two decades of critical attention; there is likely more critical commentary specifically about *The Voice in the Closet* than about any single Federman text. The book had generated attention from artists as well, including a series of mixed media collages by Terri Katz Kasimov. Images of two of these works are featured on the front and back of Starcherone's edition, also printed dos à dos for the French and English editions. Federman authored both texts, as always with his works in French and English; he often said he did not *translate* his own works, but *transacted* them from French to English or vice-versa, working in two languages in which he was completely fluent. I had founded Starcherone in 2000 by publishing my own story collection, *Endorsed by Jack Chapeau*. Raymond admired the production of this book and offered *The Voice in the Closet* to me, saying he knew where grant money could be found to finance it, through a foundation that promoted French culture in the US. *The Voice in the Closet* became Starcherone's second title, and was sized small, five-and-a-half inches square, with a white cover, like many of the books I had seen in French bookstores during my first visit a few months earlier.

While the most difficult to read of Federman's books, *The Voice in the Closet* is to me the central book in his oeuvre. *Voice* issues directly from the life-changing experience of Federman at age 14, and his role in the most horrifying calamity of the 20th century. What is known by the single, inadequate word Holocaust was visited upon young Raymond starting with the *Vel' d'Hiv Rafle*, the round-up of Parisian Jews by French police under Nazi occupation and direction, on July 16, 1942. Likely alerted by voices in the street as to what was about to occur, then hearing the police at the door of the family's apartment, Raymond's mother Marguerite pushed him into an upstairs broom closet, where Raymond escaped detection and spent the whole of a harrowing day and night before finally venturing out at dawn the next day. He would never again see his parents or his two sisters, Jacqueline and Sarah. These four were deported to Auschwitz while Raymond, the middle child, survived. Federman represents his family in *The Voice in the Closet* and in books throughout his canon with the marks of absence, "X-X-X-X."

As Gérard Bucher has noted, *The Voice in the Closet* refuses to tell this story. Instead of clear narrative, the reader finds a dense, claustrophobic, unpunctuated text of twenty pages without a capital letter to begin, a period at the end, or even page numbers to mark where one is as one reads it, as if these pages act as a sample out of a continuous voice, never-ending voice, a voice angry, allusive, and convoluted, compressing Federman's experience from 1942 with the narrative present and simultaneously creating a kind of dialogue between the two experiences. The book's first-person narration very much focuses on a dynamic inherent in memoir, or fictions that imitate memoir: the doubling of voice, where the consciousness of the actor at the time who lived the event is being told by the writer/teller in the current moment of the tale, a separate, older consciousness, relating and reflecting on the earlier time. Susan Rubin Suleiman has noted that Federman's work customarily is not discussed in accounts of survivor literature because Federman's texts don't conceive of their primary occupation as witnessing. Other writers of Holocaust literature, for instance Primo Levi, set out to document and interrogate historical evil, but "the problem as Federman sees it is how to tell the story. How to give form and shape to an experience that was in its essence chaotic and incomprehensible" (Suleiman 217). As the boy-voice from the closet confronts the adult-voice who is purporting to put the experience into words, he condemns the act of representation:

> no I cannot resign myself to being the inventory
> of his miscalculations I am not ready for my
> summation nor do I wish to participate any

> longer willy nilly in the fiasco of his fabrication
> failed account of my survival abandoned in the
> dark with nothing but my own excrement to play
> with now neatly packaged on the roof to become
> the symbol of my origin in the wordshit of his
> fabulation (Federman, *Voice*)

To tell a story of one's past is to choose details, use language to give narrative form, create symbols, and engage in other operations here railed at as "fabrication," involving "miscalculations," the entirety becoming a "fiasco." There can be no representing such trauma coherently in words, the book contends. The boy's humiliation is symbolized in his having to defecate in this dark, closed space, finding some paper with which to package his filth, keeping the parcel with him in the closet through the long night, and finally in the next day's first light pushing the package up through a skylight to the roof. Yet symbolism is also "wordshit." Federman refuses to tell a thing without the voice of the experience denouncing its representation.

So it always remained, in essence, until the end of Federman's writing career. Refusing any simple telling of the stories of his life while returning to them, again and again, compulsively, he called all of his seemingly autobiographical texts "fiction." In retelling stories in various books, Federman frequently admitted having made up this or that detail. Often, the stories were told with comedic spin, but that never made the stakes of Federman's narrative ethics any less serious. Fiction, for Federman, meant folding the most desperate, powerful realities into deliberately invented constructions, mutating any suggestion of a straightforward tale with wild machinations of typography, long digressions on seemingly trivial details, metafictional interruptions, and flights of invented fancy. Offered a substantial advance for his first book, *Double or Nothing*, by Little, Brown, and Co., in 1967, but only if he "cut all the trivia," including long digressions about cooking noodles in order to live cheaply while writing the book, Federman rebelled. "I went upstairs and locked myself in the attic. From 1967 to 1970 I demolished the novel. I created this screen of words. But I realize it was more than that. I was learning to write a novel by dismantling, by deconstructing" (Interview).[1]

My Body in Nine Parts (2005)

Whereas the other books published by Starcherone appeared elsewhere first, whether as reprints or as English "transactions" of works first published in France, Federman's second project with Starcherone was original with us. In *My Body in Nine Parts*, Federman's trademark self-reflexiveness finds a new vehicle. Federman's stepson, Steve Murez, a photographer based in Paris, took a series of nine black and white photographs of Raymond's body, each lit strategically to create play of lights and darks, the author's literal corpus against rich, black backgrounds in chapters titled "My Hair," "My Nose," "My Toes," "My Hands," "My Scars," etc. The project is playfully conceived; for "My Sexual Organ," the photo features the author's naked waist and upper legs with hands strategically cupped to conceal the eponymous body part. But even as there is whimsy in the text, such as in the chapter where Federman, one by one, in the act of clipping his toenails, names and imparts personalities to each of his toes, there is also vulnerability. Federman was 78 when the book was published. The photos show white hair and deeply creased, withering flesh: we read Federman's body as another kind of text.

Though he called this, too, fiction, as Raymond aged he also edged closer to allowing his stories a witnessing function. The "voice" had railed against the author in him in 1979 and earlier, when he began writing in the late 1960s, and Federman had responded by using words to "screen," to problematize, complicate, and interrogate. But on the opening page of *My Body in Nine Parts*, while not witnessing in the largest historical sense,

---

1 A longer version of this quote, with visuals of Federman's manuscript and the finished "concrete" pages of *Double or Nothing* can be seen in my article, "How, and How Not, to be a Published Novelist," in *Federman's Fictions,* ed. Jeffrey di Leo.

of atrocities, there is to be seen something new in Raymond's writing, even as he claimed only to be writing about his hair — quiet commemoration of a mother who would later save him, fighting everyday battles in a hard life, for her son:

> So it was my mother who cared for my hair. When I was a little boy she would wash it for me, comb it and part it to one side. The left side, I think. But I'm not sure anymore. I would have to look at an old childhood photo of me to determine which side my mother parted my hair. In any case, it was my mother who cared for my hair. She also searched in it for lice when I caught some from the other boys at school. She would snare them out with a special comb. A lice comb, with very short and tight teeth so the lice could be pulled out. Then she would crush them right on the comb with the nail of her thumb. We couldn't afford to buy the expensive powder and cream you apply to your hair to kill lice. So my mother killed the lice herself. With her nails. (12)

The unsentimentalized portrait of a mother crushing lice nevertheless has a powerful, moving quality to it. The blood cannot but signal a violence to come of which she was yet unaware but the reader is not. Marguerite, whose act began Raymond's journey to survival, appears in passing several more times in *My Body in Nine Parts*, for instance in "My Nose," which explicitly references this bodily marker of prejudice and oppression: "Okay, I'll admit I have a big nose . . . Even my mother's love couldn't do anything about that. It was pre-determined, pre-designed by centuries and centuries of insults and humiliations that my ancestors had to endure because of their noses." (34).

By the time of the publication of *My Body in Nine Parts*, Raymond had moved from Buffalo, where we had met and where we had arranged for me to publish *The Voice in the Closet*, to San Diego, having retired from teaching at the University at Buffalo. Raymond and his wife Erica had lived in Buffalo some 35 years. He had something of a legendary status in Buffalo, but he was at the same time not necessarily popular among his departmental colleagues, who grew weary of Federman's incessant self-regard. The complaints resulted both from long acquaintance with someone who every day might find new ways of talking about, and praising, himself and from the kinds of slights and frictions common among academics. That is to say, while such responses weren't necessarily generous, they also weren't entirely unwarranted. Raymond was, after all, a man capable of writing a book about different parts of his body, and routinely gave characters names like "Moinous" ("me-we" in French), "Namredef" (Federman, backwards).[2] Professionally, he might, as he once did for me while I was an undergrad, write a recommendation letter in which he credited himself for a student's achievements. Even his own self-absorption was a trait of which he seemed proud and tickled to regard in himself. He loved telling stories about himself, and loved that he loved telling stories about himself.

I knew Ray for many years, and there was a period of some years during which his solipsism became intolerable to me as well. Then, at some point, I changed my perspective on this, and toward Ray. This change for me came with the understanding, or theory, since I could not say whether or not it was actually true but only that it seemed this way to me, that Raymond was so self-involved, to the point of annoyance or worse, because there was a part of him that was permanently arrested as the 14 year-old boy who spent that day and night in a closet, losing his family to an unseen but violent fate, and then emerged to somehow survive as a Jewish teenager in occupied France — and not just survive but

---

2 Jeffrey di Leo usefully puts this self-attention of Federman into literary context: "Characters with names such as Moinous, Namredef, French, Boris, Cousin, Ace, Tutu, Homme de Plume, Penman, Dartagnan, Ramon Hombre Della Pluma, the Old Man, Faterman, Federmann, Féderman and F emerge in his narrative space and taunt one to read them as fictional abstractions of the author" (di Leo 8).

succeed, coming to America, parachuting out of planes as a US solider during the Korean War, earning a PhD and finding a beautiful bride in California, becoming at last a university professor and world-renowned novelist. The "intense concentration of self"[3] necessary to have embarked upon and sustain his way through that odyssey continued to project itself large, and yielded a residue of conceit that was hardly tolerable to a great many. Those who knew and loved him accepted this is how he was. In the late 1990s, when I had returned to Buffalo, this time as a faculty member at a small college in the city, I was visiting Raymond's house when he said to me, "Oh, wait, let me read you something." We had only just entered the house through a back door and stopped in the kitchen, and without pausing he picked up a book that had just arrived from Turkey, his essays, *The Supreme Indecision of the Writer*, and we sat down at the kitchen table and he began reading from it to me. A few minutes later, his wife Erica came in the door and frowned, "Oh, Federman . . ." It was a scene she had no doubt witnessed many times before.

"Don't worry," I said to Erica. "I know him." I had come to expect and accept this in him.

In 2008, I helped organize an 80th birthday tribute to Raymond in Buffalo, and he and Erica flew back from San Diego for a day of panels on Ray's work, an art show featuring works by artists inspired by Ray, and an evening tribute reading, which I hosted. I had gotten married to my wife Susan around this time and when Raymond came to the microphone to do the final reading of the evening, of his own work, he began with a surprise. "As many of you know," he said, "Ted recently married the beautiful Susan Moynihan." He paused for polite applause in the room, before holding up a package. "I brought with me a wedding gift for the

---

3 cf. *Moby-Dick*, Ch. 93, "The Castaway." This phrase in Melville's novel refers to the black boy, Pip, left alone bobbing on the surface of the ocean after falling overboard during a whale chase, who thereafter suffers a kind of wise madness. I don't mean to imply Raymond lost his mind, but that his intense, comedic, performative self had the ability to make one forget that he was a trauma victim. Like Pip's, Raymond's experience was visited on a young man perceived as an animal by the dominant political structure and powerfully abandoned in an experience of exaggerated solitude. "The immense concentration of self in the middle of such a heartless immensity," writes Melville, "my God! who can tell it?"

bride and groom." I was touched by this, because it seemed a different side of Raymond than I had seen before. Not that Raymond wasn't generous; he just was not the type to draw attention away from himself in a public performance. A moment later, as I opened the gift, it was all explained. It was a bronze casting of Federman's nose, mounted on marble.

Susan and I still cherish this gift.

Shhh: The Story of a Childhood (2010)

Federman's body of work shares some outward formal resemblances with that of another writer from a French-speaking background, Jack Kerouac. Each of these two experimental novelists used events in their lives as the nearly exclusive subject matter of their books, constantly and compulsively returning to moments in their respective lives and retelling the stories, and also continually altering the tales and how they are constructed. In mid-career, Kerouac began openly regarding all his books as part of one long book, "The Duluoz Legend," and Federman describes his own work in such a way in *Shhh*, his final novel, published by Starcherone the year after he died: "what I'm in the process of telling is the final chapter of the great story I've been muttering and scribbling for the past forty years" (*Shhh* 25).

Federman had been moving this way, into something like memoir, into a recounting of his life to fill in the empty spaces, in his late books before *Shhh*. In *Return to Manure* (2006), for instance, Federman adopts traits that will also feature in *Shhh*. The narrator for each book is "Federman," and unlike in many another book, this narrator is not retelling someone else's story, as had Namredef, Moinous, or many other Federman stand-ins of previous books. Instead, each book begins with the apparent task of telling a part of the author's early life in France, from which Federman emigrated at age 19. In 1942, following his closet episode, Federman made his way into the countryside in southwest France and found work on a farm near the town of Montflanquin, where he stayed until the war ended. In *Return to Manure*, Federman tells of a trip made by car with his wife Erica in search of this farm, recollecting the miserable life he'd had there as a fugitive in his own country. In *Shhh*, Federman seeks to tell the story of his childhood, prior to the moment of being put in the closet. And, in each book, Federman employs a device that disrupts the telling of these stories. Never fully relying upon chronological narrative, constantly diverting from episodes and stories to tell other stories, add poems, or create new fictions, the frequently appearing disruptions reflect presumed readerly reactions, incorporating frustration with the digressions, deflating serious moments with exasperated interjections, or urging the narrator to return to the central story, as for instance in this moment from *Manure*: "Yes, Federman, you are repeating yourself. Get on with the story of the farm. Did you find it or what?" (70).

But let us never mistake these novels, these fictions, for autobiography, as Federman (or we should say, "Federman,"), tells us in a reply to one of these readerly disruptions in *Shhh*:

> *What I'm writing is pure fiction, because, you see, I've forgotten my entire childhood. It has been blocked in me. So I've to invent it, reconstruct it. And besides, as Mallarmé once put it,* All that is written is fictive.
>
> *The blocks of words that I'm accumulating on the pages are like the bricks that are used to build a house. I'm in the process of building my childhood with these blocks of words.* (19)

More than most of Raymond's books, *Shhh* tempts us through its resemblance to a work of Holocaust survivor testimony to think of it as something other than fiction, but this passage gives us at least three reasons that it would be a mistake for us to do so. First, Federman tells us, he doesn't remember anything from his childhood. I don't believe that this is said glibly or in exaggeration. We cannot ignore that most things known of Federman's biography, even the closet episode itself, are drawn from information gleaned from his books, all of which have insistently urged us to read them as fictions. This is not by any means to suggest anything so crass as that Raymond's family did not die at Auschwitz; we may, for the record, find official documentation of this.[4] And we should also be cognizant that at the most dangerous extreme of replacing the realities of the Holocaust with questions about authenticity are the anti-Semitic lies of Holocaust denial. But Federman does insist on the role that story plays even in authentic events, and allows that his memories have long since been supplanted by the stories he's told about them between the ages of 14 and of the writing of *Shhh*, nearing 80. "I do not think that my life and history are the sources of my fiction, but that in fact my fiction is what invents my life and history," Federman was quoted as having written, in the obituary that appeared in *The New York Times* after his death. "In other words, the stories I write are my life" (Fox). Second, Mallarmé's claim ups the ante: *all that is written is fictive.* Writing about experience cannot but select, re-form, edit, (mis)represent, and all manner of other potential distortions that we remember from the "voice in the closet" and its fear of "fabrication" and "wordshit." Yet what the novelist is here talking about in terms of his art is not cast merely as loss or abdication. This is a third way in which *Shhh* is distinct from autobiography. Federman adhered to a style for many decades that emphasized the block paragraph. His architectural metaphor, where blocks of prose become bricks building the structure of his fiction, describes a process of construction toward the making of something new. Invention is not betrayal or vacating of the truth, as might be inferred from the Mallarmé formulation, but can result in its own truth, and truth that is moving, powerful, honest, and authentic — testimony of its own kind.

I am writing at length on *Shhh* because I believe it to be a neglected book in Federman's canon. There are a great many moments in this work that have haunted me since I first read it as a digital file Raymond emailed

---

4 Cf., for instance, documents in *Federman A to X-X-X-X: A Recyclopedia Narrative* (ed. McCaffery, *et al*).

me, that have both emotional power and hard-won wisdom while still retaining the playfulness Raymond always brought to his pages. One such instance in *Shhh* is in the story of the young school friend, Robert Laurent. Like so many stories in Federman books, this one begins in digression. The narrator is telling us about his father, Simon, who was a romantic and a Communist, but also a failed provider, losing much of the money that could have supported his family at the racetrack and at cards. The card game favored in those days was *belote*, and Raymond recalls waiting frequently as a boy "in a cloud of cigarette smoke in the back of the Métropole café" for his father to finish one last hand with his friends (99). Young Raymond would then play the game himself with Robert Laurent, who was also known as Bébert. Federman the writer then gives the story a hook.

> I don't know why, but I have never forgotten Robert Laurent's name. Not so with the names of the other boys in school. They have all been forgotten. But not his name.
>
> Oh, I know now why I haven't forgotten Robert Laurent's name. (100)

Only he doesn't yet tell us — not at first. First come digressions about swimming. Bébert and Raymond had both been members of a swimming club, even though Raymond's Uncle Leon had told him to avoid this friend because his parents were anti-Semites. Nevertheless, with Bébert as companion at meetings of *L'Amicale de Natation*, Raymond became a strong swimmer. Later, Raymond would swim in high school in Detroit, and then at Wayne University, almost (he tells us) qualifying for the 1948 Olympics. But this is not why he never forgot the name of his friend.

> It's because the day I went to school for the first time with the yellow star on my clothes, that day, when I asked Bébert if we were going to play

belote after school, he said, No, my parents told
me I can't play with you any more . . .

I suppose, that's a good enough reason for not
having forgotten his name. But there is a better
one also. (103)

The narrator now tells us of a time some fifteen years later when, after
Raymond has been living in the US for ten years, he returns to France.
While sitting in a café in Montparnasse, who should he see but Robert
Laurent. Instead of the two avoiding each other, Robert greets Raymond.
Of course, he heard about what happened to Raymond's family in the war,
and he extends his condolences. Then he launches into the story of what
he's been doing for all this time. In his early 20s, Robert relates, he
became the French champion in swimming the butterfly. By this point in
his own life, Raymond has had a great many experiences himself. In
America, he enlisted in the Army and fought in Korea, serving as a
paratrooper in the 82nd Airborne. Returning to the US, he went to
Columbia University on the GI Bill. He has become a writer, though he has
not yet published a book, and he is studying French literature at UCLA.
But he doesn't say this to Laurent, listening instead as the Frenchman
describes the banalities of his current life, the decent wages at his factory
job, making toothpaste tubes, and his desire to find himself a nice *gonzesse*
("broad") to marry.

Save the smile he gets from this reminder of French slang, Raymond is
indifferent to all of what Laurent says. Nevertheless, to his surprise, when
Laurent gets up to leave he invites Raymond to dinner with his family, an
invitation that Raymond is too startled not to accept.

"Let's just say," Federman writes, "I was curious to see how anti-
Semites lived now" (105).

A week later, he goes to chez Laurent and greets Robert's family, who
receive him like old friends. His father asks Raymond about his work and
his writing, and what it's like to live in America. Nobody mentions the
war. Robert's mother shuttles back and forth between the dining room

and the kitchen, readying things for the meal and then arrives at the table with a large *soupière*, announcing dinner is served. Raymond reaches down for his spoon and for the first time notices initials engraved on it, "M.F."

> And suddenly I realize that I am holding in my hand a silver spoon that belonged to my mother. Yes, my mother had a set of silverware with her initials. I believe it was a gift from her sisters when she got married. We never used that silverware. It stayed in the drawer of the buffet wrapped in newspaper. Whenever my mother complained to my father that she didn't have enough money to buy food, my father would threaten to take the silverware to a pawn shop.

This is a powerful climax to the story of a Holocaust survivor's return to post-war Europe, where trauma lies in wait to meet the subject at every turn, even in moments of seeming reconciliation. Yet this is not where Federman ends the story of Robert Laurent. In the next prose block we are back in the present of the writing of *Shhh*, and the phone is ringing in the author's house in San Diego. He picks it up and begins talking with his adult daughter, Simone. She lives on the opposite coast from Raymond, in New York. She asks him about his writing and Raymond tells her about the episode he's just written, about Robert Laurent, and asks her if she would like to hear it.

When he has finished, Simone reacts skeptically: "It's not true. I never heard that story before" (108). She rejects every part of it. She doesn't believe Marguerite Federman nor her family were wealthy enough to have owned or purchased a set of silver, and she reminds her father that his aunts were too stingy to have given such a valuable present. She also finds the discovery scene too melodramatic and doesn't believe Raymond and Robert Laurent would have recognized each other in the café, and even if they had, a dinner invitation would have been ludicrous in such circumstances. "You fabricated that whole spoon story," she pronounces.

Their conversation ends, and Raymond sums up the episode for his readers, who at this moment don't know what to believe, and are likely to think the author has been judged too harshly by his daughter. But such readers are in for a surprise:

> I should have told her that readers of fiction like to be told sad stories, as long as they appear to be true. I mean convincing, and the chronology is faithful to the principle of non-contradiction. It is well-known that testimonies cause indignation and make those who listen feel good. What I wrote in that scene is a kind of testimony of what happened at that time, not only to us, but to many Jews who were deported. Their things, their possessions were stolen. Especially the silver and the works of art. (109)

To this point, most readers of *Shhh* will have forgotten that they are reading fiction, although the work has not explicitly claimed to be anything but this. Yet implicitly Federman has been very aware of the lines being blurred, which is made clear by his evocation of Holocaust literature with the word "testimony." A genre of historical literature hovers over this scene, which witnessed the lost lives, lost possessions, and enormous historical crimes that gave rise to the petty crimes of opportunity in which many more people partook, and in which citizenries of entire nations were culpable. Such testimonies inspired and still inspire enormous indignation. Conditioned by such stories, the last thing a reader expects is that the teller of such a story is going to *falsify* (how quickly a moral vocabulary comes to bear upon acts of fictive representation in such a context!) details related to the lives of parents killed at Auschwitz.

And yet this narrator has told us he doesn't remember the things that he is now endeavoring to tell us about. Yet tell he must. The reader of the entire Federman saga begins to understand better the anger of Federman *at himself* in the two intertwined voices of *The Voice in the Closet*: part of him wants to insist on the purity of what can and can't be said, even as another part of him is setting out to develop an art form that can present invention-as-testimony, testimony comprised of invention. It is also no accident Federman's works never appeared with mainstream publishing houses in the US, but that he published all of his American books with nonprofit small presses.[5] Raymond did not create fictions to distort but rather better to embody the truths of 20th century history, even as he invented stories about his parents' lives for publication, but the result is more complicated than a public seeking testimonials of unambiguous events is after. Instead, Federman's inventions honor complex realities of representation, survivor guilt, and how trauma acts upon memory. When Little, Brown, and Co. made an offer to Federman in 1967 for his first novel, *Double or Nothing*, the author himself reacted indignantly. Of this offer, Raymond said, in 2007, "[They] wanted to buy my life for five thousand bucks" (Interview). This was part of his motivation in demolishing the more easily consumed artifact he had first produced; it was loyalty being shown by one part to another part of himself, to continue the roles outlined in *The Voice in the Closet*. The writer known to readers as a wild inventor, as one who indulged in "trivia," and who railed against the "imposture of realism" (*Shhh* 9), remained true, for the entirely of his life as a literary artist, to a deeply held code concerning the ethics and morality of acts of representation.

*

---

5 A non-exhaustive list of publishers in the US that published Federman's work during his lifetime includes these 14 imprints: Alt-X; BlazeVox; Coda/Station Hill Press; Fiction Collective/FC2/University of Alabama Press; Green Integer; Indiana University Press; Poetry Salzburg; Six Gallery Press; State University of New York Press; Starcherone Books; Sun & Moon; Swallow Press; Thunder's Mouth Press; and Two Ravens Press (UK).

Raymond e-mailed me in the summer of 2009 as I was working to publish *Shhh* and we were both in powerful moments of passage in our respective lives. Raymond was suffering the late stages of the cancer that would take his life and my wife Susan and I were days away from the birth of our first child.

> Ted
> bad news here
> I had a Ct Scan and Pet Scan
> a few days ago
> and they revealed that the two
> cancers I have in the lungs
> are growing
> the chemo pills I am taking
> don't seem to help
> I am weak fatigued depressed
>
> I asked the doc if I am dying
> he said yes — I didn't want to know
> more —
>
> I am sad — I can't write
> no courge [sic] no desire
>
> i would love to see Shhh out
> before ...
>
> no need to say more
>
> all the best
> Raymond

I wrote back:

Dear Raymond,

Susan is walking around with a very full belly right now — she is due on the 19th, officially, but it could be any day now.

I'm sorry we will not be naming her Raymond, but we do have your nose mounted on the wall in the living room!

I don't know what to say, except we will do our best to get the book done . . . So tell your doctor to keep you around for a while! (Smile.)

I'm very sorry to get this note -- I will turn my thoughts to the spirits and hope the feelings reach you. In the meantime, we have a team together that's working on getting the book completed.

Your work has touched so many people's lives — remember this when your thoughts turn to despair.

Love,
Ted (& Susan)

I had forgotten I had this email in my archives until setting out to write this essay. Raymond and Erica had been back to Buffalo the previous October for the "Federman@80" celebration. Raymond had already been taking chemo drugs, and there was worry about his ability to make it through the full day's events, which ran some twelve hours, at three different locations. Various institutions and artists wanted opportunities to honor him, and the event kept expanding. Artists Harvey Breverman and Terri Katz Kasimov joined photographer and former Federman colleague in the University at Buffalo English department Bruce Jackson in a morning opening of a show of their works related to Federman at the UB/Anderson Gallery. In the afternoon were papers by critics including Susan Rubin Suleiman of Harvard, Marcel Cornis-Pope of Virginia Commonwealth University, and Larry McCaffrey of San Diego State University, and the evening reading included appearances by poet Charles Bernstein of University of Pennsylvania, Canadian-American poet and University at Buffalo Gray Chair Steve McCaffery, Davis Schneiderman, Christina Milletti, Michael Basinski, and more.

Last on the bill, long after the day had begun, Federman came to the microphone. First, he gave my wife and I his casted nose. And then, though we knew him to be sick and weakened by the drugs, he performed his work. He had followed his daughter Simone's appearance; during her reflections, minutes earlier, whenever she began to break into tears, Raymond would exhort from the auditorium crowd — "Federman!" — as if to say to her that a Federman does not give in or break down, but continues to fight. Simone bucked up and continued.

In his own performance, Raymond gave us laughter. No one who didn't know better would have guessed he was in poor health. I have seen many writers perform their works over the past three decades, and there really aren't many who were or are as entertaining as Raymond always was.

Among many coinages in Federman's parlance there is his word "laughterature," yet another self-description from an inexhaustible man who never tired of looking in the mirror.

Works Cited

Bucher, Gérard. "To Invent You, Federman." Preface. *The Voice in the Closet/La voix dans le cabinet de débarras.* By Raymond Federman. Buffalo, NY: Starcherone, 2001. Print.

Di Leo, Jeffrey R. Introduction. "Other Voices: The Fiction of Raymond Federman." *Federman's Fictions: Invention, Theory, Holocaust.* Ed. Jeffrey R. Di Leo. Albany: SUNY Press, 2011: 1-26. Print.

Federman, Raymond. Email to the author. 9 July 2009.

---. *My Body in Nine Parts.* Buffalo, NY: Starcherone, 2005. Print.

---. Personal Interview. 14 March 2007.

---. *Return to Manure.* Tuscaloosa, AL: FC2/U of Alabama Press, 2006. Print.

---. *Shhh: The Story of a Childhood.* Buffalo, NY: Starcherone, 2010. Print.

---. *The Voice in the Closet/La voix dans le cabinet de débarras.*

Fox, Margalit. "Raymond Federman, Novelist and Beckett Scholar, Is Dead at 81." *New York Times.* 17 October, 2009. Web. 6 June, 2016.

McCaffery, Larry, Thomas Hartl, and Doug Rice. *Federman: From A to X-X-X-X: A Recyclopedic Narrative.* San Diego, CA: San Diego State UP, 1998. Print.

Pelton, Ted. Email to Raymond Federman. 9 July 2009.

Suleiman, Susan Rubin. "When Postmodern Play Meets Survivor Testimony." *Federman's Fictions: Invention, Theory, Holocaust.* 215-228.

Chouchou in the Cave: A Prehistoric Chronicle

AN ABANDONED FICTION

RAYMOND FEDERMAN

TABLE OF CONTENTS

1. The State of Erection & Other Consequences

2. The State of Excretion & Further Consequences

3. The State of Boneweeping & Other Complications

4. The State of Anticipation & the Beginning of Despair

5. The State of Invasion or How to Get Rid of the Bugs

The State of Erection & Other Consequences

None of us could remember how it happened. Who among us first cracked his ribcage to rise from a four-legged position to a biped posture and screaming with pain into the wilderness launched us into our present state of confused erection.

But erect we were. First among all the species to look up at the sky defiantly.

I was among the first. The first batch. One of the early erectus. Perhaps even a bit premature. For until my extinction I could not leak my yellow water upright like the other erectus. I had to discharge my yellow water resting my knuckles on the ground and lifting one leg up sideways. Still I was fully erect. But none of us could remember how the state of erection happened. Though all of us felt for many moons the atrocious pain in the back. Across the back from shoulder bone to shoulder bone down the spine and across the chest too. The terrible memory-less pain of ancient ignorance.

Some of us would awake in the dark of the cave screaming with pain and roam around bent in half holding on to the small of our backs with both hands moaning *Oy Weh Oy Weh* while stumbling over the bodies of our fellowcavemen curled in the little death.

Shut the fluke up and go back to your lousy smelly moss someone would shout. But then his turn would come too. And the following moon he would awake with the ancestral pain in the back. And he would be the one to be cursed for stumbling over the bodies curled in the little death.

Many suns & moons later when we set out from the cave towards the red glow in the sky we were to remember that distant night of agony when the first among us erected. And as we trampled across the swamps crawled in the mud charged up the hills and rolled down the valleys on our way to the red glow in the sky we could still hear inside our narrow skulls that horrible cry that filled the jungle when the first ribcage cracked.

By then most of us were fully erect. I was among the first. The first batch. Many of us erected all at once. Yes. Many of us. I was never alone in my state of erection. I cannot remember ever being erect alone. We were not made for solitary wandering. Always huddling together in nervous packs. Staying close together. Always rubbing elbows.

Some of us who were not fully deployed remained semi-erect. It was fear and the apprehension of the pain in the back that kept them folded in half. But it was clear that sooner or later they too would break out of their twisted bones and rise. Or else collapse into extinction.

These semi-erectus looked foolish to us. *Stand up straight you animal* we would say to them while kicking them in the rear-place where a reddish hump recalled the vanishing tail of our previous condition.

Walk like a hominid you retarded slouching lump of meat we would say to them while monkeying their clumsy hopping motions. Not that we were that agile ourselves in our simian bowlegged-ness. But at least we were upright.

We all went through the change in adult age. There were no children in the first batch. We erected in mid-course of our prehistoric adult existence. Females and males at the same time otherwise we would have been quickly extinguished. Children born of our state of erection came out fully extended.

We recorded only one case of regression. That pitiful semi-erect baby born one darkmoon in the swamps was immediately exterminated. We buried him in the mud. Though the fear of total regression was inconceivable to us we all agreed that it was preferable not to take a chance. We could not afford to stumble back into the unconsciousness of our implausible origin nor could we afford to progress on the basis of a twisted design. Since we knew not where we were where we came from and where we were going we had no sense of direction. Forward and backward was the same to us. With our unthinkable beginning and our unknown destination we were in a constant state of physical and mental stupor.

The semi-erectus were naturally more hairy than the rest of us. This compensated for their shameful retardation. For even though they suffered mentally for not having yet reached the state of full erection they did not suffer physically like the rest of us from the cold and the inclemencies of the sky. In the early cycles of our erection when our bodies were gradually losing their last patches of hair many of us would hop around in the swamps with goose bumps all over our greyish skin or spend long moons in the cave sneezing and trembling uncontrollably. After all the ice age was still just around the corner of geological ebullition. Wow did we freeze our asses during the ice age.

No one could recall who among us spoke the first word. And what that word was. How a useful and recognizable sound emerged from the primordial cry of erectional agony was a mystery to us. It was rumored for many suns & moons that this first word was a negative and that it was uttered by the smallest of the erectus when a big Upman tried to snatch his cavewoman away from him.

Ohnoyoudont he supposedly shouted raising his club furiously above his head. Immediately we all went around repeating in a happy singsong *Ohnoyoudont! Ohnoyoudont!* Thus hominid language was born. Not to communicate something but to maintain a sense of property among us. For if on the one hand we were formless fluid utterers who rejected all that was alien to the nonverbal core of our self-centered existence. On the other hand we resided in the fixed shapes and external orders of our gestures. Since we were postulated gratuitously we never learned how we came to speak or be spoken.

No one could recall either who first reached up into a tree with his foot now turned tool-hand to grab a fruit though we all agree that the fruit was a banana. An early species of bananas which we called *Bayanas.*

I cannot recall ever being deprived of Bayanas during my entire cave existence. Bayanas governed our entire system of social and private activities. They were our measure of reality as well as our condition of dreams. We dreamt Bayanas all the time. Without our Bayanas we would certainly not have progressed and multiplied.

None of us had a name. We had not yet invented nomination. From the beginning we functioned as an anonymous collective bunch just as Bayanas grow on Bayanabushes. It was much later that I was named. The first in fact to receive a name.

It was given to me by my cavewoman. The one I was humping at the time. I had taken her away from the hairy semi-erect brute who always slept in a private niche inside the big communal cave. He called it his cave-within-the-cave. He was obnoxious and vulgar. He thought he was already postcava. Nobody liked him. He beat everybody all the time with his big stick for no reason.

One moondark I don't know why he started beating me. So I bit his leg so hard he dropped his big knotty stick and while he was rolling on the ground holding on to his calf and moaning I grabbed his cavewoman by the hair pull her to my corner of the cave and pushed her down on my personal pile of moss. The big mean cavebrute understood that I meant business.

She was not fully erect yet my cavewoman. Just past the half-way mark. It made it difficult to do the good thing to her face to face. I had to give her pleasure from the rear as in the old pre-erectional moons. We did it in the swamps. I loved it in the mud. And she did too. The mud would splash all over our bodies as we wiggled and humped our primitive pleasure.

We were not very imaginative in this kind of frolicking. It took us many suns & moons to discover that imagination is in nature even though nothing in nature explains how to use imagination. That's the problem with nature. It never explains itself.

The day my cavewoman gave me a name I was mounting her from the rear pushing in deep in search of the unknown when she let out a little sweet cry. At first I didn't know what that little cry was. But then she looked up her eyes gleaming with joy and murmured *Chouchou! Chouchou more.* And Chouchou I became. When she repeated it again and again I knew I was Chouchou and so I gave her a name too. I called her Zizi. *Zizi I got more for you!* I said.

When our fellowcavepeople heard that I was Chouchou and she was Zizi they all went around trying out names on each other. Xzypo. Machin. Truc. Yetyet. Connard. Kock. Bigman. Odibil. Outt. Salaud. And many other names like these. They had no idea what these names meant or why they were giving each other these names.

Of course I knew why Zizi had called me Chouchou and why I called her Zizi. We wanted to keep it a secret that we had inadvertently invented jouissance. But the Chief [yes we had a Chief] forced us to reveal why and how we suddenly became Chouchou and Zizi.

So we demonstrated in front of the whole caveclan. Right there in the swamps. After the demonstration all the cavemen started chasing the cavewomen so they could give each other a name.

This is how we recognized that the state of erection corresponded to the emergence of nomination and playfluking. Or to put it in simpler terms. In the beginning was the little cry and then came the name. The Chief explained it to us differently [yes the Chief always explained everything to us. That's why he was the Chief].

This is what he said: *When mouthole words propagate and disseminate and everything starts to signify then the possibility of speculating on an origin fades away for lack of any guarantee of validity.*

The Chief always spoke like that. He made things so clear for us. So now we knew that nomination can serve to establish an origin. Or else erase origin. Or something like that. The moment my cavewoman called me Chouchou I acquired an anteriority and a purpose for my being however accidental it may have been. This does not mean of course that I understood where I came from or where I was going but it gave me a chance to speculate in the darkness of the cave and in the narrowness of my skull about pre-existential matters. Give a caveman a name and immediately he begins to think himself in control of his destiny.

Before this memorable moment of nomination when we needed to draw attention to one another we would shout: *Hey you! Hello there! Psiit! Coucou!* We hadn't yet learned how to whistle. The birds had not yet visited our corner of the jungle. Or else we would hit each other on the head with sticks. Poke each other in the ribs. Throw stones or mud at each other. *Hey you! Psitt! Psitt!*

It was a great joyful moment when the first among us accidentally snapped his fingers and everybody turned around to look at him. After that we all delighted in practicing the finger-snapping music. *Snapsnap! Snapsnap!* We would go at each other playing the finger-snapping music. Then came the drums and the dancing. But that's another story.

When my cavecherie called me Chouchou I thought she had said Coco. But the second time it was Chouchou she murmured. I had pulled her mercilessly into an animal state that left her quivering frantically and she fell forward head first into the mud as I pushed in deeper and further in search of the little cry. She barely moved. She stayed there arched and half-buried in the muck on the other side of abandonment until I fell out of her. My schlang was much bigger and longer than those of my fellowcavemen [a lucky abnormality the Chief declared] and consequently took a long time to reach its blissful destination.

That blue day many others were also frolicking in the mud. Jumping on top of each other. Humping as they always did on a blue day. It was a great blue day. No goose bumps. No sneezing. No running noses. No trembling. No saying *sonofacavebitch wow it's cold!* None of that.

Also no mean ugly paleolithic beast had come from the other side of the swamps to scare us back to the cave. Only a bird. A giant bird with a formidable beak and immense wings appeared in the sky out of nowhere. He landed on top of the tallest bayanabush and watched us all day with his unblinking round eyes. Our first bird. First one we ever saw. We could not tell if he was ugly or beautiful because we could not compare him to other birds since he was our first bird.

Of course we didn't know it was a bird. We had no knowledge of birds. It's much later when we were on our way to the red glow in the sky that we used the word bird for the first time. We had found an extinguished one in the jungle. A huge one. Still warm. We ate it. And the Chief shouted while chewing on a juicy thigh and drooling from the mouth: *What a delicious biiiirrrrrrrrrd!* It was not clear what he had said because his mouth was so full the name of the thing got swallowed with a piece of meat. But all of us shouted *BIIIIIIIIIRRRRRD.* And the delicious meat became bird.

Meanwhile on that blue day our first bird was still watching us form the top of the bayanabush. Suddenly he spread his wings and flew away.

We all stood there in the swamps dumbfounded with our noses up in the air following the *Archaeopteryxal* flight of this bird who beat his wings while *koaxpfing and kaaascching* in the blue sky. It was a strange sight to our eyes and a mysterious music to our ears.

Suddenly the chubby little one among us with the long crooked nose [his name was Piedenez] climbed to the top of the tree where the bird had been perched. Piedenez seemed to have suddenly recaptured instinctively his ancestral ape agility. He stood up on the highest branch. Spread his arms. Let out a wild cry. More like a squeak of the mouthole trying to imitate the bird's koaxpfing and kaassching and then he lurched upward into the air arms still spread out. We found him buried under the mud. He was extinguished. But still smiling ornithologically. None of us after that dared follow his daring act.

We were learning slowly. Painfully. But joyfully. We had not yet fallen into the great hole of culture which time digs relentlessly. We were only on the edge of the precipice of culture leaning against the onrushing wind of knowledge. We had no previous experience to draw upon. It became clear to us however that we were not made for the sky. We were stuck on the ground. The only way out of our earthly heaviness and clumsiness would have been to step out of the circle that confined us within the circumferential gravity of our obscure origin. A circle whose center would have to be our physical absence. At least that's how the Chief explained it to us. But it was too late for that. We had already evolved beyond the state of hollow bones. We were on our way to atavistic redundancy. And since our skulls were still empty spheres not yet cluttered with memories our cavexistence could only project itself forward along the curve of its own ignorance. Or what Upman, one of the big ones among us, once called: *Our zero degree of forgotten past-perfectness.*

We did however manage for a while to enjoy the pleasure of being in the sky. The bliss of aerial loftiness. By bird-proxy. This was after we reached the red glow in the sky and touched its magic power. When we domesticated some of these big birds and used them as means of transportation to go from one part of the jungle to another. For instance to go and visit the little nonose-fourfinger-unibreasted homobayana people who lived near the big boulder and the other side of the swamps and with whom we had become friendly after me and Zizi came upon them by chance during an afternoon of boneweeping.

This encounter was later. During the state of boneweeping. After the first bird. But before we reached the red glow in the sky. We often confused before and after. That's why I'm mentioning the nonose bayana people now even though they have not yet appeared.

After we domesticated the big birds we would climb on their back carefully avoiding the long vertebrate tail that could wipe us out with one blow. We held onto the neck of the bird with both hands. Also carefully avoiding the sharp teeth inside the formidable beak that could cut off our hands with one bite. And we would take off into the sky. Sometimes two of us straddling one bird.

Zizi and me we often went up into the sky together even though it was dangerous for two cavepeople to ride one bird. Many cavemen fell from the sky in mid-flight and became buried in the mud of the swamps during these dangerous flights.

These birds worked better with only one rider. But it was still dangerous for a lone passenger. So not everycavebody participated in the lofty adventure.

It was fun to rise above the jungle and watch our cavebuddies below wave at us. It gave those of us who dared to ride the birds a sense of elevated superiority. Except that for those who fell from the sky into the swamps must have felt inferior on the way down. Especially since all the cavebuddies below would scream and laffture joyfully while they were falling.

This was after we reached the red glow in the sky. But the lofty pleasure did not last long. Those dumb big birds became extinct. A new species replaced them. Little biddy birds of nothing who not only refused to be domesticated but were too small to carry anything on their backs. These little biddy birds were useless. And dirty too. They constantly dropped their kaka on us from above. But they were delicious when we ate them.

After the big birds were extinguished we went back to our primitive means of transportation. Bipedal fear. Especially when the mean ugly beast came and we had to run back to the safety of the cave.

Things did not always progress well with us. And not all progress was permanent. The process of learning had its flaws. Because we had no past to remember. And were not ready to imagine a future. We were stuck between two opposing delusions: knowing none. Known of none.

We would often forget what we had just learned. Or do it backward. We were not habituated yet to comprehension. So our gestures our attitudes and the words we were uttering would tumble into an anterior state of confused nonsensicality.

We kept repeating and mixing up what we told each other. For instance how none of us could remember how the state of erection happened.

It would come out this way: None could crack of us who rise to remember ribcage from position biped posture fourleg. Remember none us could. Us of none. Among was the I first but others the pain in less. Not leak me could they yellow fully erect at mouth of cave water.

When this linguo-chaos happened our cavelife became totally disorganized. Our utterances took off by themselves into forms that we could not control.

For instance: While yellow water to the wind in the light after darksleep they all gave me alone leaked in mud yellow and rock on all four with leg up sideways squeaking the water while them make game pissing longer higher farther but not me me in pain was they me up pull me could not pissup Upman laffture me because me not water make yellow with big leakleg up they all laffture pointing me my moving big leakleg. *Get big leakleg up* they laffture. *Get big leakleg up!*

Now me tell more disorganized scenes from cavexistence.

Moonlight is filling the cave after sleepdark. Upman is making yellow water into the wind. Upman playing with Upman little leakleg. A game. They pull me up. Me scream. Me is pain in back. Oy Weh. They laffture. The moving part cannot play. Upman piss on my leakleg. All the Upmen play with moving parts. Me drop down. Me go away from Upman on all four. Out of moonlight. Me drop. On all four into the darkplace jungle. The place of wet and cold. Inside the bayanabushes. Me have the sad water in my eyes. Me is shame.

None could us happened how remember.

We were so repetitious. So confused. And yet so anxious to get on to the next stage of evolution. But there was danger.

Here is a cavescene of danger.

Me is shoving rock. Me is pushing rock with shoulder. Shoving rock up to sleep place. Other Upmen also shoving rocks. Shoving rock up to cave because Big Stickman coming in new light to hit us with bigstick. To club body. Club head. Club back. To beat Upman with bigclub and eat Upman soft parts. Drink red water inside Upman.

Me is shoving rock. Big Stickman coming soon in new light.

When Upman making yellow water in mud after sleepdark Stickman hit Upman with bigstick. Pafff! Upman fall in big sleep.

Me is shoving big rock. More Upmen shoving rocks up to cave to roll down on Big Stickman when Big Stickman come. This big danger.

Now me tell another disorganized cavescene.

Cavewoman smell is in jungle. In cool wet place. Me move in the smell. Cavewoman is under bayanabush. Cavewoman on all four chewing soft place of jungle runner little beast. Quietly chewing yamyam. Cavewoman making smell. Me see place of smell. Me stop. Cavewoman me see. Yamyaming. She chewing quietly soft place of jungle runner little beast.

Upmen pissup on me. Me go away into jungle. On all four. Me smell cavewoman. Me go to smell. Me watch cavewoman chewing yamyam. Me am fear. Other Upmen also in jungle place watching cavewoman yamyaming. She chewing little body of jungle runner. Me watching with others. Cavewoman chewing chewing under bayanabush.

Me no more sad water in eyes. Me want smell place cavewoman.

Me now tell sleepdark in the cave.

Groaning in sleepdark inside cave us sleep in heap. Heapup. Heapdown. Groaning. Constant shifting of pack. Body slow motion all moon. Terror suffering us not know. All dark moaning. Of we Of weh! From the noise place. Skin to skin. Finger in hole. Of we Of Weh! Stickman comes with bigclub in new light at the open of cave. Me crawl out of pack. Leak yellow water on stone. Me crawl back to heap. Insert me in the pack. Get as many parts of body inside the other bodies. Them shift to permit me. Of We Of Weh! The heap shifts. Heapup. Heapdown.

Now me tell the jungle fluking scene.

When caveman gets the stiffness in the little leakleg caveman go to jungle. In jungle he get bayana. He take banana and he walk around and around. He hunting cavewoman smell. When cavewoman smell he smell he follows the body. At the body of cavewoman he give bayana to cavewoman. She drop down and chews bayana. Yamyam. Caveman go behind cavewoman and sticks the stiff part in smell-hole until soft part again. Bangbang. The fear stop in that time of bangbang. When part soft finish caveman go. Caveman sit doen. Fear come back.

It is the way of the caveman. Cavewoman chew bayana. Yamyam.

The red glow in the sky is moving across the up. Up and away.

That's how it was in our caveworld. Not always progressively.

Not the least charm of this cavelife of pure blank movement is the gression and its aptness to receive without approval but with fervent stupor the faint inscription of the outworld.

This sensitivelessness was not the least charm of our aimless roaming in the swamps. We loved it there. Splashing around. Crawling in the mud. We were full of unrestrained vigor. Even though some of us were already curiously aged and decayed in our stumbling cavexistence. Suffering from spavined feet. Impetigo. Blurred vision. Toothlessness.

Rhumatism. And of course the perpetual backaches due to the agany of erection and the dampness of the cave. And so we roamed around ill and dejected. Creepy-crawly. Yet indifferent to nature. Nature was there only to be abused. To be observed with disdain. Those of us including myself who were not prematurely aged and decayed we were living a vicarious autogamy full of lifefulness and shlangfulness. We were constantly questing. Always wandering and questing. Touching the flower. Smell the mammoth droppings. Watching the birds make circles in the sky. Feeling our little leakleg throb. Listening to it whine.

We were curious questers. Relentless wanderers. But without purpose. Without any goal. We were.

The subsequent wanderings of our descendants were supposedly ennobled by their participating in the quest motif if nothing else. So we would have deduced if the power of deduction had been ours that they would be impelled to search unendingly for an end to searching until the end of moon and sun. But not us. Us the vigorous ones. The early erectus. We had no such delusions in our static state of aimlessness. That's all we could manage. Which was more than we could. We were. That's all. [*until further notice*]

THE STATE OF ERECTION & OTHER CONSEQUENCES

nione ovus coud member how hapen ... when rection hapen ... who mong us first cracked ribcage torise from quadruped position to biped posture ... & screaaaming with hurt insid wildernesssss launchd us in present state confusd rection ... but rect us was ... first mong alspecies look upsky defiantly ...

me mong first ... me mean first wave ... first batch .. early rectus ... me maybe bit premature ... because til extinshion ovme ... me coud niot leak yelow water standinup like other rectuses ... so me do yelow leaking restin nuckles on ground & legup sideways ... stil me fuly rect ... but nione us coud member how hapen state ov rection ...

yet manyus felt ... for many moons ... trocious ake in us backs ... crosback from boneshoulder to boneshoulder down spine to biddy holeass & cros chest too ... big memoryless ake ov ancient ignorance ... ah ifus suferd lots for stature of future big standin generations ...

somus somoften come out litle death in darkcave in moonglow screaming with ake ... somus roam round all dark bent haf ... holding ussmalback with hands ... moaning oy wch oy weh ... stumbling over bodies othercavefelows curled in smal death ...

shut thefluckup go back your filtyshitymoss & jump back in smal death ... felowcavemanbastard shouted from corner rockysmelful dweling ... but then turn his come for him lousyfelowcave shouter to come out smal death with bigake in back ... & moonnext him feel ancestral ake ... yio him be oneus cursed cause him stumbling over us bodies curled in smal death ...

manymanymany suns-moons after rection ... when us set out from cave direcshion smoky redglow insky ... farway ... us were tomember distant moonglow of agony when first homo mong us rected ... & whileus trampled crosswamps ... crawled mud ... chargedup mountains ... fel down valeys ... onway to redglow ... us stil hear inus narrow skuls horible cries in jungle when first ribcage craked ...

bywhen us reached redglow insky most us erected fuly was ... give or take excepshions ... slowhomorectatus us called them niot ful deployed ... as me say ... me mong early unfiold one ... me say mong because us were gether always ... always bunched gether ... yio ... me never alone ... me canot member ever be lone ... nio us niot made for solitary wandering ... us homonids ... us always hudle gether ... us nervouspack ... us scared ... always close gether ... always elbows rubing ... smeling badsmels each others ... yio us doing lots badodors in litle hole in bigass because us grasseating lots ...

someus notfuly deployed stood demirect ... poorslobs ... by sunglow us set out for smoky redglow in sky ... many ancient quadrupedians mong us already extinguished ... maybe demirectus stayed folded half because of fear... fearaprehension oldake in back ... terible oldake in back ... me tell yiou ... but inevitable somelater moonglow them too ... slobdemis ... can break out twisted bones & rise ... or else ... us eat them ...

demis looked foolish to us ... stand up straight yiou animal ... us cry to demirectus kicking them in rearplace where redish hump made member us vanished tail of previous condition ... walk like true hominid yiou retarded lump slouching meat ... us yel to demirectus monkeying them clumsy boping motions ... niot mean this us more agile uselves in oiur simian bowlegedness ... but us at least was up & rect ...

oh bytheway cidentaly fore me forget ... me shoud mention ... those us rected all did in adultage ... samemoon ... al us change alonce ... same moonglow ... us was so hapy ... us jubilant cause us rectus now matefuck front & niot rear no more ... only us hominids in entire universe fuckmating do frontward ... us gotgot great jouissance then ... us gotgot big rection ... us homorectus never regress to quadrupedian state ... us standup tal ... us rect now ... us bigrect ... us man ... us bigproud ... but someglows sometime us fuckmate in rear ... for old glowsake ...

[*to be continued*]

Concerning the Original Mastubatory Gesture

One wonders what the first homo sapiens must have thought [if thinking he could] or did [certainly he could do] when he awoke one night in the dark of the cave and reached with his hand under his dirty animal pelt covering his groin to touch an unexpected erection [perhaps not the first but the first he reached for] to touch it feel it squeeze it rub it shake it until it made him squirm on his dirty pile of moss and then scream with this newly discovered sensation this pleasure which he could not yet name or explain and which later much later he named jouissance.

Yes one must wonder what this first one among this newly erected species felt before finding his way to the pleasure of a twat with this thing in his hand. What did he do. Did he scream? Laugh? Burst into tears? Or did he rise to his feet in the dark of the cave and shouted to his cavefellowmen lost in the little death: **Hey you guys wake up wake up you won't believe the incredible discovery I just made!**

And one can further wonder as to what took place in the dark of the cave the following night when all the cavemen reached under their filthy pelts to explore the discovery the first among them had made. Of course one should also wonder what the cavewomen did or said when the first man among them shouted his discovery in the dark of the cave.

Federman at 88: Where are You?

SIMONE FEDERMAN

Federman what are you? Where are you? You are everywhere. Federman here Federman there. My fingers type it like a quick little dance Federman without effort. It is there everywhere. It is attached to my name. Simone Juliette and then it is there Federman over and over again. All day, everyday. The rest of you think Federman now and again, sure you may even hesitate and think Federman with fondness, but then I am sure there is a sub-set of you that think Federman and feel really irritated, are sick of his shenanigans, so what with this Federman, big deal another Federman piece of shit! Federman. I carry you around with me stuck to me always, even in my sleep. Federman stuck to my eyes.

53 years ago is when our friendship began or so he said being a fictitious character it is hard to have any credibility; chronological credibility is especially dubious. Since the defining moment his mother pushed him back in the closet and told him to "ssh", "chut" in French he always insisted, at the heart of Federman is still whether in words, pictures or hyper-textual communication, the performance of his continued existence, his continued event.

My father was/is a fictioneer. As a child I thought that to be as good as a musketeer. In fact, I am sure I was told that. "Un pour tous, tous pour un" one for all, all for one.

In my living room, hangs a 'Me Too' poster framed behind glass, Federman there on the wall, I play ping pong with myself from both sides now smash smash smash our screams and laughter in the basement every night hangs behind glass, #1 and your signature makes me miss your big hands, always so smooth in the swimming pool, they would glide through the water like magic, soft but strong.

They slid over the keys with a little cha cha cha, a smile and sometimes a grimace. The IBM selectric stud with its sexy balls was your lover on the third floor in that ball room you sitting at one end by the window yes where the rock came in at you! So you paying attention, excellent.

Okay, so I know shit, I know stuff no body else knows. I know what is true and what is not although have stopped caring. I saw the broken glass and the rock that flew through the window of his study on the third floor in *The Voice in the Closet*. My hot wheels room was on the same floor. I knew that when he slid down the stairs barely touching each step that it meant that he would be there with me. I knew that sound. He knew when I showed him my quick draw in the hall mirror that I was a rooting tooting cowboy. I knew he was a trapeze artist in the circus because he could do one arm push ups and clap. My pop was the only person I ever saw do that. He knew I was in the circus too when he would grab my arms and flip me over between his legs. We are Federmans.

Now is the time I quote something I wrote before, irregardless of its quality:

"My eyes were as bottomless as his, hollowed in my tiny face peering out through the bright windshield when he picked me up after school. And my mouth was almost more jaded — perfecting the scowl of a French-movie gangster, the attitude, if not the accent, that made him so charming to women. I would have smoked Gauloise in the car if he'd let me, the way he did, with the windows rolled up so his (h)air wouldn't blow, as we cruised the town, partners in crime, till my mother got home.

My mother sparkled with Hollywood sunlight, whereas me and my pop flickered in the shadows of the place where we lived when she was not around, where all his stories and the movies he'd taken me to converged, Goddard and Sergio Leone all of them. Errands were just an excuse for a stake out; a trip to the bank, casing the joint for the big heist "the Organization" had planned. I would make drawings of the joint and we would later plan how we would spend the money. Our swarthy complexions suited our roles as the good kind of bad guys, though I was more of a cowboy than he was, with half a half gallon hat in the back seat to prove it, and he admired that about me. I was, after all, a real American, unlike him.

"Zoot, alors!" he'd say, forced to stall at a red light, and I'd take aim with my pistol finger tip, waiting until just the right moment — "Pow" — to shoot it green."

I know this is true about him being a lucky gambler because when the two of us drove across country we stopped at many many slot machines and at the last one in Nevada, the sign said so, we won a lot of money that afternoon. Although in Vegas I wasn't allowed in the casino, so he would run out to the lobby and ask me for lucky number for the roulette wheel and when 13 black came up we won lots of money on my bet but he said he would only give me five dollars and he should keep the rest, too much money for a kid.

So I know he really must have worn a zoot suit in Japan and won big on the black market. I have the gold watch to prove it and saw the pictures. There are so many pictures to prove it all, so many stories in my head. Sometimes I talk just like him with his thick accent, lots of French slang peppering my speech, sometimes his stories but mostly I channel his comments about what is happening right now in my life or he is congratulating my friends on theirs. Call me sometime if you miss him, he hasn't gone any where. Federman tous les jours.

While Waiting for the Book:
A Somewhat Disorganized Dialogue Between Two Letters

RAYMOND FEDERMAN

A: I'm putting this in my new book — the one on violence — the violence done to writers should maybe instead be the theme

B: what kind of book you're writing and what kind of SHIT you're putting in
it's not clear to me
sounds like a book in which anything can go in
all the cultural dreck detritus merde of this world the kind of book I love

A: it's going in

B: yes let it go in

A: I just started — max is home and there is so much to do here but if I don't make a start I never will —

B: how is the movie star doing

A: I began with the story of hanging the girl off the railings — writing it down makes it seem worse somehow — when I tell it there's always laughter — I mean everyone who tells me their tales laugh — with embarrassment I guess — some — most smile at the time of telling — as if they can't believe what they are about to tell —

B: a great way to start a story — hang the protagonist — hang the girl — this way she won't bug you any more — and this way you can go on without having that girl interfere with the way you tell her story thinking you're lying —

A: We went to a friends on Saturday — J. is from Ireland where he worked when he was 20 in a prison filled with murderers and rapists — he said they had to regularly beat up prisoners — he said if I didn't join in they would have beat me — the prisoners when they saw you were new would throw their food at you to get your reaction — your colleagues would wait to see what you'd do — I wouldn't have lasted — he kept saying — you know me now don't you — and yes he is the kindest of people — a sweet lovely guy — and who would think he said — who would know I could do that —

B: you must have gotten lots of good material for the violence book last Saturday
we are all born murderers
only a few remain so
and you go to talk to the happy few [fous]

A: I haven't started the letter side yet — I have to do that out of the house — the letter to the letter

B: what letter? Whose letter? Where letter? When letter?

A: I am just trying to write up others accounts and their stories — one of the worse so far —

B: the worse it gets

the better it gets
sam didn't say that
I did
but I learned to say
such things from sam
I mean the symmetry of a sentence

A: a friend who was coming out of a pub with her friend while walking to the car she saw a man sitting on the wall of the pub car park — he was with someone else — he had in his hand a large orange saucepan — as she got close she thought he had something to eat — she was a little curious but didn't really dwell on it — as she walked to the passenger door of the car — the man called out and threw the contents of the saucepan over her — she at first had no idea what it was and for a moment believed it was acid as it was burning her face — she began wiping it off and realised — as she got into the car — that it was vomit

B: since as it is said at the end of this dialogue I don't have to read everything — I skipped this paragraph — maybe you could summarize for in a dozen words

A: Seth has a great story of hitting someone with a dead fish

B: tell him to send it to me
I'll make a poem with it

A: Another friend was building bonfires with his friends — it was an annual event when they were boys — the bonfire building on the common became very competitive — their gang of boys were worried they'd not have the biggest one — the bonfires got so big they'd make small houses inside where you could sit — concerned theirs wasn't big enough they raided the house of an old lady who lived near by — she was eccentric and had a big rambling house — while she was out they broke in and took her antique harmonium — her piano — letters and photographs and they broke up the instruments and threw them on to the bonfire along with her letters and photographs. When the bonfire night came they burnt the lot — no one ever caught them or linked them to the incident.

B: I started reading this paragraph
but the phone rang
S asking
what do I think
she should get mom
for mother's day I told her here mom is dying
to have one of those
little gadget that makes
milk foam and fuzz
when you put it in your coffee
I think it's called
a milk fizzler
or something like that
great idea S said
like the one J has
yes
for how many cups of coffee
S inquires
only one I reply
and add
well make it two cups
In case your mom decides
on morning to have a second cup
but normally she's the one cup type
she's the only who drinks coffee chez nous

A: heugh

B: so that's why I couldn't finish reading that paragraph
maybe I'll go back and read it later

when I finish fiddling with Chut
I can't stop going in it
and fiddling with it
I read a passage
and immediately I start
adding words
changing words
deleting words
and even rephrasing the sentences
I am working on the style
I want this book to be
as it is said in the book
I want Chut to be pure poetic chaos
it's hard to let go you know
when you know you wrote
something that even moves
the writer when he reads it
I don't mean moves him
sentimentally
but in forcing him
to try and improve what he has already written
hoping to arrive
at the right aggregate of pure poetic chaos
the original chaos

A: Anyway I want to write others accounts in one voice as if they are telling — and with no reflection — just the tale —

B: oh you mean speak — or rather — write in tongues
a voice speaking many languages at the same time
a stereophonic voice
do it it's fun
I had so much fun doing it in some of my books
but not in Chut

Chut is so close to real life I am sure I'm going to be accused
of having deserted surfiction for real life stories
of having written plain unabashed autobiographical writing
yes that's what is going to be said of Chut
finally Federman has stopped lying and is telling the true story
Federman has stopped lying — that's a good one —
I hope those who say that
read between the lines
and above the lines
and below the lines
there is so much lying in Chut
Chut is a pile of lies more real than reality
I burst into laughter when
I read Chut — its very healthy
the best part of
having written a book
is to read
before anyone else
when it is in motion
because after that
when others have polluted the book
with their readings
then the book will no longer be yours
and if perchance you open it one day
just to remember how you did it
it becomes boring tedious emmerdant
for you to read it
I don't know why I just wrote all that
I could have written something else, living souls, you will see it all comes
out the same at the end

[sam whispering one of his old sayings in my ear]

A: slow beginnings

B: it's the beginning that is slow
then the middle
then the end
in the end it's the end that is slow
I know
I am in the slow ending period
the letting go of a book
anticipating
the praises
the abject responses
the obligatory rejection letters
and all the rest
until one day the publisher writes you to say chut just came out we are
sending you a copy express and you are all — how shall I say — excited —
yes mentally physically emotionally and even sexually as you await THE
BOOK — and you wait — you wait — a week already — two now — three
weeks — you panique — you imagine the book floating on the waves of the
Atlantic and slowly descending into the depth of the ocean pour aller
dormir dans les goemons verts — thank you Victor Alas — or else being
read by some half-drunk half-starved homeless being wrapped in
newspapers — prone on the ground on top of more old newspapers —
history in the unmaking under his ass — there in nouillorque city —
reading THE BOOK — so I send the publisher a quick email asking if the
book has been mailed and if so when and why is it that it has not yet
arrived here — I'm so impatient to see — to hold THE BOOK — and the nice
publisher says but we mailed you 10 copies on march 15 — and today is
may 3rd — oh la vache — imagine 10 copies of THE BOOK dispersed all
over the ocean — and slowly sinking int les goemons verts — or in the
hands of some 10 homeless beings reading THE BOOK with their asses on
top of history in the unmaking — what will they think of me — so the
good publisher look we're going to send you another exemplaire — yes
the book is coming from Marseille — you should get it in a few days — I
breath easily and thank the generous publisher with another email — and

I wait — I am so busy waiting I don't do a fucking thing but wait — wait for the mailman — and wait again the next day for the mail man — I want to see that BOOK I need to see it to make sure it really exists and how it looks — and if I will have pleasure holding it in my hand — reading the blurb on the back which supposedly will tell you all about the book — and you will burst into laughter read the blurb whatsisname wrote which the publisher didn't even tell you he has asked whatsisname — so misrepresentative it is from what you have written — and you'll be disappointed by the size of the print which makes it difficult for an old fart like me to read with my reading glasses — as if a transparent wall was needed to read my own writing — which I am sure it distort — for when finally the book arrives and you are determined to give it a good read — the more you read the more the book seems foreign to you — and you start laughing at the dumb things — the lies you read in this book — yes that's how it usually happens — at least with me — and today is May 15 — I'm projecting a bit forward in time but I am sure that's how it will happen — I know from experience — and still not fucking BOOK — and to make things even worse — a buddy poet from where the book was published sends in an email a review of the BOOK — a superb review that says what an incredible book this is — etc etc — ok it gives pleasure to the writer to read a good intelligent review especially when it makes more of the book than the book is — the usual extrapolations critics feel obligated to do to reveal their culture — but still you are pissed that the book is already being read discussed reviewed and perhaps even already being discarded in some poubelle — and you haven't seen the fucking thing — I have just related without realizing it — am I stoned? — the recent history in the form of a story of what happened since the day I received — way back in March — or maybe it was February — a message from my publisher saying that COUP DE POMPES was out and copies were being mailed to me — and now here we are — May 15 — my birthday —and still no COUP DE POMPES only little postal kicks in the ass —

oh well

as old sam used to say

fuck the postal system
especially the French postal system
being on strike every other day

A: I have to begin the left pages or the right pages — the letter to the anonymous other — I'm not sure which way round yet. I have to ask more random others for their tales but maybe next week when I go to the museum to write I can do that there.

B: whatever you do don't write on both sides of the page
you know what I mean
it would confuse the potential readers

A: You don't have to read all this — maybe I am simply talking to myself

B: I read as much as I could because while reading
I was also talking to myself

TIOLI

STEVE KATZ

I first met Ray Federman when I taught at Cornell. We invited him to read. That was the time of DOUBLE OR NOTHING and he gave a good reading. As we were about to enter a restaurant later he asked my companion, obviously an intimate friend, "Wouldn't you rather sleep with a Frenchman?" Federman's accent was as if on a rheostat, which for seduction he dialed to maximum French. Anyone committing to read his long bizarre (a French word) simple complicated novel TAKE IT OR LEAVE IT gets to "sleep with a Frenchman". One of the earliest gestures that the tenacious narrative voice makes is to drop several buckets from his literary frontloader—names of his novelist peers, critics, literary predecessors, theorists (mostly French), all fomenting in his purview. They string out along the line of his voice like charms on a bracelet. He translates a well known passage from Derrida, and presents it as a typographical medallion in the center of a page. He assures us from the start that the author is well-educated, and is equal to any challenge literary or theoretical as Federman presents an Epic that unfolds "Frenchy's" adventures in the 82nd Airborne, and his assimilation into USA.

The voice toggles to an expletive-packed vernacular that flings contempt at his cohorts in the 82nd, and most of the others who cross the crappy path. The acceleration and momentum recalls Céline, particularly when he punctuates with Célinesque ellipses. Frenchy intends to see the USA in his battered Buick, while he heads for an assignment at Fort Drum where a paycheck waits. He nimbly bends his expletive packed line through conflicts with the officers commissioned and non-, adventures in Jazz, sexual diversions, alcohol mischief, and other digressions, an admirable picaresque in this vernacular tour de force.

The line he grips winds through typographical adventures, perhaps too often on the level of visual pun, but showing his almost giddy pleasure the author takes casting the line of the book. Whenever the narrator whips into the revelatory or the absurd or the frivolous, Frenchy manages to hang on. The characters he condemns rarely talk for themselves. Not a scene is freed from authorial control. Though he advocates the casual he keeps a tight rein along the protracted seam of iteration. A mystery how it becomes so compelling though repetitious, and full of offensive stereotypes, and so obvious in his self-aggrandizing exaggeration and fabrication? Some centripetal force keeps us clinging.

What keeps you reading is perhaps the feeling that you witness the flailing of a man drowning in his own suds, trying to stay alive in the hidden undertow. Maybe it's schadenfreude. It's like watching Buster Keaton. The narrator grips the line to save himself. You hang on too as if a literary breakthrough is about to unspool. When he threads into WWII, his life threatened through the Vichy Government and the holocaust, an unanticipated gravitas drenches the novel, even in retrospect. You nudge closer to the narrator, on a new level of sympathy and understanding. The desperate pace has power and credibility as the narcissism becomes an assertion by Frenchy that he is still alive despite it all, and will be as long as he continues to spin the line, grasp it, and pull himself along his story as he makes it. This darkening of the voice makes TAKE IT OR LEAVE IT one of the most moving, original books of the late XXth century. It deepens the tone of postmodern self-reflexivity, and takes it beyond antics.

Federman continued to explore that material, WWII and survival during the holocaust. THE VOICE IN THE CLOSET, for instance. The material became money for him, particularly in Europe. When I occasionally saw him at conference or reading he loved to tell me how much money he got for an appearance in Antwerp, for instance.

"They paid me in cash," said he.

My last dance with Federman was at a reading I was to give at Chapman University in Orange, CA. He had retired into golf in San Diego at the time. Mark Axelrod asked Raymond to introduce me. A substantial crowd showed up. Federman's introduction took most of an hour, during which he hardly mentioned me, but spoke about Federman. By the time I staggered to the podium, and stood in the vortex of "himself", most of the audience was gone. I read anyway to a chosen few. Take it or leave it.

Jazz & Tubes

AN ABANDONED FICTION*

RAYMOND FEDERMAN

I first heard the sound of jazz — I mean really heard — in 1945 when the war was over and France was liberated and I was back in Paris after three miserable years slaving on a farm — Paris was full of happy-go-lucky American G.I.s and one could hear jazz blearing all over the city while everybody was masticating American chewing and puffing on louquuiiie streaaques chasterfeels and chamelles — that's when I heard le jazz for the first time — maybe I had heard some jazz notes before that on the radio when I was a boy — but I did not then recognize what it was — and what it would become for me — and how jazz would help me fill the hole of absence in me —

I heard jazz on my way back to Paris from Montflanquin in le Lot-et-Garonne — on top of an American tank — I swear it was on top of a tank — I am sure that if I could find Charlie — the G.I. who helped me up on the tank when it went by — I was walking — trying to hitch a ride — yes Charlie would certify that I really returned to Paris on an American tank — he was from New Jersey Charlie — that much I remember — but I have no idea where he is now — but on that tank they had a radio and it played jazz —

---

* Note in this abandoned fiction, and those that follow, Federman requested the typos remain.

a few days after I got back to Paris I found myself working in a factory where they made toothpaste tubes — one must continue to survive — one way or another — why not toothpaste tubes —

has anyone reading this any idea how toothpaste tubes are made — well let me show you how it was done in those days — those miserable days that followed the end of the war — when we were all struggling to regain our footing in life —

I started telling about jazz but we must detour jazz for a moment and talk about tubes —

imagine a factory — any factory — an ugly space — vast enough for a search to be in vain — narrow enough for escape to be in vain — sam would say — a vague structure with lots of dirty broken windows —

— unbearably cold in the winter — horribly hot in the summer — and inside — lined like a herd of bovine — or better yet — like fruit trees in an orchard — huge machines that look like monsters out of some cheap sci-fi movies — you — the machinist — stand in front of one of those machines — before you — about waist high — a shiny steel plate well anchored — in the middle of it a hole — a round hole — no it's not a hole — a cavity rather neatly carved into the steel — perfectly round and smooth — not too deep — well finished and polished — desirable in its perfection — it's called a Matrix — isn't that interesting — above that steel plate a complex metal construction holds — vertically — a rounded shinny metal rod of normal dimensions — that piece — I am almost tempted to say that phallus-like thing — is called in French un Piston — indeed it does look like a virile cock in erection —

now the action — this Piston when the machine is turned on electrically goes up and down up and down at a rapid precise pace and inserts itself hard into the Matrix — oh I should have mentioned — that on one side of the Matrix — let's say on the right side for the commodity of the description — there is like a little corridor that leads to the edge of the Matrix — like a little slightly inclined slide in a playground — no — like a little railroad track rather — well this is where I come in —

my job in this factory — for 10 hours — in those days the workday was 10 hours — what am I saying workday — for me it was nightwork — because I was on the night shift in that factory — from 8 to 8 — and sometime even overtime on the weekend — but without overpay — in this factory you worked à la piece — that is to say how many tubes you produced during your shift — weekend shifts count the same — one must survive —

my job was to slide along the little track — with two fingers — flat circular pieces of lead the size of a large coin — let's say half a dollar size — or if you prefer the size of a tube of toothpaste — not the family size — just the regular size — in those days they didn't have the improved larger family size — the lead coins were the size of a normal tube of toothpaste that feels like a cock in erection in your hand when you hold it — please excuse the directness of the language but it seems to me that to give a true picture of how the Piston and the Matrix function or malfunction I must rely on a precise vocabulary that will adequately describe how toothpaste tubes are given birth — just as good a way to see it as any other — since the technical terms of the tools used to make toothpaste tubes are in themselves erotically suggestive —

my job then — as one of the machinists — is to slide one of these lead coins — one after another consecutively — at the steady pace set by the up-and-down motion of the piston — into the little track and guide it with two fingers — delicately but as rapidly as possible — toward the matrix — and just as the coin settles in the bottom of the Matrix the Piston arrives — the blow of the Piston's head on the Matrix's bottom crushes the coin which then explodes and erects into a narrow cylinder open at both ends that clings to the Piston as it retreats upward — all the way up from whence it came — before surging again downward again — time after time — at the same pace during the entire night shift —

the thin rounded cylinder open at both ends that clings to the Piston does not however reach the top of the mechanism that holds and makes the

Piston go up and down — half way up a rounded gadget through which the Piston must go as it travels up and down — a very tight little gadget — releases the tube — for that's what the coin has become now — a tube open at both ends — and —

oh I forgot to mention the little air blower attached to one side of the machine — the same side as the little track — on the right too — which blows the open-ended tube into a box on the left side of the machine — a very ingenious system — one that requires precision and timing — an acrobatic synchronization from one box to another of the hand that slides the lead coin into the matrix just on time for the piston to crush it and then drag it back up transformed into a hot cylinder to be then blown into a box —

I said hot cylinder because these open-ended tubes when they are blown into the box after the violent blow they received from the Piston was extremely hot — so hot that to touch them without gloves causes a severe burn — however because of the delicate and precise action that the hands of machinist must perform — it is not possible to wear gloves — as a result sometimes when the blower malfunctions — and the tube is blown away in the wrong direction — the machinist must retrieve the wandering tube with his hand — the hand that is not slicing the coins in the Matrix — without thinking of the burning consequences — and he suffers yet another burn —

so now you see how toothpaste tubes are made —

this is the machine I had been trained to work — other machines performed other functions — for instance a machine twists one end of this cylinder to close it while another machine carves the little screw crevices where one screws the top — but before the machine that twist the bottom and close it one must fill the tubes with toothpaste — this is done by another machine that looks like a giant toothpaste tube — a really big tube — but with a very small opening through which the white paste is injected into the tubes — the filling of the tubes must logically be done before the twisting of the end upon itself — somebody had to think of that — otherwise how could the toothpaste be put into the tube when both ends are closed —

the filling of the tubes with toothpaste was done in a different part of the usine where I worked — in that part all the ouvriers wore white tabliers — and they were mostly women — many of them quite sexy in their tight white tabliers — in the summer when it was unbearably hot in the factory many of them wore nothing under their tablier —

how do I know that — because during the ten minute breaks we had every four hours — I would sometime wander in that part of the factory to admire the little beauties and even fool around with them — the other guys in my part of the factory also did that — during the ten minute break — but when le contre-maître saw us fooling around in the other part of the factory he would chew our asses and tell us to get back to work — or else — in those days one connerie and you were out —

in my part of the usine we wore grey ugly worn-out working clothes full of stains — the stains did not all come from the oil that we had to use every ten minutes to make the tube machines work better — but also from occasional sperm ejaculations — excuse the digression within the digression — but to give you a good sense of how it was to work in a factory in those days — doing the same gesture for ten hours during the night — women and men — yes there were women machinists too — most of us of a tender age still — sometimes — well no need to go into little details — let me just say that les cabinets de toilette were ideal places to relieve the tension of working on the machines for hours — especially the ladies' toilets — doing the same gestures at the same speed — again and again — the French call that kind of work travail à la chaîne — we call that on the line — whatever it is called it creates a lot of tension in the body — in the muscles especially — and in the head too — for if for an instant the hand that feeds the coins into the Matrix slows down or hesitates and the coin arrives too late then the piston hits only a piece of it or the empty bottom of the Matrix it explodes — burst into an ejaculation of steel fragments that fly all over the place — or rather I should say — splashes all over —

this brings me to describe the most crucial part of the machinist's job — it requires precision — the more the piston humps the matrix — I cannot see another way to explain that — the hotter it gets — and as is well known heat makes metal expand — so that the person working at that machine — in this case me — must check regularly with a little ruler the diameter of the Matrix — which also expands each time the Piston penetrates it — but not as rapidly as the Piston — I mean the heating up and the expanding — and the machinist must also measure the diameter and circumference of the Piston to make sure it still fits perfectly into the Matrix — otherwise if the Piston has grown larger than the Matrix — because of the heat — an explosion can occur when the over-heated piston hits the matrix which is not wide enough for the piston — even though the Matrix itself has expanded somewhat — but not enough to receive the violent blow of the enlarged piston — yes a big explosion —

when this happens — and it happens repeatedly each working night in the factory because there are — as I have already mentioned — many tube machines in that big factory — sometimes even several pistons explode at the same time on different machines — then the factory is full of dangerous bits of steel flying all over — and this is why we machinists have to wear a big plastic mask over their faces when working the tube machine —

by the way did I mention that this factory was in Vanves — just outside of Paris — I had to take the metro to Portes de Vanves to get there — and then walk a good 20 minutes in Vanves to get to the factory because the metro did not go beyond Portes de Vanves — and there was no bus line in the direction of the factory —

but to come back to the pistons — when one of the pistons exploded like that with a violent ejaculation of steel fragments all the other machinists — male and female — would explode into laughter and applaud sarcastically the one who had just failed to measure his or her tools properly — of course le contre-maître would immediately come rushing to the malfunctioning machine and chew the ass of the poor machinist for having again fucked up — and wasted time and production —

you may ask what does the machinist do when he finds that the Piston had become too enlarged to perform properly because of the heat — no the machinist does not wait until the piston cools off to start working again — that would have slowed down production — and production was the key word in that factory in Vanves — a new piston is quickly inserted in the proper place and the work continues while the over-heated piston is cooling off so that it can be used again in case of need — we had many Pistons de rechange in this factory —

speed was essential in those days — you would get paid according to how many boxes of coins had become tubes — there was an old guy with a little chariot who kept bringing more boxes of lead coins when the box you were working with was almost empty — and he would take away the box with the hot tubes —

you were paid by the number of tubes in the box — there was a machine that counted how many tubes were in each box — now if your machine malfunctioned and some of the tubes were fucked up you were not paid for the fucked up tubes — usually when the Pistons and the Matrix exploded there was always a tube implicated — and if during one shift you had several Piston explosions then you also had several fucked up tubes — that's how it went in that factory

by the way did I mention that I spent almost two years in that factory — until 1947 — when finally I left for America — where — two weeks after I arrived — I started working in a factory in Detroit — it was a Chrysler factory — I was making springs for the car seats — but that's another story — and a different technique —

but let me finish the toothpaste tube factory —

by the way I should mention that we did not wear gloves to do the work — it was a delicate type of work to slide those coins into the slot — it required a certain finger dexterity to measure the Matrix and the Piston — I learned a great deal working in this factory — a great deal I quickly forgot after I got out of there —

I also learned a great deal about the pleasures of sex in that factory — it was not unusual to get two or three blow jobs in one night —

well back to Le Jazz —

so here I am back in Paris in 1945 — 17 years old — working in a factory at night — so during the day I slept for a few hours after I got back to my crummy one room shit hole in the wall in Montparnasse — and then I would just wander in the streets discovering a city which to tell you the truth I really didn't know well — until 1942 I lived with my parents and sisters in Montrouge — a suburb of Paris — not too far from La Porte d'Orléans — but still outside the city —

[see *Aunt Rachel's Fur* for details]

and there was a place on one of the grand boulevards that sold music disques — in that place you could go listen to music — standing close to one of the walls you could put a coin in a slit and through a little speaker in the wall you could hear music — you had to put you ear close to the wall to be able to hear well because other people were listening to other music against the wall —

well me it's there — against that wall — that I listened to jazz almost every day — and understood that jazz was going to save my life — or at least help me survive —

the first record I listen to was a recording by Coleman Hawkins — ah Coleman Hawkins — he has remained my master in jazz — Hawkins on tenor sax — one of the great improvisers — there is one piece he plays called I'll Get By that is almost as good to me as an orgasm when I listen to it — then one day I heard Billy Holiday sing through the wall — and that day I didn't cry even though her song was so sad — it was called Gloomy Sunday — but during the night 5 or 6 pistons were pulverized at my machine — I was not really there — I was making love to Billy Holiday's voice inside the wall —

after that I kept returning to Billy Holiday's voice especially when she sang Lover Man for me — and I could hear in the background Lester Young making love to her with his saxophone — ah Prez — another one of my first loves on the sax — then Charlie Parker came along — but that's another story I have already told —

with my ear close to the wall in the music place on Le boulevard des Italiens in Paris I knew then that I was destined to go to America where I would find real jazz — where I would live real jazz — where I would even play real jazz —

[more might be told one day]

Raymond Federman's Ecological Self in Return to Manure

SERPIL OPPERMANN

When Raymond Federman wrote to me from his hospital bed in 2009, saying "Serpil, hurry up I am about to change tense," I was trying to formulate the ways in which his fiction could be read ecocritically.* I regret that he changed tense without seeing the ecological exploration of his novels, and never forgot his last famous words in that short e-mail I received. In this essay, I argue that if "identity and self-awareness are ecological in essence" (Jagtenberg and McKie 124), Federman's playfully constructed, polyphonic surfictional self can also be read as an ecological self embracing his memories that are diffusely enacted in a postmodernized landscape. *Return to Manure,* in particular, signals a more emphatic sense of an ecological self than his other novels do by focusing on Federman's childhood experiences in a farm in France. What emerges from the process of writing the story of his poignant relations with nonhuman natures in this novel is the idea that "the co-extensive materiality of humans and nonhumans offer multiple possibilities for forging new environmental paths" (Alaimo and Hekman 9). The farm environment with all of its details about domesticated animals in this decentered postmodern text, or surfictional autobiography, contests

---

* See *"To Whom It May Concern*: Reading Metafiction Ecocritically." *Canary Island Journal of Literature* (*Revista Canaria de Estudios Ingleses*) Special Issue on "Ecocriticism in English Studies," guest-edited by Juan Ignacio Oliva and Carmen Flys Junquera (April 2012): 95-110.

traditional environmentalism committed only to wildlife preservation. As Tom Jagdenberg and David McKie observe, "Life and meaning are fundamentally ecological" (122), which Federman would also acknowledge; but he would also add that this ecological dimension cannot always be framed in arguments about nature as a transcendent realm of plenitude for aesthetic contemplation. *Return to Manure* enables us to rethink nature in terms of the ongoing drama between species by highlighting the mutual destiny that unfolds in Federman's life story of suffering, injustice, violence, and survival.

Federman's Storied Life

Raymond Federman always believed that life gathers its true meaning in narrative forms, when it is storied; but this storied dimension of life emerges most meaningfully in what he calls "surfictional" mode of writing. In his definition, surfiction is "the kind of fiction that constantly renews our faith in man's intelligence and imagination rather than man's distorted vision of reality [...] This I call SURFICTION. However, not because it imitates reality, but because it exposes the fictionality of reality" (*Critifiction* 37).

According to Federman, "rather than serving as a mirror or redoubling on itself, fiction adds itself to the world thus creating a meaningful relation that did not previously exist" (*Critifiction* 38). "To write fiction today," he avers, "is before all an effort to create a DIFFERENCE, and not to pretend that fiction is the same thing as reality" (*Critifiction* 38). His fiction, therefore, is never an imitation of reality, but a re-creation, an invention, an imaginative foray into the depths of his memory about his traumatic experiences during the second World War. On July 16, 1942 his father, mother, and two sisters were "arrested and eventually deported to Auschwitz where they died in gas chambers. There are records of this. I escaped and survived by being hidden in a closet. I consider that traumatic day of July 16, 1942, to be my real birthdate, for that day I was given an excess of life" ("A Version" 64). This is the story

Federman rewrites and reinvents in all of his fiction. In *The Twofold Vibration* (1982), for example, he states: "Well you invent yourself as you go along, re-invent what you think really happened, this way you can survive anything" (51). The ongoing reinvention of himself begins with his first novel, *Double or Nothing* (1971) where he tells the story of a nameless writer who comes to America after losing his family in the death camps and struggles to write the story of the boy who survived. *Take It or Leave It* (1976), told by a nameless voice, is also the story of a survivor who is drafted into the U.S Army in the early 1950s. His third novel, *The Voice in the Closet* (1979) is a painful rewriting of the day when he hid in the closet while his family were taken away. The boy wants to tell the truth of what happened, but the story refuses to be told in coherent language, so the entire text is an uninterrupted sentence that constitutues the novel. Similarly, in *Smiles on Washington Square* (1985), *To Whom It May Concern* (1990), *Aunt Rachel's Fur* (2001), and *Loose Shoes: a life story of sorts* (2001) Federman searches for the traces of his own story of survival. The subsequent surfictions, *The Twilight of the Bums* (2002), *My Body in Nine Parts* (2005), *Return to Manure* (2006), and *The Carcasses: A Fable* (2009) all transcend and subvert traditional autobiographical voice to explore how one invents the story of one's life, and how imagination gets indelibly wedded to reality in the process of writing.

Integral to his reinvention of self is the fact that Federman never considers language as a disembodied human sign system, but as an embedded activity grounded in the very fabric of life itself which, he believed, is inseparable from the reality of language: "Everything (life, history, experience, even death) is contained in language" (*Critifiction* 89). Fiction writing for Federman is part of *being*: "fiction is above all an effort to apprehend and comprehend human existence played on the level of words" (*Critifiction* 38). Such an understanding of existence signifies the most intimate entanglements of life and its expessions — a continuum between language and the material world. It is this focus on the porosity of language and reality in his surfictions that enables him to merge linguistic constructionism in his bodily engagements with language. "I write with my entire body," he says in an interview. "My body, is I hope, in the text too [...] I am very tired when I am finished writing because I have used my body" ("Discussion" 383). In a way, Federman travels "through the entangled territories of material and discursive, natural and cultural, biological and textual" (Alaimo 238).

Inner and Outer Ecologies in *Return to Manure*

In *Return to Manure*, fusing the natural and the fictional worlds, this entanglement emerges through his bodily engagement with the manure-filled, rain-drenched fields, farm animals, gardens and flowers, with earthly organisms, as well as with debris and dirt. Evidently, the farm illustrates what Timothy Morton calls "dark ecology," which is "realistic, depressing, intimate, and alive and ironic at the same time" (*The Ecological* 16). That is why, Federman's surfictional autobiography in *Return to Manure* does not endorse "a celebratory poetics of nature" (Buell, "Literature as Environmental(ist)" 23); but renders a sense of a "a horizion of lost security and broken trust" (Beck 28). In such a context, his mode of speaking the modalities of the self does not prescribe to the vision of a harmonious ecological self. Rather, his ecological self traces how a sense of self works itself out in a dark ecological setting filled with inequities, injustice, and repression. This self is also played out in the discursive frames of reference to what Marina Schauffler calls inner and outer ecologies. Inner ecology, according to Schauffler, is "the spiritual beliefs and ethical values that guide our actions," while outer ecology is "a collective web of life and elemental matter in which we participate" (3). In the postmodern context, however, inner and outer ecologies take on diferent meanings as showcased by Federman's inner ecology relying on a relational logic of inhabiting both language and the world.

The process of Federman's storytelling embodies the formative effects of his past experiences, his memory, and his now-absent homeland. This is a psychologically inflected process in which reality and imagination exist in mutuality rather than as binary opposites. Federman's outer ecology — similarly configured upon a web of mutual relations between the ontology of place and its discursive constructions — is a recourse to a land that cannot anchor the vagaries of his real and invented selves, as well as the dispositions of identity and memory which are rendered ambiguous. Land here is more than a physical landscape, encompassing both the living environment and Federman's fictional reinventions of it in a dark ecological setting, which emerges as what we can call "Federmanland." Conceived this way, fiction writing becomes a constitutive experience of existence, and the environmental implications of this paradoxical ontology in Federmanland remain inevitably ambivalent. From a traditional ecological point of view, Federman's outer ecology problematizes environmental-ethical concerns mostly found, to quote Buell, in "impact-oriented thinking" and writing ("Literature as Environmental(ist)" 24); but from an ecological-postmodern perspective, it is suffused with playfully rendered environmental perspectives contesting the utopic visions of romantic ecologies through the author's existential struggle to capture the emotional and moral sense of an inner ecology that both shapes and is shaped by his outer ecology, which remains a typical site of dark ecology "alive and ironic" to repeat Morton's words. As Federman expresses it in his poem 'Among the Beasts', included in the first part of the novel: "Barefoot I ran on the cold earth/ and fell into a hole full of bees/ and all the trees laughed at me" (35).

The permeable boundaries between the inner and outer ecologies in *Return to Manure* indicate that the outer process is inextricably shot through with inner valuative significance. Thus, for Federman writing is synonymous with being, for it is the only means of coping with loss, displacement, pain, suffering, horror, and death. Therefore, his storied self is told, retold and, in a way, untold in many fragments. It emerges from this provisionality of a postmodern identity that highlights the impossibility of producing coherent self-knowledge. Thus, rather than seeking to demonstrate the importance of vitalizing relations with nature, Federman's account in *Return to Manure* presents an ambivalent relationship of the human self to its immediate environment by suspending the moral vision in self-nature connections. Enmeshed in postmodern complexity and a dark ecological setting, Federman's life writing here cannot paint an accurate picture of that to which it refers, precisely because that referent has been lost forever. Therefore, to quote Jakki Spicer, his writing negotiates "among the seeming contradictions between truth and accuracy, memory and history, objective and subjective truth, and so on" (388). It represents the process of struggling through writing for self-realization, and along the process providing an interesting fusion of dark ecological and surfictional modes of writing.

At the outset, *Return to Manure* traverses the spheres of inner and outer ecologies, focusing on the sustained intensity of Federman's childhood memories in a farm near Montflanquin in France. As a "displaced storyteller" Federman problematizes the ecological issues invested by ethical considerations, and plays with the borderline between the past associated with the lost homeland and the present, which is marked by absence. He does, however, easily negotiate the tensions between fiction and fact, and human and nonhuman natures, moving his writing beyond the irresolvability of the distinction between postmodern and ecological autobiographical modes even if his surfictional mode deconstructs the voice of homogeneity that the ecological concept of self usually generates. Using a surfictional self in ecological contexts actually transforms the boundaries of ecological discourse, and works over the limitations of logocentric approaches to the concept of an ecological self, which is often criticized for having little "grounding in practical hands on living" (Booth 7). It is quite clear that *Return to Manure* does not attempt to forge imaginary links between surfictional and ecological life writings, but discloses the experience of a surficitional self within a dark ecological setting whereby the ecology of a surfictional self provokes alternative articulations of ecological discourses of identity. This is to conceptualize the self as that in which the writer rethinks his relation to the physical environment and speaks from a discursive point of departure without totally abandoning his connections to the real world in his writing. This use of the self is obviously incompatible with the notion of some transcendent integral self one finds in ecological life writing. But, although it poses a direct challenge to the holistic concept of ecological self that seeks to produce coherent self-knowledge, the surfictional concept of self offers a more pragmatic sense of living in the world in its worst conditions. Here the issues of dejection, death, manure, shock and sexuality, traumatic sense of displacement, and forced dislocation play an essential role in the unfolding of an ecological perception that radically challenges and critically subverts the realist and naturalist traditions promoted by ecological life writing.

The question, then, is how to construct a language of an ecology of a surfictional self that is able to speak to ecocriticism within the framework of common principles. *Return to Manure* focuses on the ways of making that language matter—a language that invests in the necessity, as Federman puts it, of "producing meaning, and not merely reproducing a pre-existing meaning" (*Critifiction* 38). In an interview with Charles Bernstein, Federman also said: "I wanted the box of words not to say what it was, but *to be what it was*" (my italics, 74). In framing language ontologically in fiction writing, Federman claims that "rather than serving as a mirror or redoubling on itself, fiction adds itself to the world thus creating a meaningful relation that did not previously exist" (*Critifiction* 38). The "distinction between the real and the fictitious, the imaginary and the factual," he also says, "disappears when I contemplate my life and when I write" (Qtd. in McCaffery 291-92). Environmental attention here is only implicitly present; instead Federman discloses an ironic ecological self "forever displaced into fiction" ('Displaced Person' 100), but which is never distinct from the body. "I write with my entire body," he says in an interview included in *Autobiographie and Avant-garde*. "My body, is I hope, in the text too [...] I am very tired when I am finished writing because I have used my body" ('Discussion' 383). His ecological self is, therefore, a highly existential agency which can neither be separated from his real life experiences, nor totally linked to his real life personality. As he tells McCaffery, "it's this act of fictionalizing my life which has given me the chance to make sense out of my life [...] my life is not the story, the story is my life" (291).

Barry Lopez, the prominent American nature writer, states with good reason that "Human imagination is shaped by the architecture of the world it encounters at an early age" (3), which especially holds true for Federman, as this architecture set the direction of his self-writing in terms of the cycles of life and death that could only be expressed in a surfictional mode of writing. Despite his metafictional self-consciousness, one could say that for Federman the sense of being "emplaced" and/or feeling "displaced" constitutes the major narrative question in many of his novels. Referring to himself in the third person, he writes that

> one must accept the fact that what makes up his fiction is not necessarily what is there [...] but what is not there [...] In other words, what is important to notice in Federman's fiction is what is absent. And indeed, the fundamental aspect, the central theme of his fiction is ABSENCE (*Critifiction* 86).

The loss of "the sense of being environed" pervades Federman's narratives, entailing a "self-conscious sense of an inevitable but uncertain and shifting relation between being and physical context" (Buell, *The Future* 62). This relationship takes on a deeper and a more complex meaning in the self-reflexive medium of Federman's autobiographical surfictions as the problematic connections between imagination, memory, and place fuse with the logic of metafiction. Since the continuity with place has been shattered when he was a child, Federman turns to imagination to mend the broken link, but he always suggests this loss cannot fully be restored in language. Therefore, his surfictions highlight a conscious problematization of conventional autobiographies through an ironic subversion of the rhetoric of self-revelation. However, in the middlepoint between life and fiction where the multiple voices of the writer's self struggle to reinstate the world he lost, one finds an unusual acceptance of the unruly sides of both inner and outer ecologies. The search for the lost connections with the land and the exploration of self gradually crystallize into questioning of the divide between inner and outer ecological relations. Federman's life writing, for this reason, evinces a highly existential narrative ontology that highlights the felt absence of an embodied connection to place, giving an intensity of meaning to what happens when one feels placeless.

The Story of the Farm

Return to Manure epitomizes this problematic link between inner and outer ecologies through a sustained intensity of Federman's painful childhood memories during World War II in a farm near Montflanquin where he witnessed the frightening aspects of animals' life, and their suffering. Following his family's arrest in 1942, the 13 year old Federman finds a way to escape on a train and jumps off in the southwest of France. He finds a farm where he stays for three years shovelling manure until France is liberated. "I was only thirteen when my parents were taken away," he writes, evoking a keen sense of sadness:

> A shy scared city boy who had never seen a cow
> or a pig up close, who didn't know anything
> about plucking a dead chicken's feathers, or how
> animals climb on top of each other to fornicate.
> But there I was with manure up to my knees,
> milking cows, cultivating the land with a pair of
> oxen hitched to a plow, feeding the pigs, the
> chickens, the rabbits, the geese, the goats. (33)

In his attempts to retrieve the unspeakable past Federman indulges in a digressive storytelling practice filled with perplexities and complications as it is told in a mixture of French and English. As he reminds his readers in *Critifiction*, "A voice within a voice speaks in me, double-talks in me bilingually, in French and in English, separately or, at times, simultaneously. That voice constantly plays hide-and-seek with its shadow. Now there is nothing unusual about that" (76). Since he thinks and dreams both in English and French, it is not unusual for him "to have a voice within a voice. It means that you can never separate your linguistic self from its shadow" (77). Similar to his other novels, *Return to Manure* is a perfect surfictional exercise in voices within voices that play hide and seek with Federman the writer. The novel opens with the real couple—Federman and his wife Erica—traveling in France to locate the Louzy farm, a journey one expects would lead to an idyllic natural countryside, but it leads to its "absolute opposite," as Christian Moraru in his review has also noted, dehumanizing the boy and "pushing him closer and closer to the other 'brutes' (animals) and into their scatological world" (18). The French farm is a world of absolute torture steeped deep in refuse which he recalls as "*une histoire de merde,* " mirroring the Jewish boy's dejection by the world. The farm animals, and in particular the cows constantly produce and literally live in manure. The brutal farmer Louze tells him: "Manure is the essence of life [...] and each time he would hurl a pitchfork full of manure in my face" (85). The 13 year old Federman hates the job of getting the manure out of the barn:

> Up before the sun to shovel the manure out of the barn, milk the cows, feed the pigs, the chickens, the ducks, the rabbits, the geese, the whole damn zoo of those so-called domesticated animals who spend their life doing nothing but eating and crapping all day and all night, until we kill them to eat them and defecate them in turn. Man is there ever a lot of shit on a farm.
>
> Yet nature is a damn good system. It's amazing how it functions, how it keeps renewing itself with shit. That's right, with shit.

> [...]
> And so it goes until the end of time. What a
> beautiful system nature is. It keeps jump-
> starting itself with shit. (78)

As a "displaced storyteller" Federman finds himself entangled in a problematized relationship with the immediacy of the farm environment. By drawing close anologies between the animals in the farm and his own suffering, he begins questioning the borderline between the human and the animal. "I didn't suffer from hunger," he writes, "[b]ut I suffered watching how the animals suffered in order to become food for us" (121). So he imagines "a revolt of the domesticated animals against people who eat them"(121) and says: "Even the non-carnivorous animals would eat the farmers's meat in the story I invented for myself" (122). Because Federman at age 13 cannot comprehend the animals' status as things to be consumed as the ultimate Other, he makes an innovative gesture of bringing to the forefront an invented fictive world where the Other takes revenge for the wrongs it suffers. In view of the past sufferings the 13-year-old Federman endured, however, the need for a solid ethical foundation in his relations to the animals, does not seem to fulfill his ontological need for a univocal meaning of his loss of family in the concentration camps, the symbolic consumption of humans. The implicit reference to humans as expendable resources complicates the moral space in which Federman asks us to rethink our value judgements and human behaviour to develop an ethics for the future that will affirm values and "open up the possibility of reciprocity between humans and the rest of nature" (Weston 335). But as the novel suggests, all forms of domination, exploitation, oppression, and violence are wholly interconnected in this world; and therefore Federman's sarcastic aproach undermines and radically disrupts the conventional idea of a neat ethical intertwining of the human and nonhuman animals. The text revolves around the question of the conditions of morality pointing out the stress on the author who apparently suspects but vindicates the shaky ground of developing affective ethics in a violent world. Paradoxically, however, this critical outlook is what fosters moral responsibility and urges him to develop an "affective perception" (Fox and McLean 159) in relation to animals. "We can be ethical, as Aldo Leopold also maintains, "only in relation to what we can see, feel, understand, love or otherwise have faith in" (251). But Federman's experiences in the farm complicates the rooting of self in the natural world as he finds hardly any space for aesthetic contemplation in his hard labor, simply because he witnesses and experiences suffering around him all the time. His narrative is constantly interrupted by questions framed in boxes, supposedly asked by his wife Erica, and implied readers, one of which is: "Federman, if we may interrupt. Since we are talking about natural things. On the farm being so close to nature did you appreciate it?" (165). Federman's response is telling: "You must be kidding. Mother Nature on the farm was not on our side. But neither was she against us. She was indifferent to us" (165). And he adds: "Nature and I, we didn't get along too well. I have all kinds of scars on my body from my struggle with nature. One in particular on my left knee. I must tell you how I got that one" (166). What is manifest here is not an image of nature as a form of refuge and a place for self-revelation but a rather brutal environment with daily challenges. It does, however, reshape the essence of Federman's early self through different forms of "embodied activity" in farm work, shovelling manure, plowing the earth, killing pigs, chickens, and rabbits for dinner, washing the cows and the bull, cutting wood, activites which are performed routinely every day producing feelings of anger: "One thing I do remember is that on the farm I was always angry. Angry about everything. The people. The tools, the weather. The animals. The geese especially. They would always come chasing after me trying to bite me, even though I felt sorry for them" (174).

Far from being "a pristine wilderness of pure meaning" (Morton, *Ecology* 122), nature here signifies the earthly condition of suffering and death. Federman explains more vividly:

> The crude and vulgar mode of existence of the
> people and animals had gradually taken over my
> whole being. I was confused, and could not
> understand the indifferent violence of
> reproduction and of death which surrounded
> me. Every day animals were born, died, or being
> killed. And as I participated in this incessant
> process of birth and death, I became accustomed
> to its violence and simplicity. ('A Version' 70).

In *Return to Manure* nature is a critical appraisal of the conventional concept of wilderness transmitted in the narratives of ecological life writing. With its unending cycle of death and violence, the French farm turns into an covert signifier of a Nazi death camp with its unspeakable horrors. "Death was always around us" (36) he recalls. That is why Federman cannot tell the story in the representational form of traditional realism, and therefore "narrative experimentalism is not a luxury but a necessity" (Moraru 17). "I went on telling Erica, or myself," he says, "why the story of the farm should be self-reflexive. I can't help it. I cannot write it if I do not watch myself write" (89). It is the unspeakable itself that necessitates this form of writing, the very material condition of it that prevents realistic representations. Only a discontinuous, fragmented style can, in Federman's view, provide an understanding of the fractured and tortured lives of the voiceless. As he notes at the end of the novel, "Life on the farm was a struggle without an issue. Not only for me but also for everyone else" (176). The stories embedded in such environments associated with dark ecological tenor can hardly provide romantic notions of nature; their significance lies in designating the landscape as "an embodiment of stories" (Mortimer-Sandilands 283). When Federman returns to the farm, he realizes that the landscape here, though now deserted and decaying, "continues to embody, support, and create memory" (Mortimer-Sandilands 283). In this sense writing the farm becomes an embodied practice, which is both physically located and discursively constructed in the process of telling the story.

The story of the farm and Federman's storied self are co-extensive and involve all the stories Federman has been telling in his fictions to fashion a narrative ontology for his life: the stories of the untellable, the silenced dead, and absences. Christian Moraru writes that "Federman's narrative ontology [...] always borders on voicelessness, on silence, stems from it and risks ending up back in it, to things unspoken or unspeakable" (17). Returning to manure, therefore, is an existential problem for Federman, for it means going back to the realm of the unspeakable to re-invent it in fiction. Hence when Erica asks him, "How can anyone ever believe what you say? Or what you write. You can never separate your memories from your inventions," his answer is: "I've said it many times before. I make no distinction between memory and imagination" (180). Since this context of permeable boundaries between imagination and memory is also extended to human and nonhuman natures in the novel, it compels us to maintain a non-romantic sense of ethical responsibility toward the nonhuman environments. This context can also be read as a consideration of the fact that there are other beings and they have a right to occupy a moral space just like the surfictional forms of expressing the self do. It must also be considered as another form of meaning making aspect of the world. At the end of the novel Erica says: "Look at this beautiful landscape. The hills, the meadow, the river, the trees. It's charming. I could live here." "You must be kidding," Federman answers, "What would I do here? Relive all the suffering?" (194). In this way Federman presents a different sense of inner and outer ecologies, and discloses their unruly aspects that are often left unexplored in ecological autobiographies. The ecology of a surfictional self, for this reason, is more realistic than the ecological self cultivating a sustained link with beautiful natural landscapes offering divine revelation and wholeness. By incorporating life and language, the real and the discursive, the ecology of a surfictional self, however, reveals how the world is at the same time both fictional and real, dark and light, and how both sides often merge in a relational rather than an oppositional paradigm. For example, although the landscape got on his nerves, especially in hot summer days when he was toiling there, Federman also mentions fruit trees which gave him pleasure: "We grew apple trees, pears, plums, peaches, apricots, cherries, plums. We could have survived on fruit alone. And I shouldn't forget the wild berries in the hedgerows" (182).

It is important to note that Federman does not abandon the real in favor of the discursive, but redefines them in terms of what Timothy Morton calls a "mesh" that is a "nontotalizable, open-ended concatenation of interrelations that blur and confound boundaries at practically any level" (*Ecology* 275). Conflating the discursive and the material in a mesh also indicates a new way of understanding the relationship between self and nature, which allows Federman to come to terms with the story of his life. He discursively constructs it, while showing at the same time how the discursive construction is inextricably related to nondiscursive experience of the world. Anticipating thus the new "onto-ethico-epistemology" (in Karen Barad's terms), which suggests "a fundamental inseparability of epistemological, ontological, and ethical considerations" (Barad 26), Federman eloquently notes: "The subject is no longer enclosed within the frame of the observer's vision. Instead there is a field of energy — usually a self-reflexive energy — whereby observer, subject, frame, and medium merge and interact" (*Critifiction* 55). Accordingly, Federman's approach points not only to the epistemological inseparability of the observer and the observed, but more importantly, to borrow Barad's words, to "the ontological inseparability of agentially intra-acting components" (33), which signifies a mutual entanglement of both discursive and nondiscursive engagements of participating with/ in the world. It is in this framework that Federman's surfictional fusion of inner and outer ecologies offers negotiable pathways between postmodern and ecological approaches to self-nature relations.

Endnote:

This essay is a thoroughly modified and re-written version of "An Ecology of a Surfictional Self: Raymond Federman's Inventions,"published in *Ecology and Life Writing*. Eds. Alfred Hornung and Zhao Baisheng. Heildelberg: Universitatsverlag Winter, 2013. 353-374.

Works Cited:

Alaimo, Stacy. 'Trans-Corporeal Feminisms and the Ethical Space of Nature.' *Material Feminisms*. Eds. Stacy Alaimo and Susan Hekman. Bloomington: Indiana UP, 2008. 237-264.

Alaimo, Stacy and Susan Hekman. 'Introduction: Emerging Models of Materiality in Feminist Theory.' *Material Feminisms*. Eds. Stacy Alaimo and Susan Hekman. Bloomington: Indiana UP, 2008. 1-19.

Barad, Karen. *Meeting the Universe Halfway: Quantum Physics and the Entanglement of Matter and Meaning*. Durham and London: Duke UP, 2007.

Beck, Ulrich. *Risk Society: Towards a New Modernity*. Trans. Mark Ritter. London: Sage, 1992.

Bernstein, Charles. 'THE LINEBREAK INTERVIEW'. *The Laugh that Laughs at the Laugh: Writing from and about the Pen Man, Raymond Federman*. The Spec.Issue of *Journal of Experimental Fiction 23*. Ed. Eckhard Gerdes. New York: Writer's Club, 2002. 69-78.

Booth, Annie L. 'Who am I? Who are you? The Identification of Self and Other Three Ecosophies.' *The Trumpeter: Journal of Ecosophy*. 13.4 (1996): 1-10.

Buell, Lawrence. *The Future of Environmental Criticism: Environmental Crisis and Literary Imagination*. Malden, MA: Blackwell, 2005.

---. 'Literature as Environmental(ist) Thought Experiment'. *Ecology and the Environment: Perspectives from the Humanities*. Ed. Donald K. Swearer with Susan Lloyd McGarry. Cambridge: Harvard UP, 2009. 21-36.

Federman, Raymond. 'Displaced Person: The Jew/The Wanderer/The Writer'. *Denver Quarterly*. 19.1 (1984):85-100.

---. 'A Version of My Life: Early Years'. *Contemporary Authors Autobiography Series*. Vol. 8. Ed. Mark Zadrozny. Detroit: Gale, 1989. 63-81.

---. 'Discussion: Joseph Schöpp and Timothy Dow Adamas Papers'. *Autobiographie & Avant-garde: Alain Robbe-Grillet, Sergei Doubrovsky, Rachid Boudjedra, Maxine Hong Kingston, Raymond Federman, Ronald Sukenick*. Eds. Alfred Hornung and

Ernstpeter Ruhe. Tübingen: Gunter Narr Verlag, 1992. 377-384.

---. *Critifiction: Postmodern Essays.* New York: State U of New York P, 1993.

---. *The Twofold Vibration.* Bloomington: Indiana UP, 1982.

---. *Return to Manure: a nostalgic tale.* Tuscaloosa: FC2 of The U of Alabama P, 2006.

Fox, Michael Allen, and Leslie McLean. 'Animals in Moral Space'. *Animal Subjects: An Ethical Reader in a Posthuman World.* Ed. Jodey Castricano. Cultural Studies Series: Environmental Humanities. Waterloo, Ontorio: Wifrid Laurier UP, 2008.

Jagdenberg, Tom, and David McKie. *Eco-Impacts and the Greening of Postmodernity. New Maps for Communication Studies, Cultural Studies, and Sociology.* Thousand Oaks: Sage, 1997.

Leopold, Aldo. *A Sand County Almanac.* New York, Ballantine, 1966.

Lopez,. Barry. 'Conference Excerpt: Barry Lopez'. *ASLE News* 9. 2 (1997): 3

McCaffery, Larry. 'An Interview with Raymond Federman'. *Contemporary Literature.* 24.3 (Fall 1983): 285-306.

Moraru, Christian. 'Scatologikon, or Federman's Return'. *American Book Review.* 28.4 (May/June 2007): 17-18.

Mortimer-Sandilands, Catriona. 'Landscape, Memory, and Forgetting: Thinking Through (My Mother's) Body and Place'. *Material Feminisms.* Eds. Stacy Alaimo and Susan Hekman. Bloomington: Indiana UP, 2008. 265-287.

Morton, Timothy. *Ecology Without Nature: Rethinking Environmental Aesthetics.* Cambridge: Harvard UP, 2007.

---. *The Ecological Thought.* Cambridge: Harvard UP, 2010.

Schauffler, Marina E. *Turning to Earth: Stories of Ecological Conversion.* Charlottesville: U of Virginia P, 2003.

Spicer, Jakki. 'The Author is Dead, Long Live the Author: Autobiography and the Fantasy of the Individual'. *Criticism.* 47. 3 (Summer 2005): 387-403.

Weston, Anthony. 'Before Environmental Ethics'. *Environmental Ethics.* 14 (1992): 321-38.

Ramona

AN ABANDONED FICTION

RAYMOND FEDERMAN

Ace! SoS!* Something disturbing happened. I don't know if I should be overjoyed or frightened, or if I should panic, kill myself, or simply forget it. Perhaps just a passing thing. A dark cloud.

The situation is serious. The next novel is here, the one I must write now. The book I must now commit myself to for who knows how long. I say novel, but who knows what new genre this one will invent as it writes itself, or unwrites itself.

The subject? What it'll be? The form & content of my father.

Just as you some time ago, not so long ago reconstructed and deconstructed your father postmortem, I think my father . . . papa, I should say, because I always called him, papa, or else I would say mon père when referring to him — the word father sounds alien in my mouth, I never had the occasion to say father à mon père. I never could call papa father or dad in my borrowed tongue, he changed tense too soon, or rather they changed the tense on him, before I went into exile into my borrowed tongue . . . papa is asking me to write this book.

That's the subject then: Mon père. Papa.

---

*   George Chambers.

As for the form. Well, that will take shape as the story unfolds.

No. This one will be written in English, not in French, the last one was too hard, too painful to do in the frog language, but there'll be a lot of French mixed with the English in this one because I always remember my father. It's always papa I think about. Does that make sense to you?

The book will be called Ramona. Yes Ramona.

Why?

Here, why don't you listen to the opening pages, you'll understand why Ramona. That's all that's written so far. Just a few pages. But I think the whole book is there already. Tell me what you think. Here is the beginning.

*

RAMONA

My father's favorite song was RAMONA. It goes like this, *Ramona je t'aimerai toute la vie, Ramona je t'aimerai . . .* In French, because I only know the words in French. But I think that song also exists in English.

My father always listened to the French song, that's why I know it only in French. *Ramona je t'aimerai toute la vie . . .*

My father, the dreamer, l'artiste manqué, le romantique, the Trotskyist, the gambler, le coureur de femmes, the Brudny Zyd, my tuberculous father, who never achieved his vocation, my father while listening to Ramona on the scratched disque playing on our vieux dusty phonographe with the big speaker and la petite manivelle, my father, papa, mon père would dream.

La petite manivelle! Hah! That's funny. I don't even know what you call that in English, la petite manivelle, you know the thing you turn to rewind le phonographe. You know. Sometimes towards the end of the disk, when the phonograph was running out of gas, when its was unwinding, the voice of the singer would linger into distortions, the voice of the singer would become . . . so slow, slow and sad too.

I never knew who was singing the Ramona that my father loved so much. It was a woman, a young woman I think, with a beautiful deep sad raspy voice. She died young. My father told me that one day when I asked him if maybe someday we could go listen to her in person . . . She had tuberculosis. Like my father. That's all my father told me about. I don't even know her name, or perhaps I knew it once but have forgotten it. But even me when I listened to Ramona with papa, I could feel tenderness for her. Yes, that's what it was, tenderness . . .

No, not passion. I was too young then to know what passion was.

I did mention that my father was tuberculous. That he had a lung removed. I think it was the left lung. He spat blood all the time. I'll have to say more about that later.

It is possible that I felt passion while listening to Ramona avec papa, but I didn't know that it was passion. Papa, of course, knew what passion is. I am sure he knew. Papa was a very passionate man. He loved women. Il était coureur de femmes. That's what all my aunts and uncles always said about him. Un coureur de femmes. Un fainéant. Un rien-du-tout Papa.

So what. So he loved women. Maybe that's what he left with me when he changed tense. His passion. His passion for women. For love. Sex? Look, it's not because I am writing about my father that I have to become puribond.

Yes, even me, while listening to the sad voice of the singer singing *Ramona je t'aimerai toute la vie* . . . I would feel tenderness for her and I would imagine her being petite and fragile, with very long black hair, and very long curly eyelashes. That's all I could imagine about her then. Today I could imagine her much better if I could listen to her sing Ramona again. Today I know how to imagine a beautiful woman. A woman one desires.

But how I can I find the record with her singing? I don't know her name.

When papa listened to Ramona there was dreaming in his eyes, I could see that, and I know he was dreaming about his failed vocation. And about his failed loves. He was dreaming, there in our squalid one room apartment, ce misérable petit taudis where papa and maman, and my two sisters, Sarah et Jacqueline, and me too of course, lived, if one can call the sordid kind of existence we had, living.

When papa listened to Ramona, sitting in his old fauteuil à moitié défoncé, facing le phonographe, I could tell he was dreaming, I could tell he was making up stories about how he could have become un grand artiste if ...

Ah oui, if ...

I could see it in his eyes, but I could also feel it in the tips of his fingers, in his fingernails gently scratching my back when I would say to him, as we listened to Ramona, papa gratte moi le dos, s'il te plaît, ça me gratte là, près de l'omoplate gauche ...

I had just studied human anatomy à l'école des garçons rue de Bagneux, that's why I could tell my father that it was my left shoulder blade that itched.

Anyway, as I sat on the floor at papa's feet, next to his fauteuil, an old beat-up fauteuil vert à moitié défoncé, me too I listened to the phonograph play Ramona, while papa's fingers scratched my back dreamily, and that's why I can say now that I knew he was dreaming, dreaming the great works of art he wanted to create and knew he would never create.

Not because he was lazy, like my aunts and uncles always said, not because he was sick all the time. Because he was not ready yet. They changed tense too soon on him. I am sure he would have created something immortal. A masterpiece if they had given him the time. I could feel it in his fingers.

Papa, il avait de très belles mains, with long fingers. Very white hands. I think I have my father's hands.

He had done some paintings that may even have had artistic value. Who knows. His friends, most of them foreigners, struggling artists, starving artists I should say, always said good things about his paintings, they looked up to him, but deep inside my father knew he had failed, failed to achieve the vocation inscribed in him by his father, or some remote ancestor.

I think my father was the first one in our family to become an artist. Or at least the first one to fail as an artist. All the others before him, his father, grand-father, great-grand-father, and those who went before them, all of them were schlemils. Except it is said that one of them, way back in the 16th century, was a conquistador who became very rich in the new world. But he was a mean bastard. He killed a lot of people in the new world. His name was the Baron Nicolas von Federman. Yes, he was nobility.

Whether or not my father was a descendant of that Federman may never be authenticated, but me I believe he was. There was something aristocratic about my father, even if he was a Trotskyist, and never achieved anything. He always dressed elegantly. He was good-looking. He had gray eyes. Women walking by in the street would turn around to look at him. I often saw that when I went out with my father.

I once wrote a poem about that. I mean about the nothing, le rien-du-tout that my father was. I'll put it here, for whatever it's worth. It's called . . .

BEFORE THAT

Some say, can say: my father was a farmer,
and his father before him, and his father
before that. We are of the earth.

Others say, can say: my father was a builder,

and his father before him, and his father
before that. We are of the stone.

And others can say: my father was a sailor,
and his father before him, and his father
before that. We are of the water.

They have been farmers, builders, sailors,
no doubt, since the time earth, stone, water
entered into the lives of men, and still are.

I am a writer, but I cannot say: my father
was a writer, nor his father before him,
nor his father before that. I have no antecedent.

My father, and his father before him, and his father
before that were neither of the earth, nor of the stone,
nor of the water. The world was indifferent to them.

I write, perhaps, so that one day my children can say:
my father was a writer, the first in our family.
We are now of the word. We are inscribed in the world.

I feel I could write on the earth, on the stone.
It seems to me that I could even write on water.
I write to establish an antecedent for my children.

Five thousand years without writing in my family,
what can I do against this force which presses
behind me? Say that I write to fill this void?

Say, I suppose, that of my father I cannot say anything,
except what I have invented to fill the immense gap
of his absence, and of his erasure from history.

No, I am wrong, you see, because I can say: my father
was a wanderer, he came from nowhere and went nowhere.
He came without earth, stone, water, and he went wordless.

While contemplating his failures, and absentmindedly scratching my back, my father was perhaps thinking that his son, I mean me, would someday achieve the vocation he had failed to achieve. And so, gently, with the tip of his fingers . . . already aware that his tuberculosis would soon kill him, or that some unforgivable enormity would erase him from history . . . yes, as he listened to *Ramona je t'aimerai toute la vie* my father knew that soon he would change tense or the tenses would be changed for him in spite of himself and he would never achieve his vocation . . . and so while gently scratching my left omoplate he would try to make me feel this yearning for greatness, he would try to transmit with the tip of his fingers this vocation into my body, into my skin, my flesh, my bones, and up here into my head.

As my father and I sat together listening to Ramona, papa lost in his dream, me slowly dozing off under the gentle touch of papa's hand, he would infuse in me, transfer in me . . . ah, shit how shall I say it! . . . he would give me my inheritance. His vocation. That's all he gave me. Yes, there in my head, papa put the dream he was dreaming while listening to a sad woman's voice sing *Ramona je t'aimerai toute la vie, Ramona je t'aimerai* . . .

*

Ace . . . SoS! Shall I burn this? Or do I take the risk . . . the risk of having to contemplate yet another failure. Like my father. The risk of stumbling into sentimentality.

The other day, while taking a shower, I caught myself humming *Ramonaaaa je t'aimerrrrai toute la viiie* . . . Dragging the words into the soapy water.

I told you the situation is critical.

*

MON PÈRE L'ARTISTE MANQUÉ

C'est ainsi que je travaillais tous les jours, plus ou moins absent du monde et de moi-même. Comme si j'étais coupé des espoirs naturels de la vie. Mon existence stagnante dans le vide du non-sens.

Il y avait nulle part pour faire marche arrière. Nulle part pour aller de l'avant. J'étais coincé dans une condition temporaire et chaque jour je m'enfonçais encore un peu plus dans l'incompréhension. Ma vie, n'était pas devenue un tas de cendres, mais un tas d'émotions désordonnées. Je me sentais insignifiant.

De tels sentiments contrastaient radicalement avec la confiance en soi et l'imprudence de mon père. Mon père l'artiste tuberculeux, dont les belles mains avaient été transformées en parchemin pour filtrer la lumière.

Mon père, l'artiste manqué qui pensait que tout finit toujours par l'échec, et que l'on doit alors faire de l'échec une occasion. C'est ce qu'il m'a dit un jour, quand j'étais encore tout petit. Il me l'a dit quand je le regardais travailler sur un de ses tableaux, et que je lui ai demandé de quoi il s'agissait. Et c'est qu'il a répondu. Il faut faire de l'échec un succès retentissant J'ai pas très bien compris ce qu'il voulait dire. Dans la peinture qu'il était en train de faire y avait rien de reconnaissable pour moi. C'était que des grosses taches de peinture. Je devais avoir sept ou huit ans. Je suppose que j'étais bien trop jeune pour comprendre ce que mon père faisait, et pourquoi ma mère lui disait tout le temps, Pourquoi tu peins pas quelque chose qui remplirait le ventre de tes enfants au lieu de peindre ces taches de peinture si laides que personne n'en veut. Mais mon père répondait, Tu ne comprends rien. On est en train de changer la façon dont les gens regardent les tableaux, et la façon dont ils regardent le monde.

Une fois de temps en temps mon père m'amenait avec lui dans le garage où lui et quelques autres artistes travaillaient. C'étaient tous des étrangers. Des russes, des polonais, des hongrois, des roumains, et des autres étrangers encore. Ils parlaient tous des langues différentes. Je sais pas comment il faisait mon père, mais il comprenait toutes ces langues. Mais en plus de faire de la peinture, tous ces artistes étrangers s'engueulaient tout le temps pour la politique. Mon père il gueulait le plus fort. Il était communiste mon père.

L'un des artistes qui travaillait dans ce garage avec mon père était déjà célèbre. Il venait aussi de Pologne comme mon père. Je crois qu'il s'appelait Marcoussis. Oui, c'est çat. Louis Marcoussis. Les autres artistes l'appelaient toujours Loulou. Il était devenu connu. Il était plus âgé que mon père, mais ils étaient copains. Ils parlaient tout le temps polonais ensemble. Ils passaient beaucoup de temps ensemble à jouer aux cartes dans les cafés.

Comment tu sais ça ?

Je le sais parce que souvent, quand mon père rentrait pas dîner, ma mère m'envoyait le chercher au Café Métropole à la Porte d'Orléans. C'est là où les artistes de Montrouge passaient leur temps à jouer aux cartes. Ils jouaient à la belote. Mon père m'a même appris à y jouer. Oui, c'est à la belote qu'ils jouaient dans ce café enfumé, tout en discutant la politique.

Au café Métropole mon père et ses amis jouaient pour de l'argent à la belote. Je le sais parce que, quand j'allais chercher mon père et que je lui disais qu'on l'attendait à la maison, il me disait d'attendre la fin de la partie, et c'est alors que je voyais que les perdants devaient payer les gagnants. Parfois mon père gagnait. Souvent il perdait. Quand il gagnait ma mère était heureuse pour les enfants parce qu'il lui donnait quelques sous de plus pour acheter de la bouffe.

Je crois t'avoir dit que mon père avait la tuberculose, mais ça l'empêchait pas de fumer cigarette après cigarette quand il jouait aux cartes ou travaillait à ses tableaux. Des Gitanes. A la chaîne il les fumait. Je m'en souviens. Des Gitanes sans filtre. A cette époque les cigarettes avaient pas de filtre. Quand mon père avait plus de cigarettes, il m'envoyait acheter ses Gitanes chez Marius, le café au coin de la rue où on vivait.

[Pour plus de détails sur la tuberculose de mon père, lisez *La Fourrure de Ma tante Rachel*.]

Mais revenons au garage. C'était un garage abandonné dans la zone pas loin de l'endroit où nous vivions à Montrouge. Il y avaient des poutres pourries au plafond. Je m'en souviens parfaitement. Je veux dire des poutres au plafond, parce que les artistes qui travaillaient là, chacun dans un coin du garage, disaient souvent en plaisantant qu'un jour ou l'autre le plafond s'effondrerait sur eux. Et je me souviens de ce que mon père leur a dit un jour, et nous tomberons tous dans l'immortalité. Incroyable que je me souvienne encore parfaitement ce qu'il a dit.

J'aimais bien aller au garage. Mais c'était pas souvent parce que mon père il était pas souvent à la maison. Parfois il dormait même pas à la maison.

Au garage, mon père me donnait une feuille de papier et des crayons de couleur, et je dessinais. J'étais pas très bon pour le dessin. Et encore aujourd'hui, je suis incapable de dessiner un trait droit, et encore moins un cercle. Mais dans l'atelier de mon père, oui c'est comme cela qu'il appelait le garage où il travaillait, son atelier, je m'asseyais par terre dans un coin, et je gribouillais mon papier tout en regardant en même temps ce que mon père faisait. Il avait l'air heureux, content de ce qu'il était en train de faire. J'avais une grande admiration pour lui, même si je le connaissais pas très bien.

Mes tantes et mes oncles disaient toujours que c'était un fainéant, un bon à rien, un flambeur, un joueur, un coureur de femmes, un communiste désenchanté, un mauvais mari. C'est ce que mes oncles et mes tantes arrêtaient pas de dire sur mon père, mais moi j'adorais cet homme imprévisible qui avait dans ses mains, au bout des doigts, tout un univers de beauté et de plaisir, avant qu'on l'efface de l'histoire à l'âge de trente-sept ans...

To All Who Might Be Interested

G.N. FORESTER

You welcome summer as the months of turbulence.

How about . . . if this fiction commenced in a train station . . . say Sam were to have missed a connecting train and had to wait for the next one . . . stuck in that vast bustling hall where Sam and Ray first said good-bye . . . years after they first arrived there, after the long escape from the place of nerve gas bombs and flying shrapnel slicing flesh . . . just think . . . Sam could sit at a table in one of the gallery cafes overlooking the platforms . . . a breathing space . . . a place to muse, gather thoughts, consider the rendezvous with Ray in the kingdom of angels following that lengthy period of being apart . . . how much time has passed . . . more time than Sam and Ray were together . . . if that could work . . . following the usual tussle with parts of speech that are never spoken but written, I'll close the scrapbook and wait for the facts that are fiction to deny falsity and coax verity onto the page.

So I imagine the fiction's outline, topography. Think of the equator separating Sam, dwelling on an island of illusory opportunity for . . . say a decade . . . and Ray, settled as long on another island equally robust with the rhetoric of egality. The one a place of harsh sun and stark contrasts, the other of misted moors and pragmatic aristocracy, the former a landscape reminiscent of those where Ray and Sam were born, the latter its ecological opposite. The country of their birth, defined by these two extremes and its unfortunate location as playground of international egos, where the unpardonable is still being perpetrated in the name of human freedom. That country is a placeholder, a qualifier, the first wash on the canvas of their lives. They escaped. Sam towards the sunrise and Ray towards the sunset.

I've named them both. And yet . . . is Sam Samantha, or Samuel? Sami, Sameh? Perhaps Sam is both? The burden imposed by a name, bequeathed and never sought, of nationality, language, culture, religion . . . otherness or sameness . . . still a gender will out, if a preposition appears. Likewise for Ray . . . Raylene, Raymond, Raya, Raj? Maybe masculine. No. Momentarily, either or.

The train Sam missed hisses its arrival at dusk. Ray and a companion of some years have driven to the capital with time to spare, and are now far too early. Such a circumstance as Sam and Ray seeing each other again merits merriment, perhaps an impromptu parody sketch of long-lost brothers, sisters, cousins, lovers, or trying to imagine Sam's impressions on seeing them, two tillers of young minds, teachers shaping the island's future. But rather than laughing at how absurd their small welcoming party will seem to Sam, renowned archaeologist and curator of indigenous artifacts, they are subdued, disturbed by the news of another terrorist attack.

Earlier the same day, suicide bombers had exploded themselves and dozens of shoppers in one of the capital's most popular malls. No details have yet been released, but the media is already surmising the origin of the attack, already the calls for stricter border control and segregation and special monitoring are mounting. A mournful evening for a greeting: scenes of carnage blazing from electronic billboards. Horrendous kismet. How will Sam react?

The toll of maimed and lifeless is uncertain. Some media sites speculate almost one hundred in all, with school children numbering at least fifty percent. Others put the figures higher, as more victims are found in the wreckage. The initial blasts had shattered shop front windows, a centre-piece hanging garden, spraying bloodied bits of human and plant as high as the building's domed glass roof. It could have been even worse, had the ceiling collapsed. Anti-terrorist forces were stationed within minutes, adjoining streets and thoroughfares cordoned, CCTV footage examined minutely for fleeing collaborators. No arrests yet, but already pictures of persons wanted for questioning circulate. International gateways are heavily guarded, security increased, processing of incoming and outgoing passengers has slowed to a crawl.

Somewhere else, in the city of goodbyes, Sam may not yet have heard about the tragedy awaiting. Sam has been people-watching, wondering about the lives of those walking past, some with eyes meeting Sam's only to slide away, others intent on large screens, small screens, ubiquitous devices of communication. But Sam prefers to avoid Twits and chats, likes and selfies, instead the dying medium of a newspaper sprawls across the table beside an empty coffee cup. Ray will tell Sam about the attack, and Sam will murmur disquiet, hearing in Ray's voice and seeing in Ray's eyes memories of that long escape, of the atrocity whose genesis is older than either of them.

Unrelated and yet not at all, inside a drab building in the capital where streets are paved with false economy, Ray's younger sibling, dressed in air force fatigues, is sitting before large high-definition screens, beside a colleague grasping flight controls, and waiting for the target coordinates to be relayed. The screens display rustic images: mud-brick walls and tin-slated roofs of a shanty-town in a desert, figures scurrying along dry-earth streets, some leading animals, some riding bicycles, between jeeps laden with artillery driven at uncaring speed around blind corners. One street is filled with seated and standing figures, tables covered with flat disks of bread, vegetables, fruit, mobile phones, buckets, the carcasses of animals. One house along that street is the intended target.

Ray's younger sibling, when asked about occupation, states air force technician. Drone pilot invokes animosity, since engaging with a hostile force from the safety of an office thousands of kilometres from danger is dishonorable. Ray wonders at that tag, air force technician, wonders why the younger sibling rarely speaks about work, spends hours training in the gym, exudes an air of privilege and righteousness at odds with Ray's own sense of fractured self. More than age separates them, for Ray still looks exotic, foreign, with dark skin and hair and eyes and an accent to match. The younger sibling is paler and has refused to speak in the language of their childhood since their arrival, has adopted the mannerisms, colloquialisms, clothes of the adopting country. Its prejudices as well.

Seated in the train terminus, observing the ebb and flow of travellers and feeling equally scrutinised, with patrolling police stopping every once in a while a little distance from Ray's table outside a well-known coffee shop chain, Ray swings between elation and worry. Elation at the thought of meeting Sam again. Angst about the younger sibling, who works near the bombed mall, and has not returned calls. Not unusual, since the younger sibling is never available while at the office. But still, Ray would feel calmer with a text message.

Ray doesn't know the younger sibling fell deeply in love with Sam all those years ago. A hopeless teenage crush, made even more desperate because Sam and Ray, enduring the agonies of survival in a city torn by local forces pursuing ethnic cleansing and international interference X-hairing ideologically defined targets, found an improbable solace in the arms of the other. Returning from what semblance of school still existed, they were confronted with the rubble of the building where their families had once lived. The three of them were the only survivors of the missile strike in their quarter that day.

Have you twigged to the gist of this set-up? Stasis. Sam stuck at the train station in the city of farewells, outwardly serene, inwardly cringing at recalled embarrassments, anxious about seeing Ray after so long, and after the way they parted, and trying futilely to forget the desolate disintegration, still perpetuated, of the country that birthed them. The panic of not knowing when the next airstrike would come, only the certainty that it would, or that ground armies from either side regarded the besieged inhabitants at first as encumbrance, and finally as shields. That was when they fled.

Ray tapping fingers on the table, lower leg swinging like a metronome, not quite quarrelsome, almost regretting bringing the partner of now to meet the partner of then, reliving the last acrimonious weeks before the bitter decision to separate, to put the past, in all its enormity, behind them, and to go their separate ways. Sam to study history in a country steeped in dreaming, Ray to turn the nightmare of the long escape to the hope of a tolerant future.

Can you picture what I'm creating? All that time of Sam's existence spent on an island refusing acknowledgement of its internal conflicts, its external inconsistencies, maintaining an illusion of freedom derived from cant and not from action. Ray, as many years whittled away on another island denying its deep roots of insularity, its commitment to uphold noble conventions while undermining the requisite foundations.

And loitering in the shadows of their lives, the place of antiquity rent then as now by warring tribes proclaiming possession of ultimate truth, economic interests masquerading as factional support, resource hungry despots annexing peasant lands, this place that was home that became a death zone, from which they escaped on the accelerated cusp of adulthood to the place of temporary refuge before its foreignness and peculiar customs leaned too heavily on their fragile unity. What caused such an irrevocable dissolution? Let me explain.

Ray and Sam and Ray's younger sibling, they escaped. But their families—parents, younger sisters, older brothers, aunts, uncles—perished. None of them were present during that long exodus. They died as charred husks, or crushed beneath concrete, or suffocated with their bodies' nervous systems in chaos. Obliterated. Images attest their annihilation, their tombs twisted lumps of rock and brick.

Perhaps that is why Sam will become an archaeologist, digging in the remains of graves for the presence of humanity.

It's seems to fit, doesn't it? I could make Sam a mortuary doctor, but have no plausible reason for Sam to visit Ray's island. On the other hand, as a gravedigger, a collector of human remnants, Sam can represent a delegation requesting the return of precious artefacts to their rightful indigenous owners. International, high-profile, this lends Sam a certain gravitas, no? And Ray is impressed, whether wanting to admit it or not. Sam was always controversial, idealistic, ready to champion a just cause, yet with a perverse streak suggesting narcissism, even a certain cruelty. Ray has never seen the collections Sam has curated, but rumours have circulated occasionally about Sam's methods of finding significant objects. Ray would prefer that Sam wants to re-establish contact after so much time has passed, that the latent longing to be together exists as much in Sam as it does in Ray. They had clung so passionately to each other in the aftermath of their families' destruction, each a limpet to the other's rock. And yet . . . how virulently they had fought at the end. The force of their sundering had propelled each to the opposite ends of the earth.

Is it Sam or is it Ray who asks why the other bolted, and so far away? Which of the two thinks that the other acted in haste, that they still belong with each other? They felt as twinned souls, united by the hopeless disunity surrounding them, sharing the same sufferings, the same questions, the same worry about Ray's younger sibling, who remained mute for three years after the long escape.

This fiction undeniably supposes Ray and Sam enduring a brutality foreshadowed in history. While neither evil is the principal focus, the latter must be highlighted. You groan, of course. It's been done to death!

To which I reply we have not sated our desire for acts of violence as a subject of discussion. Pick your choice of catastrophe. A multi-car pile-up, a suicidal pilot, a government's downfall, leaked intelligence, mass shootings, a nuclear explosion, a sinkhole in a crowded city. What a plethora of possibilities, and now we have multiplicities of media to echo the next news item. Yesterday's leftovers served piping hot as today's *plat du jour*. The same old is different new, it's just a question of spin, the thesis has never changed, only the angle of view.

So, yes, the latter must be highlighted. By what means did Sam and Ray and Ray's sibling overcome adversity, and what precipitated Sam and Ray's split before meeting again. This preoccupies my tale.

But to return to matters, I'm not concerned with the tale. It is, after all, unvarying. The quality and contours interest me. What frame is appropriate for Ray and Sam?

The dilemma, as always, is the beginning. To narrate the key elements shorn of unnecessary schmaltz, but engaging enough to effect a response. To establish the stage and the performers, so that events unfurl without guidance. I've no shortage of examples, re-worked to achieve my purpose. But to no avail. At least not yet.

I tried this yesterday:

[Character] stood beside the bread-seller waiting for the freshly baked mounds of crusty loaf to cool in the afternoon breeze, when the storm of [character's] troubles erupted. The baker's lean-to folded inwards, scattering rounds of bread, while across the street the wall buckled, swayed, and collapsed in a huge wave of sound and dust clouds.

Urgh. Can't imagine wanting to read that myself. And that good old chestnut OUAT no longer cuts it. Only the magical realists write fables, and this is a tale without faery. A fiction that when told is nothing but fact.

Conceivably I could start in the middle, and return to the beginning. Character description, but should it be Sam or Ray? Description is limiting, but provides the basis for imagination, it's what I don't write that allows inspiration. Paint a word picture of facial features, hair-style, body morphology (careful to avoid image issues), favourite sport, favourite author, favourite hobby (sex, like everyone), favourite food (chocolate for him, oysters for her). Not nondescript, but not remarkable either. Except in a crowd of ethnically other.

Sam is journeying, but now stuck. Ray journeyed, and is now waiting. Both are delayed, in effect. What justification to choose the one over the other as the opening character? Horoscope? Weekday? Thursday's child has far to go. Suggesting Sam should feature first in the narrative, having travelled from one hemisphere to the other, with a stopover in the land of farewells, for reasons known only to Sam. To combine fact and fiction, it is Thursday, December 20th. Or January 20th. Either of those dates are significant since events that occurred on those dates are intrinsic to events that affected Sam and Ray. On the one, a dictator became the head of state, on the other, a dictator was beheaded.

Arriving in the middle of the continent and after visiting some illustrious museums, the character misses the scheduled train. That twist of timing potters the tale, since that stasis is the bowl in which the tale is poured.

The character grimaces at the overhead digital display, searching for the next train to the intended destination. Jetlag has yet to crinkle the corners of the eyes, increase the pallor of the skin, flatten the tangles of hair. On the mezzanine level, the character locates a quiet café, selects an obscured seat with a view across the huge hall, and orders a specialty coffee and version of torte beloved by Ray. Rustling open a newspaper, the character reads desultorily. Fatigue perhaps, but more likely trepidation disturbs concentration. Thoughts like moths fluttering against a candle-lit pane, unordered, ungrasped, unrelenting, memories of what has gone before, of the arrival in this land of unspoken guilt, of the long escape from the horror arisen like a phoenix from the horror unleashed in this wide-gazing land in times so recent and yet already fast forgotten.

In that first period of military action, on May 15th, or June 5th, or March 20th—to render it genuine—the black morning of another invasion, repulsion, justification, the families of Ray and Sam and thousands of others innocent of the arguments in favour of conflict were caught in the X-fire of intervention. They did not know of their status as orphans, nor as inferred or even prospective oppressors, until turning the corner of the dust-blanketed street in which they lived and finding only smoke and rubble. Ray and Sam and Ray's sibling roamed more streets like the one left behind them, until the decision that leaving was no more dangerous than staying. All three suffered intensely, and guilt for having lived grapples with the impulse to embrace existence.

Once when the three of them arrived at a border, guards began spraying bullets at the lines of people. The sound of shots sent them scurrying back to the stony dunes, joining another group, with whom had they remained, Sam and Ray and Ray's sibling would have become yet another drowned statistic. That was not the only border at which inhumane acts occurred. People were herded like cattle inside security pens and left without food or water, women disappeared at night, children were molested outside makeshift lavatories, some sold as slaves. Ray's sibling has watched countless documentaries itemising these barbarities. Unlike Ray and Sam, Ray's younger sibling seeks reminders of those years, grows colder and harder and more determined. But to achieve what, Ray is unsure.

Ray sometimes wonders if someone, anyone of their families might have survived. Sam's older brother, preparing for his wedding the following week. Ray's baby sister, just learning to crawl. Could they have ended up somewhere else, processed in another land across the oceans, and even now be searching for Sam and Ray? Ray sees a parent in the long stride of an unknown man with curly dark hair, or the smile of a woman pushing a pram in the park, the cry of a child resembles that of a cousin. Ray has dreamt of a girl who looks like Ray clutching at Ray's hand and saying, in the language of their childhood, I am your sister, I looked for you everywhere. And Ray knows that lost sister with the same mouth, same nose, same eyes as Ray, it is like looking in a mirror.

Ray supposes Sam must also reanimate the dead, but which sibling? Or maybe parents? Sam was close to a cousin, but Ray cannot remember her name. Pretty, always with kohl-limned eyes and swaying hips. Ray teaches art to disadvantaged children every week in the local community centre. So many studies of family faces no-one mourns except Ray, used to teach the children proportion, symmetry, shading, shapes. Ray once sketched an imagined family portrait and on finishing it, wept suddenly, sitting alone on the floor of the room shared with Sam and Ray's younger sibling in the city of first processing. Sam came home and wiped away Ray's tears, Ray's sibling, still mute, tore the portrait to shreds.

Would any of Ray's lost siblings have responded like that? Why is Ray, settled with a job and partner, still among the living, and not among the dead?

That day in school, before the first rocket blast, Ray had painted the ruins of an ancient tomb outside the walls of the city. The teacher seemed particularly pleased and offered to buy the painting. Ray's family, like most in the neighborhood, were poor, and Ray agreed to the suggestion. The coins felt warm and heavy in Ray's pocket while walking home from school, and they stopped at the honey shop and purchased crumbly slabs of sticky honey comb. They had been sucking sweet liquid from the wax as the first of the rockets hit the ancient tomb Ray had painted. Ray's painting, intended to be sold by the teacher at tourist prices in a bazaar elsewhere in the country, is now one of the spoils of war, hanging in the private gallery of an arms dealer.

So, an adequate start, yes? I've been so slack with writing to you. Every so often I ascend from the pit of my own making and think of something to share, before sinking in the blackness of that gloom. At one point, I thought . . . but then I read that Primo Levy probably didn't die by executing himself. It was an accident. As it always is, the line between life and death.

Summer is arriving. The days are growing longer, the trees are dressed in green, the birds are making merry with each other, every creature is restless and urgent, marking territory, enticing mates, fighting the competition. You welcome summer as the months of turbulence.

My agent's office called me earlier. You've met my agent, Fede, do you recall? We had dinner together when you were here, and you chased that handsome waiter round the bar. Anyway, I'm still on their books, but they're reassigning someone else to me. Nothing on my side, in fact I had no idea. Fede had changed tense. A heart attack, very sudden. Poof. Too much of a good time. The agency emailed me about the cremation ceremony. Let me quote you some of the obituary:

Fede was distinguished amongst Beckettian scholars, born May 15th, 1928 in the Parisian suburb of Montrouge to a poor Jewish family. Fede's mother Marguerite was a charwoman, her husband a philandering artist. During the infamous Vél' d'Hiv' of July 16th, 1942, the family was incarcerated. Only Fede escaped the gas chambers at Auschwitz.

One version, as related to Beckett, describes how during a break in the deportation journey east Fede noticed a neighboring wagon full of tubers, and climbed from the holding train to the vegetable wagon. When the train rolled off, being stuffed with tubers Fede missed catching it. Fede recounts elsewhere that just before the family was taken away by French police, Fede was pushed inside a closet by Marguerite. The following three years were spent shoveling shit on a farm *dans le midi.*

Located by a benevolent uncle in Paris at the end of the war and shipped to the US in 1947, Fede integrated, but never assimilated, always remaining Gallic in word and tone and deed. Several jobs later, Fede enlisted in the army and was active in Korea. With an honorable discharge in 1954, Fede completed a Bachelor of Arts (Columbia), a Masters, and a PhD (UCLA) by 1965. Between representing avant-gardistes and penning several novels, Fede continued collating criticism on Beckett and introducing students to postmodern literature, first at Santa Barbara (1960-64), and at SUNY Buffalo (1965-99) before retiring as Distinguished Professor, Melodia E. Jones Chair, National Arts Endowment Fellow, and holder of the *Palmes académiques.*

The industry awarded his services to publishing with Literary Agent of the Year Medal (1965, 1970, 1971, 1974, 1976, 1985), and Agent of Best Debut Fiction (1980, 1986, 1990). Fede championed stories deliberately obscuring fact and fiction, appending the labels 'surfiction' and 'critifiction' to such literature, characterised by typographical innovation, self-reference, comic deployment of language, stratified narration, sly winks at the reader, fluctuating perspectives, in short, 'difficult' works with a 'profuse' style.

Well, better to be labelled profuse than obtuse, I suppose. Not that it's common knowledge Fede helped place my work. I'll miss that black humour and ready wit.

Have I been writing? Nix, null, nada. Not since spring of last year. Nothing inspires, nothing lures me inside tales of a floating world. My novels of the last few years are the offspring of another writer. Collector's items when I'm dead, perhaps. There's an epitaph waiting to be written: still available second hand.

The new agent asked for some 'commercially oriented' work, as though a book is written to a formula, produced on a factory assembly line. Have you heard about the software that writes news articles? How long until fiction?

I've tried out a few ideas, but everything dead ends. I'm overtaken by the voice of the reader, querulous, demanding rigour, exactitude, action, emotion, clarity. A critic recently said ambiguity is the hallmark of a lazy writer. Yes, I miss Fede.

So I ploughed on, and here we are. Let me know your thoughts on Sam and Ray. Could I carve something from that? Word-obsessors such as we, to quit writing would be a fate worse than . . . well, you know what I mean. Help me out with this next journey. And let me know how you are doing, the family, the animals, the garden. That novel you started working on, about the summer of their malcontent. More anon.

Report From the World Federation of Displaced Writers

RAYMOND FEDERMAN

We had never known Federman to be that violent, on the contrary, more like him to talk or double-talk his way out of a fight, either in French of in English, or both simultaneously, except once, in 2028, the day of his birthday, yes May 15, imagine that, premember the future if you can, our old man getting into a fight at his age.

Yes now I premember, it was in Sofia Bulgaria, Moinous exclaims, when he kicked a guy in the ass, a critic, and then punched him in the mouth.

That's right, it was during a literary conference, a huge international conference on the future of literature, in Sofia, Namredef confirmed, *The World Federation of Displaced Writers,* the **WFDW**, we were there with him of course.

All the literati in the world were present, some already dead, others half-dead, others on their way out, they had gathered urgently in the Dimitrov Great Hall of the People to discuss the critical situation of contemporary literature at a crucial moment in history when literature was seriously and painfully questioning its *raison d'être,* was on the verge of becoming a mere supplement of culture, when the very act of writing was being challenged and displaced from all sides by technological substitutions and all sort of creepy gadgets, artificial languages and computerized intelligence, as the western civilization was dwindling away into scientific technocracy and pseudo-mystical fantasy.

The critic in question, the guy who got kicked in the ass and punched in the mouth, was some pitiful entremetteur of literature, for every cliff there is always someone to jump off, Moinous cut in, a pushy pimpled juvenile cacademic critic in his early twenties, an embryonic mind from John Hookers University, at least that's what the name tag on his lapel said, a typical file-card PMLA scholar, yes PMLA was still going on, who stood up in the middle of an animated argument about the present and future morality of the novel, that stubborn moribund genre which was still, even then, refusing to die.

John Gardner and his clique and Larry McCaffery with his clan were tackling each other, moralizing on the one side and demoralizing on the other, when that pushy asshole of a critic jumped right in to take side with the moralizers and complain, in twisted xylophagouscacademic terms, that fiction today has become totally unreadable, that it has lost touch with reality, imagine that, as if that dead horse, that carcass of reality was still something to be concerned with, because, he went on, too many writers are indulging in egocentric logomachy.

He was obviously referring to Federman's work and to the little speech Federman had made earlier, quite eloquently, in defense and illustration of what Federman calls the leapfrog technique in digressive fiction, yes definitely referring to Federman and to some of his contemporaries even though he did not mention names, that little shit pot, writers such as Ronnie Schlunick, Clarion Vapor, Stove Klotz, Warner Abolish, Dave Plush, Morbid Caillou, Ludovic February, Bill Gasoil, Phillipeau Soleil, Tudor Les-Oies, Oswal Bartender, Johnny Vulture, Giorgo Bedroom, to name only a few, and others of that generation with whom Federman had been associated for decades as a daring disruptive subversive experimentalist, all of them present of course that day in the Great Hall of the People, and who were still at the center of the lively controversy about the validity and superiority of post-future fiction versus neo-antediluvian fiction, that endless quarrel of the post-ancients and the supra-postmoderns.

That dumbass critic was complaining, whining rather, that all these so-called sursurfictioneers are masturbating their futile experiments without any regard for communication and existential gestalt, wallowing instead in self-conscious solipsism, destructuring and desyntaxing language for the sake of playfulness and dislogotraction, ludique laughterature, oh he had some vocabulary that puny critic, he paused a moment to admire his little pun, and consequently, he went on, these superegoisticalnarcissists are deserting their moral responsibility toward Man, with a capital letter he emphasized, and Society, also with a capital letter, can you believe that, one still argues on such a pathetic basis, in 2028, doesn't that little fizzle of a critic understand that these avant-garde writers neither think a kick because they fell a kick nor feel a kick because they think a kick.

But he went on, that intellectually retarded paraplegic parasite of mediocrity with his squeaking effeminate voice which kept rising as he spoke, saying that the concern of most of these elitist collectivists today is only with language, language and nothing else, but a theory of fiction as mere logos doing its tricks is an outlandish notion, I am quoting him *verbatim*, Namredef pointed out, and he continued, he was endless that criiiitic, explaining that reading fiction should not merely be an act of looking at words distributed on the pages, but rather should be like falling into a dream that foregrounds reality, and that after reading a few pages of a novel the words should simply disappear, what an idiot, language disappear, yep vanish, just like that, pssitt, muscade et voila, what a cretin, and only images should unfold pleasurably in the mind of the reader, unbelievable, like a private television show, mental cinema.

Roland Barthes was sitting a couple of seats away from us and I heard him mumble, how stubborn these illusionists can be to still want to peddle *leur cinéma intérieur en 2028* as the primary function of the novel, but what about *l'émotion, pourquoi serait-elle antipathique á la jouissance, c'est un trouble, une lisière évanouissement, quelque chose de pervers, sous des dehors bien-pensants, c'est même, peut-être, la plus retorse des pertes, car elle contredit la règle donnée á la jouissance une figure fixe, forte, violente, crue, quelque chose de nécessairement musclé, tendu, phallique.*

At this point Federman stood up, he was sitting directly behind that constipated critic from Johns Hookers University whose name of course will not be revealed here, and turning to Roland Barthes he said, *t'as raison Coco colle-lui ton phallus dans le cul*, and as he said this he kicked the critic in the ass, and I mean hard and right on target, the critic almost fell forward over the people sitting in front of him, you pompous pederastic pedantic punk, he shouted letting his lips explode scornfully into the alliterations, don't you understand that a concern for the dignity or decrepitude of language is, after all, a concern for the dignity and decrepitude of man, for a writer to disdain to do anything more questionable with his art than explore relentlessly the nature of his own medium, in this case words in extemporaneous arrangements, the question of human dignity can not present itself in any other terms than those of the dignity of human language, even if language was originally *une erreur de la nature*, and as he said this Federman waved to Antonin Artaud who was seated a few rows back.

Half of the audience applauded with dignified enthusiasm while the other half booed and hissed nervously, it was indeed a very mixed literary crowd representing many tendencies and movements and schools and cliques and clans, from all extremes, passionate avant-gardists, breakthough fictioneers, surexperimentalist, paracritics, social neoreligiousrealists, antipostsymbolists, neoprehistorians, superpastirrealists, and even a few aposteriornaturalists.

The pushy critic meanwhile turned toward Federman fuming with rage and still rubbing his ass shamefully, he tried to grab Federman by the neck, and that's when Federman punched him in the mouth, a perfect solid right uppercut to the jaw.

Immediately the participants split into two camps, the postancients with their critics and their theoreticians on one side, and the postpostmoderns with their paracritics on the other, and everybody started punching, scuffling in the aisles of the Great Hall of the People, throwing books at each other, pamphlets, dictionaries, even unpublished manuscripts, pens and pencils, portable typewriters, laptops, scriptodictos, erasers, anything they could get their hands on, they were spitting at each other, pulling each other's hair and beards, yes there were many bearded participants as is always the case at literary conferences, scratching each other's faces with overgrown nails.

It is well known that writers are noted for being dirty fighters, as when Charles Perrault and Nicolas Boileau scratched each other's eyes out during the famous Querelle des Anciens et des Modernes in 1693, amazing how the world of *littérateurs* vibrates in a twofold manner every two or three hundred years, or better yet when Norman Mailer gave Gore Vidal one of his resounding knee-in-the-crotch publicly at a fancy literary cocktail party in 1977, what a scandal that was, we were there that day, the three of us, Federman, Moinous and I, specifies Namredef, standing only a few feet away from Mailer and Vidal when the blow happened, and we even heard what Mailer said, My dear Vidal there are those who kick balls and those who get kicked in the balls, I am sure you know in which category you belong, and when Gore Vidal tried to scratch Mailer's face, the latter shoved his knee up Vidal's testicles who folded at the waist and shrieked, Oh you animal, big brute, it was quite a scene indeed, amazing how history always repeats itself, as it was happening in the Great Hall of the People, but on a much larger and much more violent scale.

And so here in Sofia Bulgaria we were in the middle of another historic brawl, the battle was raging, Namredef and I were watching from a corner of the conference room standing on top of a table, trying to duck the blows and the flying objets d'art, cowardly as we are we preferred to stay above the melee, fantastic, Moinous said as he caught a copy of *The Divine Comedy* in full flight, we had lost sight of Federman in the commotion, but finally caught a glimpse of him buried under an angry pack of neo-classic gothic novelists, he was flat on his back and these burly fellows were pounding at him with their fists, but it was impossible for us to go to his help, all avenues of approach were blocked, so we remained on our observation table, keeping track of the skirmishes, recording individual and collectives victories.

Finally someone managed to crawl to a microphone which had toppled over on the floor and screamed into it, in Polish, I think it was Polish, or perhaps Slavonic, the official language of the conference, Hey you idiots, stop that, we are translating here for the commodity of this report what that person said, we didn't come here, he continued, to have a literary riot, especially now when half of the planet is still starving for knowledge, obviously the speaker was an erudite social realist, but it was useless, and now the sirens and whistles of the Bulgarian militia were screeching in the streets and in the corridors of the Great Hall of the People as the battled raged on until a raucous authoritative voice came over the loud-speakers in the ceiling.

Achtung, Achtung, it was the voice of Günter Grass who was then President of **WFDW**, *Bitte meine Damen und Herren,* I must say the women participants were just as active and belligerent in this confrontation as the males, using their innate feminine agility to overcome their more loutish male assailants, at one point Moinous and I watched Joyce Carol Oates flip Gabriel Garcia Marquez over her back in a neat judo move while next to her Margaret Atwood was twisting Alain Robbe-Grillet's arm behind his back.

Bitte meine Damen und Herren, the voice of Günter Grass insisted, *beruhigen Sie sich, lassen Sie uns mit Würde, besonders jetz wo dies ganze Welt uns beobachted, besonders wenn did Bletchtrommel des Opposition heult wie die Hundejahresoldaten der Vernunft muss standhaft bleiben un nich umfallen, nich Katze und Maus spielen, ja, muss nich flappen, Bitte kehren Sie zu ihren Stühlen zurück und lassen Sie uns in Ruhe fortsetzen,* and these powerful rational Germanic words worked like magic, instantly everyone stopped fighting, there was an embarrassed moment of silence while the audience regained its composure.

Then Harold Pinter, who had just been awarded a second Nobel Prize for literature, and well he deserved it, approached the microphone on the main platform, he stood there for a full minute staring at the audience while shaking his head in a gesture of reprimand.

Behind us we heard in a Japanese whisper someone say, *Amenokado hitotsu hirakete mae ni ari utsukushiki kana yama ni tatsu niji,* Moinous turned around, *Sssh,* he said, *Oh so sorry, so sorry, my name is Yosano Hiroshi, I am a poet, who is that speaking now, can you tell me, so sorry.*

That's Pinter, Harold Pinter, the famous British playwright, the only one to ever received two Nobel Prizes, I informed the Japanese poet, *Ah so, there before our sight one of the gates of heaven swung wide and how beautifully stands the bright rainbow on the mountain brow,* recited the Japanese Poet in broken English which is difficult to imitate here, *Can you please be quiet,* Moinous said, *and skip the poetry, Oh yes yes, ah so. So sorry,* the Japanese poet said bowing to Moinous.

Pinter began to talk, pointing to Federman while marking each word with deliberate Miltonian emphasis.

I do not know this gentleman personally, or perhaps yes we did meet once, a long time ago, in a pub, but that's not important, I have read his books, I have read and reread them, and let me tell you, the farther he goes the more good it does me. I don't want philosophies, tracts, dogmas, creeds, ways out, truths, answers, nothing from the bargain basement, he is the most courageous, remorseless writer going and the more he grinds my nose in the shit the more I am grateful to him, he's not fucking me about, he's not leading me up any garden, Right on that's the way to go man, someone shouted from the back of the conference room, Ah shut the fuck up you jerk, someone else shouted back, Pinter banged his fist forcefully on the podium and continued, *he's not slipping me any wink, he's not flogging me a remedy or a path or a revelation or a basinful of breadcrumbs, he's not selling me anything I don't want to buy, he doesn't give a bollock whether I buy or not, he hasn't got his hand over his heart,*

Well, ladies and gentlemen, I'll buy his goods, hook, line and sinker, because he leaves no stone unturned and no maggot lonely, he brings forth a body of beauty. His work is beautiful . . . he paused and stared haughtily at the young critic who had been the cause of the disturbance, the room grew restless, Pinter leaned forward over the podium, **beaut-ti-ful**, my dear Sir, he repeated detaching each syllable, even if it is **un-read-able.**

Samuel Beckett who was sitting quietly in a remote corner of the great hall stood up and started applauding, all eyes turned to him in deep reverence, *honni soit qui symboles y voit*, he said in a soft tone of voice and he sat down.

Federman was deeply moved, visibly moved, he had difficulties holding back the tears of appreciation, and we did too, it was the first time, as far as we know, in the many many years he had been scribbling words, working uncompromisingly in the lonely semi-darkness of unrecognition, that someone, no not just someone but a world-renowned writer whom he greatly admired and respected had praised his work in public, he stood up, blew his nose in a large handkerchief, walked over to the platform tipping his head slightly to Samuel Beckett as he walked past him, and shook Harold Pinter's hand with marked emotion, Pinter embraced him while half of the audience applauded its warm approbation and the other half whistled and hissed it vicious objection, and so it goes with literature, always split down the middle.

It was May 2028, now some people might say that such a report is not very encouraging, but one must reply that it is not meant to encourage those who say that, after all literature is an endangered species.

Raymond

ECKHARD GERDES

After I moved to Macon, Georgia, in 1998, I began putting together the *Journal of Experimental Fiction*. It was an idea that went back to 1986, when I started publishing on a small scale and developed Depth Charge, a book publishing house. My wife, Persis, suggested that I do a literary magazine in conjunction with the press, but I really couldn't figure out how to go about that until we landed in Georgia.

The first anthology issue drew from classmates of mine at the School of the Art Institute of Chicago, students of mine from Roosevelt University, acquaintances from other small presses, and a colleague from Macon State College who had written on the work of John Barth, whom she was trying to bring to campus. The second issue was published after John Barth came to lecture at a conference at Macon State, when I asked him for permission to publish his lecture text, which he kindly let me do for a nominal fee. Most of the rest of that volume was made up of student narratives about their experiences coming to the Barth lecture and their impressions of it. They included stories about seeing one another in cars on the highway, mooning each other en route, and being shocked by each other's moons — very amusing stuff.

For a third volume I decided to research what other experimental fiction writers were doing out in the world, and one of the first names I came across was Raymond Federman. I remembered Raymond Federman. When I was 18 or so, I was working in Wilmette, Illinois, in a small bookstore owned by two very kind women, cousins, who had started the business some years earlier. That summer they had to put together a wedding for one of their daughters, and they left me in charge of the shop. I had to run the day-to-day operations of the place, which included seeing sales reps. One morning, I had an appointment to see a rep who had several publishers' lines. One of the publishers he represented was George Braziller, whose Meyer Schapiro book *Modern Art* had been a big bestseller in our store. Braziller also distributed to the trade books published by a literary house called the Fiction Collective.

I had never heard of the Fiction Collective, and the rep was rather dismissive, saying we wouldn't need those titles and that they were for a very specialized market of people interested in experimental fiction. What the rep didn't realize was that I *was* that market, for I was writing experimental fiction myself. And I looked at the titles in his catalogue: *Meningitis* by Yuriy Tarnawsky, *98.6* by Ronald Sukenick, *Babble* by Jonathan Baumbach, *Twiddledum Twaddledum* by Peter Spielberg, *Museum* by B.H. Friedman, *Moving Parts* by Steve Katz, *Mole's Pity* by Harold Jaffe, *The Secret Table* by Mark Jay Mirsky, *Holy Smoke* by Fanny Howe, *Null Set* by George Chambers, and on and on, book after book of amazing innovative fiction. It was a new world to me, and I wanted in. I told the rep to send me one of each, which came to over forty titles at that point. I couldn't wait for them to arrive. I told the ladies that the books were coming for me, and they let me pay the invoice myself so that I wouldn't have to pay the store's mark-up. When the books finally came, I opened the box immediately and eagerly, for they held magic that I wanted to get my hands on right away. Most of them were rather modest volumes in size, some of them with uniform cover art, the way great European literary publishers like Reclam and Les Éditions de Minuit have. But one of the books was different. It was much longer than the others. The cover was blue and had white parachutes and little cartoon illustrations all over it. And it was unpaginated. That really took my attention. That was Raymond Federman's *Take It or Leave It.*

So, when I came across Federman's name again, I looked online to see what I could find for him, and I found his email address. I emailed him about the *Journal*, told him we'd published Barth, and that I would love to publish something of his in an upcoming anthology.

Raymond emailed back very quickly, said he'd been a colleague of Barth's at SUNY Buffalo, and that he'd be delighted to contribute something. They had been colleagues, along with Charles Bernstein and Leslie Fiedler, back when the English department was a building's basement with bright yellow walls, the so-called "Yellow Submarine." Raymond, of course, was in Foreign Languages, but he knew the folks in the English department well. If fact, he said he'd routinely beaten Barth at tennis when they were colleagues together.

Raymond, in a subsequent email, suggested that what would be even better than contributing a piece would be an entire volume of the *Journal* devoted to his work. He said he could have friends of his send in writing about his work and that we'd be able to fill a good-sized book if I was game.

I was already charmed by him, so I agreed. Our long and delightful friendship was begun. Before I knew it, I was receiving submissions from friends and colleagues of his from Germany, France, Turkey, Belgium, and even the United States. Jan Baetens sent his in French, and I published it like that. The great critic Jerome Klinkowitz kept himself off the grid, so I had to correspond with him via snail mail. One of Raymond's old friends dragged his heels so long in getting a piece in, that Raymond finally told me to tell him that if he didn't send me something right away, Raymond would no longer be his friend. Through Raymond I met and corresponded with some of the best minds in the world of innovative writing, people like Lance Olsen, Doug Rice, George Chambers, Mark Axelrod, and many more.

The issue took beautiful shape. The next thing was to invite him to Macon State College for a reading. I got the funding together, and we had him come and read to a packed auditorium. His humor, his delightful French accent, and his charm won over even the most dubious of my colleagues. Raymond additionally volunteered to come into my classes and speak directly with my students as well, who included everyone from advanced creative writing students to freshman composition students to high school connection students. He addressed them all wonderfully according to the levels at which they read and wrote, but encouraged them all to reach farther. I had assigned *Take It or Leave It* as a text, and the students found the book to be very funny (albeit a bit dirty and disrespectful of Southerners). Everyone loved him. He had a natural ease in speaking with students and a charm that let him get away with stuff no one else could. For example, when he came into the high school connection class, which was a class I taught at a local high school on behalf of the college, he was eager to show the students how he'd discovered software that would read his work out loud in a wonderful British accent. He had to hook up his laptop to the school's overhead, and when he did, his wallpaper of a naked woman went up on the wall. Worried that I'd just violated some code of conduct, I looked at the vice principal of the high school, who was there to observe. Raymond, however, just said, "Oh, sorry, but isn't she just so beautiful," and then went on with his demonstration. The vice principal just smiled at me, amused at this charming Frenchman.

I wanted to introduce him to my wife, who had been diagnosed with metastatic breast cancer and was undergoing chemotherapy, but she wasn't feeling well enough. So we skipped it that time. He understood that Persis was very sick. We had corresponded about it, and he was one of the few people I knew who really had the ability to cheer me a little during this long and dark period in my life. Persis had been given dronabinol, which was synthetic cannabis in pill form, but she couldn't tolerate the feeling it gave her. Instead of discarding the prescription, though, she kept it and gave me the pills. I found that they were very uneven in quality. Some would really zonk me, and others did nothing, as if half of them were placebos mixed into the batch by an unscrupulous pharmacist. Raymond had asked me if I had any weed because he wanted to smoke a little in the evening before retiring. I gave him a couple of the pills and met him the next morning for breakfast. He said the pills were duds and had done nothing. He asked if I couldn't find any smoke from a student. I told him I daren't ask a student. I didn't want to be fired. This was Georgia. So I asked a colleague who was trustworthy, and he found for me one marijuana cigarette.

Not long thereafter Raymond and I had to leave for Atlanta to take him to the airport to catch his flight. We smoked the doobie on the way, and Raymond became completely animated by it. We discussed Sam. Raymond had written the first dissertation on Samuel Beckett's fiction in English, focusing on Beckett's use of language rather than symbolism, which too many critics looked for in Beckett's work, and which really bothered Beckett because he wasn't trying to use any symbolism. When they met in Paris, Beckett said to Raymond, "Finally someone has learned how to read my work!" Sam thereafter was permanently perched on Raymond's shoulder, whispering in his ear, guiding him. And Raymond spent the hour-long drive in a very excited exegesis of *The Unnamable*, the culmination of Beckett's great trilogy of novels. When Raymond spoke about Sam, his voice was as excited as that of a boy explaining his favorite sport. I was grinning and laughing the whole way to the airport.

The ensuing years were difficult ones, but Raymond's friendship really helped me through. When Raymond told me he was lecturing up at Virginia Commonwealth, a friend of mine and I drove up there together to see him. Raymond was lecturing on and was defending, as always, the primacy of voice over all other writerly concerns. One hotshot young faculty member there thought he'd try to make a name for himself by challenging Raymond: "You are contradicting what you said in your books *Critifiction* and *Surfiction* . . . [blah blah blah] . . ." Raymond just smiled at him and said, "Federman reserves the right to contradict himself." That cracked everyone up. That was Raymond. When we went out drinking together afterwards, he told the servers they were in the presence of great literary figures and laid it on so thick they asked for our autographs by the end of the evening. He was an absolute delight.

When he fell ill, I was devastated. I came to California as a guest lecturer at the John Fowles Center for Creative Writing at Chapman University, and hoped to see him again. He was supposed to introduce me but couldn't make it. When he knew he was dying, I sent him a set of WC Fields movies, including my favorite, *It's a Gift*, to watch to take his mind off his pain. Cancer, that cruel mistress, had already taken my wife, so I knew that any brief respite would be welcome. He thanked me profusely for the films and thanked me for being such a true friend.

He asked me to contribute a chapter about him as metafictioneer for a book on his work that SUNY was publishing, which I happily did, although it was only published posthumously. The book meant a great deal to him, and he was very happy with my chapter. He was also able to see the little poem for him that I eventually gave to *ABR*.

Raymond's on my shoulder, and Sam's on his,
naming the unnameable as we race toward Atlanta
like American cowboys in my red Taurus.
We're shooting the bull and smoking ourselves
brain-deep into Okefenokee Swamp grass,
and he's GO personified. He's skipping
stones from Sam's pocket, bouncing them
fifteen times across the pond, running around
to the other side and skipping them back,
showing off for my precious wife, who's dying
in the arms of morphine but determined
to see our first son graduate high school.
Raymond skips stones in a pattern of roses,
French charm and a kiss. Her lips, tight with pain,
curl into a smile for the first time in a month.
Charlie Parker's spit is still on his tongue,
surrealist paintings course through his veins,
and the pain of the universe is in his pocket,
along with flat chunks of concrete
because he's run out of skipping stones,
having given all he could in the naming
of the unnameable: that rare and beautiful

ability to erase misery wherever he goes.

My last communication from him, two weeks before he died, was in response to the poem:

Dear Eck
That fine poem touches me deeply
yes I remember that ride
and the smile on your dying wife
that was so long ago.

Almost seven years have passed since Raymond died, but I think of him almost daily. I miss him. But he stands on my shoulder forever, telling me a joke, laughing, explaining something especially beautiful he notices in language, generous with his time and affection. As with Cousin Vit in Gwendolyn Brooks's famous poem "The Rites for Cousin Vit," ultimately only one word can describe Raymond: *is*. Forever he *is*.

FAR
EAST
AIR
FORCES
AIRMEN'S MESS
TOKYO
JAPAN
1953

Out of the Foxhole

AN ABANDONED FICTION

RAYMOND FEDERMAN

"A Possible Beginning"

Hey Federman what were you doing upstairs in your closet? You've been in there since early this morning.

We often call each other Federman Erica and I.

It might not be too far————fetch to say I was masturbating with words. That's what my aesthetics is when preparing for a new book.

You started a new book?

I have something going. But I'm not sure where it's going. In fact, it started last night. Yesterday evening when you had that meeting at the club, I was sitting in my rocking chair watching Serena and Jennifer go at each other on the tennis court, what thighs these girls have, when suddenly the entire story came to me. I heard the whole thing in my head. I even heard how the book should be constructed.

You heard?

Well, you know what I mean. Maybe I was a bit stoned.

Oh, you got stoned last night while I was at the club. That's when you do it. When I'm not home. Who gets you the stuff.

Nobody. No, I wasn't stoned, I just said that to establish to tone of the story I'm going to tell. The story of the three years I spent in Tokyo. Those three years were so incoherent, I was living them as if I was stoned all the time.

Oh that story again. I've heard it so many times.

But this time it's going to be different.

How different? Don't tell me this time you're going to tell it straight, without any of your exaggerated self-reflexive circumvolutions.

I'll try. But let me explain.

You remember the discussion we had the other day about what the next book should be. And how we decided that it should be the story of Moinous in Tokyo.

So it's Moinous again. Why haven't you written it yet?

I tried a number of times. All false beginnings. Something is bothering me. I can't decide how the story should be written. To simply tell what Moinous did or imagined he did in Tokyo is not enough. That would be just another banal army story. The Story of a G.I. in Tokyo during the Korean War involved in the black market and fucking the cute little bowlegged Japanese girls. That story has been told so many times.

Yours is different. How many Jewish frogs like you were in the Korean War? Write it from the point of view of that Jewish frog.

All my stories are written from the Frog point of view. I don't know about the Jewish point of view. I never consider that one. Though sometimes it creeps into the book. In fact, one of the Tokyo stories I'll have to tell is how Moinous was invited for Passover to a Japanese Seder. It was amazing.

Why don't you tell it now, and get it over.

I can't. I have to establish the form and the tone of the book first. Otherwise it won't work.

Here we go again. Form, form, always form. You're incurable.

I know. But this book needs a form. And even more than that. It needs a backdrop. A lower level of the writing. Something else going on underneath the surface of the story.

So what else is new.

No. Listen. Remember the other day when Larry and I were working on the Federman-Tashima letters, it occurred to me that perhaps Tashima should become a major figure in this story since he was there in Tokyo with Moinous in the same outfit.

It's a good idea. This way you won't be talking only about yourself your usual narcissistic way.

To be a writer one must have the courage of one's narcissism.

I heard that one before too.

So you like the idea of Tashima being in the book since he was there. After all, later in New York, after Moinous got out of the army, Tashima played an important role in helping him become a writer.

That's true. OK, so go on. I'm listening.

Well, last night while watching tennis on TV, I scribbled on a pad everything that was going on in my head. Just the way I was hearing it. I got so involved with what I was writing, I don't even know who won the match. Here listen to what I wrote.

after Moinous is out of the foxhole in Korea and now in Tokyo assigned to the 510 military intelligence group he meets Tashima and one day Tashima says to Moinous how did you get into this fucking army how does a Jewish frog like you left over from the unforgivable enormity end up in Tokyo as a member of the 510 military intelligence group the most crooked outfit in the far east sounds like a bad joke

it is a joke Moinous says a sad joke waiting for a punch line

well tell me that joke Tashima says

it's a long story that deviates in all directions

good I like deviations replies Tashima my whole life has been a long deviation from my ancestors

if you tell me about your deviation I'll tell you about mine

you first

it might take a long time

we still have two more years to do in this stinking army we have all the time in the world so you tell me your story and I'll tell you mine the story of an American gook without an identity

mine is a long sad story good

I like sad stories

so Moinous and Tashima agree to tell each other the story of their life and how they landed in the 510 military intelligence group in Tokyo and how they became friends

at first Moinous doesn't know which parts of his story he should tell some parts are more difficult than others to tell and some as so confused that Moinous doubts he can make sense out of them so he asks Tashima where he should start

Tashima tells him start anywhere whatever you tell will be the first chapter of your life story and then I'll tell you the first chapter of my life we'll alternate

why don't you start

no you first

let's flip a coin

ok

Tashima won and so he started telling Moinous the first chapter of his life it was about how when he was a little boy his mother would fix his lunch to take to school usually rice wrapped in vine leaves the typical Japanese lunch but Tashima was so ashamed to come to school and eat his rice while all the other kids the real American kids were eating regular American sandwiches he would throw in a garbage can the lunch his mother had prepared the moment he left his house

Tashima told that story in a café in Shimbashi where he and Moinous often went on their free time

they liked that place because of its name C'est Si Bon

the owner Mister Arakawa had studied in Paris at the Sorbonne before the war and was fluent in French and that's why he called his café C'est Si Bon.

Mister Arakawa loved everything French and he considered himself an existentialist he and Moinous who also considered himself an Existentialist had great discussions in French and that's how Tashima who at first knew no French got to learn some French by listening to Moinous and Mister Arakawa argue over Jean-Paul Sartre's concept of freedom they each had a different interpretation of that concept but I am digressing I was saying that Moinous and Tashima always went to C'est si Bon not only because of the name and the owner but also because Mister Arakawa played French songs on his pick-up which could be heard in the café Moinous' favorite was the one when Mireille Mathieu sings un jour tu verras on se rencontrera.

so here they are in Tokyo the displaced frog and the displaced jap telling each other's life story in the café C'est Si Bon which Moinous had discovered soon after he arrived in Tokyo and when he saw that name he went in and introduced himself to Mister Arakawa saying that he was so happy to find a café with a French name because he was French and etc.

So you see, this is how the novel will be constructed. First a chapter about what Moinous and Tashima did in Tokyo. The black-market, the fucking of the cute Japanese bowlegged girls, the skibi [sic] shows, the night clubs, the off-limit places, the transvestites, more skikbi shows, the massages, more black-market, the chopsticks, the massages, the hot barth, the fucking, etc.

Then a chapter of Tashima's story. Then another chapter of Moinous and Tashima in Tokyo. Then a Moinous chapter. And so on.

The chapters alternating. Or let's call them scenes. The scenes in the forefront on the surface: Moinous and Tashima in Tokyo. The present of the narrative written in the present tense.

The alternating scenes of Tashima's and Moinous' life below the surface written as sub-narratives in the past tense.

Well, that's what I scribbled last night on a yellow pad while watching the tennis match. It all made sense to me. Especially the underground stories.

To tell only what Moinous did in Tokyo may be interesting, even funny, and très sexy, but it would be just a straight-forward old-fashioned story.

Now the Moinous-Tashima stories will be like echos inside the writing. A stereophonic effect. And this way the book will have a double dimension.

A double life, in other words.

Exactly. And as I thought of this double level of the book, it also became clear to me that while on the surface Moinous and Tashima were living the good G.I. life in Tokyo, in their minds they were constantly reliving, or rather replaying the sad events of the life that had led them to Tokyo. And that's what they will tell each other, exactly as it happened.

But when Moinous begins telling the story of his life, he emphasizes that he will only tell the facts. No gruesome details. Just cold facts without explanation or interpretation. without emotion even. And without long intricate sentences. No digressions. No adjectives. No adverbs. A straight-forward story written in a straight-forward language.

And last night, while toying with all that in my head, I remembered that marvelous novel by Georges Perec called **W *or the Memory of Childhood*.**

In **W**, Perec alternates chapters from the story of his childhood with the story of what takes place on an island where athletes train for some kind of Olympics games, but if they fail to win they are executed.

An incredible metaphor for the Nazis camps and the Holocaust.

The **W** of the title is the key to this double narrative. When you pronounce **W** in French you says **Double Vé** — which sounds like **Double Vie**. Yes, Double life.

So what I'm going to write now is the double life of Moinous in Tokyo. And the title of the book will be:

The Double Life of Moinous in Tokyo

I was so pleased with what I had scribbled, but also exhausted from all that thinking, I fell asleep in my rocking chair. I didn't even hear you come in.

Sounds good. So you're going to write it like that. Pieces of your story and pieces of Tashima's story.

Well, that's what I thought last night. But this morning, it felt all wrong. Including the title. The title should simply be:

Tokyo — the Missing Years

Good. No more Moinous. But why the missing years?

Yes. No more Moinous. You see, it's not going to be the story of Moinous this time. That fake being. It's going to be my story. Federman's story. That's why Moinous dropped out of the title. Out of this book. No Moinous in this one.

Good riddance. I think your readers were getting fed up with him. He is such a schlemiel.

This is going to be my story. But I'm going to write it in the first person. This will be the story of the **I** who speaks in the book. This way I cannot be accused of having invented most of the story. Only the **I** speaking in the book will be responsible for everything that is told.

So another one of your real fictitious stories.

Yes. But now let me tell you what else happened today, and how the story goes now.

I also dumped Tashima's story. I mean the scenes from his life. Tashima will be present in the book since he was in Tokyo at the same time I was there, but not his story.

You see Tashima was a very secretive guy. He never really revealed anything about himself. Except what I told already how he was ashamed of what his mother prepared for his lunch. He wanted to be a real American. He wanted to look like a real American. That was his big hang-up. And in Japan he wanted so much to look and act like a real Japanese. When we want bumming in town, especially in the off-limit neighborhoods of Tokyo, the G.I.s were not allowed to go in some parts of the city, it was never made clear to us why, and in fact it was also preferable, we were told, to wear civilian clothes rather than our uniforms when going into town on our free time, so when Tashima and I were bumming around he always dressed like a real Japanese, you know those pants that are loose on top and get tighter at the bottom, and a blouse that look like a tunic, shit it's not easy to describe what the Japanese wore in those days, very few of them dressed the western style, at least not the Japanese with whom we associated then, except for Pepito, that's what everybody called him, the crook with whom I did most of my blackmarketting, he dressed like a typical Chicago Gangster, black suit with thin white stripes, and he always wore a white borselino. But I was telling you about what Tashima wore, a typical Japanese outfit, and he always tied a scarf around his head, he really looked like a real Japanese, and yet all the japs would pick him out immediately as an

American, he could never win, he was a Nisei, and he could escape that.

Here let me tell you something else that happened while Tashima and I were in Paris. That was a few years after Tokyo after we graduated from Columbia. Yes both Tashima and I went to Columbia University, but that's another story.

In any case, Tashima went to Paris after he graduated, and in 1958 I went back to France for the first time. That too is another story.

What I want to tell to illustrate how Tashima suffered from a crisis of identity, is how one day the two of us went to visit Le Père Lachaise cemetery where all the famous French writers are buried.

We wanted to see especially the graves of the famous poets. One of the attendants took us around from one famous grave to another. He must have spent a couple of hours with us. He told us all kinds of interesting stories about the dead writers and who came to visit them. When we left we thanked him and even gave him a pourboire, and as he shook hand with Tashima he said to him, c'était un grand plaisir pour moi monsieur de bavarder avec un chinois. That's what he said to Tashima. What a pleasure it was for him to talk to a Chinese.

But I was telling you how secretive Tashima was. So that I really didn't know much about his life before we met. He did tell me once that he and his parents and his younger brother had been interned during the war in one of those camps for American Japanese in Arizona. But he never went into details of his life in that camp. And he never mentioned it again. Never. That's about all I know about Tashima. He was so evasive. All the guys in our outfit suspected that he was CIA. He was often sent on special mysterious assignments. Sometimes he would be flown back to Korea for a couple of days. But he never told me why. And when I questioned him he would say, to get stuff at the PX. It's true that the PX in Korean had more stuff and better stuff than the one in Tokyo. Tashima always came back with lots of stuff which we would sell on the black market.

What kind of stuff?

Oh you know, cartons of cigarettes, bottle of booze, watches, things like that he had gotten cheap at the PX in Korea. But I'll get into the black market stories later.

Right now I'm trying to set the geometry of the narrative. Unless I have the design of the book, I cannot get going.

Concerning Tashima, why can't you invent his story?

Invent his life! You must be kidding. I have enough trouble inventing my own life.

Too bad. Maybe Tashima's story is more interesting than yours. You could even work out a parallel between the camp where he and his family were interned and the German concentration camps.

I don't want to go into that. That's not what I want this story to be.

OK. So go ahead. Tell me what it will be.

Well, first I must explain how I got to Tokyo from Korea.

Oh, by the way, you never explained why the missing years in the title.

That's right. You remember when we had that discussion about what my next book should be, you said that I had never written about the time I spent Far East. And these three years were very important. They were like I was given a second surplus of life.

You see, I was sure I was going to get killed in Korea. In the long and endless story I've been telling about my life, this part fits between the end *Take It or Leave It* and the beginning of *Smiles on Washington*. And these are the missing years.

Oh, I see. Frenchy eventually is shipped to the Far East even though at the end of Tioli it looks like he will never make it. And he reappears under the name of Moinous in Smiles. Makes sense.

Exactly. And that's why Tokyo represents the missing years. OK. So now the story begins. How I got from Korea to Tokyo.

Let's call that part **Out of the Foxhole.** By the way, this part is told to Ace. You know George Chambers because he was in Korea too about the same time I was there. So I thought it'd be interesting to have him here as a silent interlocutor.

You always have to stick everybody in your stories.

Why not. I need someone to listen to my stories.

I am listening.

Yes, I know. But the more listeners I have, the better I can tell my stories.

OK, go ahead.

— The Bullet —

Ace, have I ever told you what happened in Korea when I found myself in a foxhole with some kid from Jersey?

Here, let me start from the beginning. You were there too, I know, freezing your ass off in the rice paddies, so I know you'll understand.

But first let's backtrack to when the boat to the Far East arrived in Yokohama full of fresh anxious recruits, most of them hillbilly puceaux [look that up in your French dictionary]. I think we came one USS Grant, but since memory is always deficient I cannot confirm that it was the USS Grant, for all I know it could have been some other stinking tub. What's for sure is that after three fucking weeks of vomiting in the Pacific, we were all glad to set foot on firm ground.

Immediately upon arrival in Yokohama, a few were selected to stay in Japan with the vacationing black-marketing Occupying Forces, while the rest was shipped directly to Korea to participate in the so-called Police Action. Me, I got the Korean vacation. But not for long, not for long, as I'll explain in a moment.

But before the ship sail to Korea we all got an overnight pass. We didn't have to go very from the ship to find what we needed. A good fuck. The giggly girls were lined on the quay when we disembarked. That night many of the dumb recruits lost their virginity.

Me, well, I had lost mine a long time ago, but that night I did get my first taste of a Japanese pussy. It was okay, but I had better ones after that.

The next morning back you should have seen the eyes of the recruits as the ship sailed to Korea and we all stood at attention in front of the American flag. We were on our way to the war.

OK, I'll skip now directly ahead now to a particular night on the front line, because it's the story of Tokyo that I want to tell. The six weeks I spent in Korea where are not that important, except for that one night.

Here I am in a foxhole somewhere beyond one of the parallels — I can't remember if it's the 38th or the 36th or the 42nd — in the middle of a rice paddy, and it's cold like hell, 20 below, and over there, across from us, less than 100 yards, on the other side of the rice paddy, some fucking Gooks are shooting at us. I can't tell you how they look because we can't see them. They're buried in the mud like us. But they are Gooks. That's what everybody calls them. And I assume they were also freezing their asses like us.

It's the middle of the night. My feet, my hands, my nose, my ears are frozen. I'm with this kid from Jersey in a deep muddy foxhole. He's smaller than me, and scared. Me, I tell him, I'm not scared because my death is behind me already. What the fuck you talking about, he says with his Jersey accent and a puzzled look on his face. I can see the puzzled look on his face because for just a moment the moon comes out from behind the clouds. Yes, it's a cloudy night. It might snow any moment. I forgot to mention, it's winter, February, and what a stinking winter it was. So I start telling Jersey the story of my life. You know, the same old sad story you've heard so many times. Meanwhile the bullets are flying over our heads in all directions, as we crouch inside the foxhole, clutching our rifles. Why the fuck are they shooting at us. We didn't do anything to make them angry. We're just two dumb G.I.'s doing our duty. I'm really pissed at those motherfucking Gooks for shooting at us like that. For no specific reason. We didn't do anything to them tonight. We didn't shoot first. We didn't insult them. We're just doing our duty. Except I forgot to mention that the foxhole in which Jersey and me are hiding is an outpost in front of the main line. We're supposed to be observing the enemy movements. We have a radio but were not supposed to use it. The main line, where our buddies are probably jerking off or snoozing up while waiting for the next attack, is about 300 yards behind us.

Maybe the reason the Gooks are shooting at our foxhole is because the little asshole Jersey just lit a cigarette. A Chesterfield, or maybe a Camel, I'm not sure, I'm not a smoker. That stupid Jersey lit his fucking cigarette without covering the flame of his lighter with his hands, like we were taught in basic training, and so the Gooks when they saw the light started shooting, and now the bullets are flying all around us, some of them with little lights attached to them, you know, tracers, so they can see us better. We're keeping our heads tucked down low in the hole.

Suddenly I have a premonition. This is it, I tell Jersey, my excess of life has run out of excess. Tonight is the night I join the angels. And I say to Jersey, give me a fucking cigarette.

I never smoked before, that's because of the swimming, but fuck it. I could have told Jersey to go and read *Take It or Leave It* to find out what a great swimmer I was when I almost made it to the Olympics, but there was no point in that since the story was not yet written, and may never be written if my premonition comes true. But, as you see, I survived that onslaught of bullets from the Gooks, otherwise I wouldn't be here telling you all this.

Anyway, at that moment, when the moon came out from behind the clouds, I was sure this was it. So I say to Jersey, give me a fucking cigarette, my first, and my last. One of these fucking bullets has my name on it. Excuse the frequent repetition of the word fucking, but I'm trying to be as realistic and as close to the truth as possible, this is an army story, and it was a crucial moment in my life.

So I take a deep drag on the fucking cigarette, and I almost choke. I start coughing like I have tuberculosis. Jersey is slapping me on the back, and screaming at me, shut the fuck up, they're going to kill us. He hands me his canteen full of, you won't believe this, full of sake, where the fuck did he get sake out here, and I choke and cough even more, and the bullets are flying even more. The whole sky is full of them. I take a second drag of the cigarette, but this time the smoke feels good inside. Feels warm. I remember, I even let some of the smoke come out slowly through my nose, my big crooked nose, just like I've seen actors do in the movies. I'm all grown-up suddenly. I feel like a man. I could fight those fucking Gooks barehanded.

I raise my head a bit above the ledge of the foxhole, up to my nose, put out my M1, and fire at will, northward towards the Gooks while shouting obscenities at them. Jersey climbs up next to me from the mud at the bottom of the foxhole and starts shooting too, but he's so short he has to stand on top of his backpack [full of cans of monkey meat and cigarettes — Jersey is a chain smoker] to reach the edge of the foxhole, it's a deep foxhole, so his head sticks out of the hole more than mine — above his chin — and the bullet destined for me hits him. No, not in the face, not in the eye, but on the wrist which was outside the security of the foxhole since he was holding his M1 above the ledge. The bullet hits the wrist, but not the flesh or the bone of the wrist — I think it was the left wrist, if I remember correctly, but since I make little distinction between memory and imagination, it could have been the right wrist just as well. In any case, the bullet with my name on it doesn't hit the wrist itself, so to speak, but Jersey's wrist-watch. I'm not kidding. And the whole fucking watch gets pulverized in his arm. I think it was a Bulova he bought at the PX in

Tokyo during his R&R, but I'm not sure. It could have been a Rolex. All I know is that it was a big round watch with a gold bracelet. He showed it me when he got back from R&R, and I said to him, wow what a fucking good-looking big wristwatch, you must have payed a fortune for it. That's exactly what I said.

Anyway, when the bullet hit the watch the whole fucking mechanism got disseminated in Jersey's entire arm, from the wrist to the elbow. The little springs got under his skin, the screws, the numbers, the hands of the watch, the rubies — yes, his watch had twelve rubies, that's what it said on the back, he showed me — got dispersed and encrusted in his arm, and Jersey is screaming like a pig being slaughtered, and I am screaming too, MEDIC! MEDIC! where the fuck are the fucking medics. Meanwhile the fucking Gooks, when they hear all that screaming and shouting, start shooting again. I get so pissed, I take a grenade out of the pocket of my field jacket and throw it northward — with my left arm [I was a lefty then] — and I hear little human squeaks. I burst into laughter. Meanwhile Jersey is at the bottom of the foxhole squirming and whining and weeping with pain, and fear of death of course. I take his flashlight [we had flashlights] out of my backpack and examine his wound. The bullets start flying again. He's not going to die. I reassure him with a tap on top of the head, and tell him, Jersey you're a fucking lucky sonofabitch, it's nothing, just a flesh wound, they gonna send you home with that, you gonna get a purple heart and a pension for life, and you know what, you'll be a celebrity, you'll have the time in you forever. You'll be a human clock. You'll get a job in a circus or freak show. You'll be rich and famous.

Just then two medics, crawling in the mud, reach our foxhole. They grab Jersey, who is still screaming and weeping and whining, and drag him back to the main line. Be careful with him, I tell them, the guy is precious.

— The Reprieve —

And me? What do you think? I'm not gonna stay in this fucking foxhole alone. I'm outta here. I'm not gonna fight the Gooks by myself. So I crawl out of the hole and retreat to the main line.

The next day the sergeant tells me to report to Captain Cohen. Yes, Captain Cohen, a Yid like me. On my way to his tent I say to myself, shit he's going to chew my ass for having deserted my post. Maybe I'll get busted. I was a PFC then. I walk into Captain Cohen's tent, give him one of my best military salute as I stand at attention.

At ease, Federstein . . .

Federman, I correct him politely . . .

Oh yeah, Federman. PFC Federman get you gear together you're flying to Tokyo.

Oh shit, I thought, they're going to court-martial me for having deserted my post. Why Sir? I ask anxiously, coming to attention again.

Not the foggiest idea. Just when I need every fucking man I have for the big push. It's an order that just came in from Central Headquarters in Tokyo.

Central Headquarters! Hey, maybe they gonna decorate me because of my heroic action last night. After all, Jersey and me we stood our ground during that ferocious attack on our foxhole, and I saved his life.

Must be important, Captain Cohen says, so get your ass moving, there is a plane leaving in ten minutes.

Yes sir!

Yes sir! I shouted militarily, when I heard they wanted me in Tokyo, and rushed to pack my duffel bag and expand my War Zone activities to Japan.

Up in the B25 fighter flying me to Tokyo, I sat next to the pilot, and he even let me hold the steering wheel for a while — ah what a sweet sensation I suddenly felt — free at last — out of the mud — once again I had outsmarted my death. I should have kept the bullet that pulverized Jersey's watch as a souvenir.

Somehow I knew I was leaving that ice box of rice paddies for good. I'll do anything in Tokyo so they don't send me back to the foxholes, I told my co-pilot as I steered the B25 to a higher altitude. I'll do anything. Even suck a dick? asked my co-pilot, and suddenly I felt a frisson pass through me. The fucking co-pilot is queer and is proposing to me, I thought [not to myself]. Suppose the cocksucker aggresses me, right here up in the sky, and demands a blow job, even though I don't do these sort of things, and he pulls rank on me and tells me it's an order [my co-pilot is a captain, and me just a one stripe PFC] but nothing ensued [hey nice choice of words here — en-suce] of that proposition, and I landed safely in Tokyo.

— On Special Assignment —

Sir! PFC Federstein reporting! I shouted to the Commanding Officer of the 510 Military Intelligence Group, Major Grandcon. [I was ordered upon landing in Tokyo to report immediately to Major Grandcon for special assignment. Me! A special assignment — I suddenly felt very important, and very alive].

Sir! PFC Federstein reporting, I said clicking in the Nazi style the heels of my superbly spit-shined paratrooper boots now cleaned for good of the mud of the rice paddies. [Yes I was a paratrooper. 82nd Airborne Division — see *Take It or Leave It* for details].

I said Federstein instead of Federman in case the Major decided to send me back to the rice paddies. I figured, this way Federstein would go instead of Federman.

At ease Soldier! Major Grandcon said holding out his hand, as if I were some kind of very special agent. Yes, this I will never forget, Grandcon called me Soldier, and shook hands with me, as if I were a national hero. It made me feel so proud to be serving my adopted country in the Far East, even though I had not yet been officially adopted [poor little orphan that I am] by my new country [that will happen later in Tokyo — see *Smiles on Washington Square* for full details of the adoption ceremony].

So I put myself at ease. Dropped into the luxurious leather armchair facing Major Grandcon's desk — after all I was a Special Ass, I had privileges — and I said, while relaxing my tired ass in the softness of the chair, all my life my feet have been killing me [see *Loose Shoes* for clarification]. Grandcon smiled and said: Me too, I have the same problem, but we're not here to talk about our feet. There is a fucking war going on, and we fucking better get it over soon because the fucking Russians are waiting in line to start the next war, and one war at a time is enough. That's exactly what Major Grandcon said.

Damn right Major! I said, speaking as one officer to another, while puffing on the Cuban cigar Major Grandcon had offered me, and reclining deep into the safety of the armchair. Not another war, I thought. Suppose they draft me for that one too, even though I'm not officially a citizen yet. And suppose the fucking Russkoffs capture me and I'm a prisoner of war, and one day while taking a leak the Russkoffs notice my circumcised cock, and immediately want to exterminate me, even though I keep waving my dog tags at them as I stand before the firing squad, naked, except for the dog tags around my neck, on which it says **P** for religion and not **J** [yes another typical army goof when they indoctrinated me — see *Take It or Leave It* for details of another army goof].

Well, let me summarize quickly what happened next, which I now recall as being a relaxing and comforting moment, when I was informed by Major Grandcon that I would be attached to the 510 MIG as a Liaison Officer [without any specific rank, however, since you are not yet a citizen, Grandcon specified] between our forces and the French speaking forces now involved in this United Action. Suddenly I remembered that I know French [in this fucking army, I didn't have much use for my French, that other language in me was, so to speak, dormant] and it all became clear to me.

Inadvertently, the fucking French, who tried so hard to have me exterminated jadis, were now saving my life because of my knowledge of their language.

The American forces need a frog to interpret — to explain to them what's going on. Wow! was I going to interpret and explain. Man, I'll make a fortune here in Tokyo interpreting and clarifying. I'm not going to do that kind of essential job, for nothing.

So I tell the Major that I accept the position on the condition that I receive a retribution of sort, and a medal to show the important role I played in the United Action in the Far East. Grandcon didn't flinch. He gave me 500000 yens right there on the spot. He took the money out of a Japanese lacquer box on his desk [I remember the lacquer box very clearly because it had a picture of Mount Fuji on the cover]. Of course, at the then current rate of exchange, it was worth about 100 bucks, but enough to buy me my second piece of slanted ass in Tokyo. And also a carton of cigarettes. Chesterfields.

You see, after that first [and fortunately not last] cigarette in the foxhole, I became [see *La Fourrure de ma Tante Rachel* for Federstein's favorite brand of cigarettes].

OK, to make that special moment even more climatic let me sum up what Major Grandcon said.

You, Federstein, Liaison Officer of undetermined rank and nationality, will serve as an interpreter for the French speaking forces newly involved in the United Action in these parts. You will reside in the Imperial Hotel in a special suite, already reserved for you, a jeep with a boysan driver will be at your service, 24 hours a day, and another boysan will take care of your needs, 24 hours a day. When I heard about the second boysan, I requested politely that the second boysan be a girlsan — a matter of taste,

I explained to Major Greatcon.

But there is a little problem to solve first. According to our records you have only five more months to serve in this army. We need you for more than that. The way things are going, this freaking war might go on for a while. Will you be willing to re-enlist for another two years? I not then we'll have to find someone else, I am sure there are other frogs like you out there, and we'll send you back to your outfit in Korea.

Less than half an hour later [after having agreed to re-enlist for another two year of service, so glad I was to be out of the fucking rice paddies], I was soaking in a steaming hot bath at the Imperial Hotel, soon to receive [after having been wiped and oiled] a deliciously slow and sensual massage by a private girlsan.

The next day .... or perhaps it was the same day, after the massage, I went strolling in the streets of devastated Tokyo. And man did it stink in that fucking city. You too must remember the canal running through the whole place. It was so infected with all the shit and piss and garbage the people threw in it. Took me seven weeks to get used to the smell, but I never got used to the dead rats floating in the canal. The day I arrived in Tokyo and was promoted to special Liaison Officer, and got my first Japanese massage, I bumped into another G.I., a corporal . . . no not Tashima Soome other guy. Tashima I met a few days later. I bumped into this corporal who looked totally stoned and drunk, and lost too. It was in a Shimbashi bar. The guy slapped me solidly on the back when he saw me come in, as if I we were old buddies, and shouted, So here you are you Old Bum, as if he had expected me, still alive, come on, man! let's booze it up.

On you, of course, my dear Fellow-Bum, I said embracing him to show my appreciation. You see, I didn't want to blow 100 bucks Grandcon gave me too soon, I wanted to save it in case later the right pussy came along. So I was willing to let that guy treat me. What the hell.

That's how The Dawn of the Bums started ..... but that's another story. Let's see if there is another way to approach this story.

— Another Possible Beginning —

Yesterday at the pedicure, while Amy was massaging my feet and it felt good. Amy is my Vietnamese pedicurist. And while she was doing my feet, I closed my eyes and bang I hear a voice in my head telling me that I should write the story of Moinous in Tokyo now that I finished the story of Moinous on the farm.

And as Amy dreamily continued to massage my feet, it occured to me that it would make a nice sequence to *The Farm* because if *The Farm* was a portrait of the artist as a young boy in shit up to his knees *Moinous in Tokyo* will be the portrait of the artist as young man finding his vocation.

You see, it's in Tokyo that Moinous wrote his first poem. Yes a poem. Before Tokyo Moinous had never written a poem. In fact, he had no idea what poetry was. Moinous read a lot while in the army mostly adventure novels or war novels, and now and then a porno novel. But he never read poetry. He had no feeling for poetry. But day in Korea, in a foxhole [the novel will be Called *Out of the Foxhole*] a french soldier gave Moinous a book — a copy of the *Méditations* of Larmartine in the popular petit classique larousse series.

Let me explain how this happened.

On the front line, near Inchon, there were the Americans foxholes in the middle, on the right the Turks' foxholes, and on the left the foxholes of the French.

At night, the American foxholes were very quiet. We were ordered to be quiet, otherwise.

On the right the Turks didn't give a shit about noise or about the gook. Some of them would crawl across the rice paddies to the side of the Gooks catch one of them and cut his ears. I can prove that because I often went to visit the Turks soldiers in their foxholes. I found them funny. And they were scared of nothing. And the way I knew about the Gooks' ears is because some of them wore necklaces made of the ears. And the one who had more ears on his necklace was considered the most courageous.

On the other side of our foxhole. The French side, it was quite different. These frogs were always singing and playing the accordion. And could they smoke. They smoke these cigarettes with dark tobacco they call Gauloises. I used to go visit their foxholes just to smoke their cigarettes. And there was one guy there, a blond, I remember, cute guy, a bit timid. A bit effeminate even. He was from southern France. Not one of the rough Parisian Titis, as they are called. I became friendly with him. He was not one of those who sang dirty songs all the time, usually when I crawled over to his foxhole, that's when the Gooks were not firing at us, and us at them, I would find him reading a book. He has a musette full of books. Most of them from the Classique Larousse series.

So one day I asked him, qu'est-ce tu lis là?

I am forced to tell that in French.

And he answered, J'suis en train'd lire du larmatine ses méditations, c'est d'la poez, and he handed me the book and I flipped the pages and even stopped to read one of the poems, it was called le lac, I don't know why this particular poem stopped my attention, maybe these lines:

Oh temps, suspends ton vol ! Et vous, heures propices

Suspendez votre cours!

This Lamartine guy thinks like me, I told the French solider. Or mabye its me who thinks like him. Because me too I wanted time to suspend its flight, and for these propitious hours to suspend their course.

Tiens si tu veux tu peux le garder, j'ai fini d' le lire ce livre, c'est pas mal. And the guy gave me the book. I still have it after all these years. So back in my foxhole, I read the book from cover to cover, and it changed the course of my life. Right there in a foxhole in the Korean mud, I decided to become a poet.

I wrote my first poem in Tokyo. I even wrote it in English. I kept it.

It was called

Travel

I Swan the Ocean under the Water
A Long Swim Years Ago Skin Tight to My Bones
As I Came up for Air I Shouted Obscenities
An Old Man Grabbed Me by the Shoulders
And Hurled Me into the Ground
I Shouted America America Here I Am
No One Answered They Were Too Busy
The Subways Were Full of Sweaty People
I Felt Too White Too Small Too Insignificant
But a Fat Woman Touched Me All over
And I Thought it Was Love
I Looked up at the Sky
The Moon Had Spread Her Legs
No One Saw Me Blush
In the Dark I Sneaked out
Of the Window and Climbed
Behind a Cloud to Look for God
But All I Found There Were My Own Footprints
Tired of the Stars and the Flying Saucers
I Came Back among Men in Straw Hats
I Had a Hot Dog Smoked a Pall Mall
And Then They Put a Green Costume
On Me and Shipped on the Other Side
Of the Other Ocean Far Away
I Had Myself a Few Chinese
Screwed a Few Japanese Girlsan
And Back Across the Ocean
In My Lonely Garret

The Light and Gas Had Been Turned off
I Waited in the Dark in the Cold
Until One Day I Found the Answer
In an Old Laundry Bag

That's When I Started Writing Poetry

Without Punctuation

I realized how easy to was to write poetry. All you had to do was write lines of words more or less the same number of words in each line, capitalize the letter of the first word, and you had a poem.

After I wrote that poem I realized I had capitalized the first letter of all the important words instead of just the first letter of the first word of each line. But to me, what I had written really looked and felt like a poem. My first poem, which I wrote because of Lamartine.

Or which Moinous wrote, if I decide that's it's his story.

In any case, that how Moinous recognized that he wanted to become a poet, a romantic poet like Lamartine. This may not be what he has become, but there in Tokyo Moinous started writing what he thought were poems, since he was alining the words on the pages just like Lamartine. But what Moinous was writing was not about the sadness of nature, and the tormented lacs, and the languishing mountains, and the weeping clouds. His poems were about what he was seeing and experiencing in Tokyo, the black market, the prostitutes, the transvestites, the skibi show, love Japanese style, poverty, fear devastation, humiliation, gratitude, envy, hatred, and of course the military crap — and so on.

And so, *Out of the Foxhole* will be the portrait of the artist as a young jerk wondering what the fuck he is doing in the fucking army.

What do you think, shall I pursue that?

Perhaps the opening sentence of this new beginning should be spoken by someone else than the Moinous.

Somebody asks: Moinous, how important was Tokyo to you?

And that somebody keeps asking questions to Moinous about his life in Tokyo and how it transformed him, and moinous invents the answers.

I say invent because much of what happened to Moinous in Tokyo has been forgotten.

But what is important is that, Tokyo was for Moinous another resurrection. Another excess of life was given to him. That's the premise of this story.

The story ends when Moinous, on stormy night, standing on the upper-deck of the ship taking him back to America, while all the other G.I.'s are snoring below deck or masturbating [never forget the central theme of your oeuvre Federman] Moinous throws into the sea the little black book in which he had written the names and addresses of people he knew before being shipped oversea to fight the war. He wanted nothing more to do with these people now. He wanted to cut himself from the past. A very symbolic gesture the throwing of the little black book into the ocean. A new start. But that gesture brought a touch of panic to Moinous, and for a moment he thought of throwing himself into the dark ocean, so as not to have to face the his unpredictable future, but instead he went below deck to where all the others were asleep, quietly took out a notebook he had in his duffle bag, and a flashlight, and back on the upper-deck, the wind blowing in his hair, he wrote his first short story, for there on that ship, that night, Moinous decided that his vocation was not poctry, but fiction. The poems he had written in Tokyo made him realize that poetry tries desperately to tell the truth, but always fails, whereas fiction is made of an accumulation of lies that become the truth.

He called his first story: *You Can't Go Home Again.*

Yes, Moinous had read Thomas Wolfe.

Well, what do you think? I have the beginning and the end, the rest should be easy to write. Just a matter of filling up pages.

I'm excited.

Of course, I'll have to do some research [geographical and sociological] to re-situate Moinous in the Tokyo of the early 50s.

Yes certainly. Those were the days indeed — but you seem to have forgotten so much my friend — we need precise details — for the sake of historical veracity — for instance how did Sumikosan hold IT — did she also do the balls — did she check the head to make sure it was not dripping — in those days my friend it was not unusual for young naive G.I. to catch the clap and not know that the stuff dripping was the clap — and what about morpions — did you ever have any — and did the girlsan suck it too —

these are details that need to be recorded —

as for Sumikosan — did I mention that she was a model for a kimono manufacture — that tells how shapely she was — but narrow — very narrow and tight — that much is understood — we used to go have tea in the afternoon at a little café called SANS SOUCI [in those days the japs were deep into existentialism] and there we listened to classical music — Sumikosan was very cultivated — she came from a good japbourgeois family — I dined chez elle once — you want me to describe that or can you visualize frenchy the Yid G.I. acting japanese chez Sumikosan — the worse is that at that time frenchy had not yet acquire the necessary chopstick dexterity to keep up with the Sumikosan family [we all ate out of the same pot chopsticking as much as each could — I think I managed one little piece of meat and twelve grains of rice — with my clumsy chopstick action — but Sumiko seeing how frustrated I was gave me chopstick lessons the next day while I was fondling her tits [she had rather voluminous tits for a Japanese] —

yes tell me more — because so far I've been doing all the fucking work —

you just give order — remember I'm a special agent on a special assignment —

this is what we have so far — and we barely scratched the surface

in Korea back then there was this woman I would always see no matter where I was an asian but in uniform military field stuff but always her eyes on me here and there

I have a question: was there a charge to fuck bareass as we used to say meaning without a condom?

was there an extra charge & if so how much????

once afternoon I was out on patrol in the half track me butter & mclaren & we got superbored as usual and stopped by these grouping of huts where girls were for sale we rented some & got fucking up and then they invited us in to the family meal wives husbands kids grand-folks all into the rice bowl & hot kimch & some weird fucking gooey drink so soon someone is shouting GOOKS & we're out side unloading our sidearms into the shadows!

likewise my medal for GOOD CONDUCT ist verlorenkaputski.

When we went ashore I got scared I thought I'd fallen off the ropes into the sea what with all my gear rifle helmet etc. so I never got ashore at Inchon I was in the brig on ship one scared ass teen let me tell you & enshamed by the fear there I was in the brig in Inchon Harbour with everyone else storming ashore Ike McArthur Tojo Geo the guy who played … yes sir! I shout militarily and rush to pack my gear and expand the war zone to Tokyo and up there in the B25 fighter flying me to Tokyo I sat next to the pilot and he even let me hold the steering wheel for a while what a sensation I suddenly felt so free once again I had outsmarted death somehow I knew I was leaving that frigidaire of rice paddies for good I'll do anything in Tokyo not to get back here I told my co-pilot anything even prostitute yourself asked the co-pilot and suddenly I felt a frisson pass through me the fucking co-pilot is queer and is proposing me suppose he agresses me right here up in the sky and asks me to give him a blowjob and it's an order the co-pilot is a captain and me just a sergeant not even first class but nothing ensued [nice word there] of that proposition and we landed safely and still hetero in Tokyo — end of the preamble

[*more to be told one day*]

A Memoir of a Delusional Sentence

DOUG RICE

Once upon a time in 1979, innocent and pure reader that I was, I randomly pulled Raymond Federman's *Double or Nothing* from a shelf in the Slippery Rock State College library. Expecting little more than, as Marcus Klein stated in his blurb, "a furious and comic scheme . . . [of a] hero becoming a citizen," I opened the oddly shaped 8.5 x 11 book. I thought I would read the first few sentences while taking a break from an essay I was writing about Shakespeare or Chaucer or Joyce for one of my undergraduate literature courses, but Federman's first sentence went on and on, spilling off the page, turning and twisting, disappearing and reappearing, refusing to stop or pause, fighting against itself in nearly psychotic ways as if the sentence was afraid of making sense, of being calm, of simply saying what needed to be said, and then putting an end to its own desire and meaning by the writer (or the narrator or the publisher or a copyeditor or anyone with a compassion for sanity) inserting a period, an endstop, and moving on to the next sentence. But Federman, incest-tually invoking Beckett's "You must go on. I can't go on. I'll go on.", kept going on. He pushed his sentence beyond obsessive exhaustion into liminal territories of possibilities that Federman himself had clearly lost control of. This sentence, escaping Federman's pen, like a river that does not know where it is flowing, combined and erased moments of biographical truth with lines of flight in ways that disrespected the ontological purpose of sentences written by other writers who feared what might become of a sentence if a sentence refused to obey the laws of grammar and common sense, if a sentence was set loose upon unsuspecting readers, without a clear destination, without uttering a defined (or divine) purpose. Federman's quirky (and somewhat inappropriate, while appropriated) parenthetical digression after parenthetical digression and digressions inside digressions assaulted the common decency of civil readers of sentences and turned themselves inside-out against the forward movement of Federman's sentence. These seemingly innocuous parenthetical tremors invaded his sentence and repeatedly (if not rapaciously) derailed the sentence and the reader. (Years later I would learn that this is the most common way the Federman virus infects innocent readers like myself and unvirgined our reading (and, dare I say, our writing) habits as we could no longer protect our "own" readerly identity from the critifictional chaos of a man named Federman, who claimed to be writing what I was reading, but who also claimed to be unable to remember if he had written all of what he had published, or if he had not written any of what he had signed his name to but had only read what he wrote somewhere in a book written by some other man with a pen, most likely books written by Samuel Beckett, and had copied these words in his own hand, or had stumbled upon these words scattered along the streets of Paris or Buffalo or Detroit and made them into sentences that he then claimed as his own; or, if Federman himself had truthfully (in a verifiable way) been locked in a closet, or if he had merely read about some other character who had been locked in a closet somewhere in France; regardless of the autobiographical truth (any truth has a deeper emotional resonance than a mere fact ever will be able to convey) of that closet and that bag of sugar, the Federman I walked with in Buffalo and Pittsburgh and in other cities in America carried that closet and that bag of sugar with him in his skin, marked, X-X-X-X (the constant reminder of four pebbles placed on the tombstones of Jewish graves), and that closet is in every sentence that Federman ever wrote, and every Federmaniacal sentence becomes, whether the sentence wants to or not, a playful and terrifying attempt to open that closet door. Federman, the Federman locked inside his sentences, struggled with this fear and this desire to open this closet door and to, somehow simultaneously, keep this real or imagined closet door locked. And those footsteps outside the door. The ones that echoed in the hallway on that fateful day and that echoed in Federman every day that he lived on this earth. (The night he went to see *Schindler's List* and could not stop writing and writing, as if he believed language could undo loss.) It is for this reason that every Federman sentence may have a beginning, but no Federman sentence ends. Ever.) Before I began this parenthesis, it was 1979, and I was, like a virgin, reading Federman for the very first time, and Federman's narrator was losing himself inside the opening sentence of *Double or Nothing*, a sentence becoming something other than a sentence, (becoming *becoming* as Gilles Deleuze would say, if he were nearby the utterance of Federman's maddening sentence falling off thousands of plateaus down a rabbit hole and becoming entangled in rhizomes of noodles and closets, and Charlie Parker playing his saxophone on street corners, as Federman, like that ancient mariner of yore, grabbed people by their shirt collars and told them stories of walking into clubs in Detroit and playing with Bird, and all of us believing (or at least wanting to believe) Federman because Federman was a man as much imagined as imagining), and Federman himself refused to stay out of that sentence or any other sentence he ever wrote. He refused to keep his distance, and this Federman character became Federman, and Federman appeared to become the narrator, and then a mirror reflected Federman's name back against himself giving birth to Namredef (although it would take years for this reflection to be given a voice) (and Federman himself, in Buffalo, in the snow, there was always snow in Buffalo, years before he, like Beckett, changed tense, gave me permission to play with his name, (and Larry McCaffery witnessed Federman giving me this permission, so we can separate truth from fiction, fact from myth, because Federman loved his name and protected his name from evil) and so, on rare occasions, such as this one, I do play with his name, because there is no true way to know where a Federman sentence ends and a Rice sentence (or anyone else's for that matter) begins, and there is no stopping this moment of supreme indecision without one pla(y)giarizing the other, and without the other knowing the one has committed such a fraudulent act of original creativity and inspiration, "for one never knows," as Federman(?) himself claims, "where one's thoughts originate, and when these thoughts merge with those of others, where one's language begins and where it converges with that of others within the dialogue all of us entertain with ourselves and with others"—addenda: these quotation marks cannot mean all that they are cracked up to mean and to protect. In the end, who "owns" language? And what sort of person claims that they are speaking in their "own" words? (Be careful when you speak. You never know whose mouth those words were in before you uttered them.) Style is the only true quotation marks. Should I quote Jalal Toufic?), and this maniacal narrator of *Double or Nothing* became the writer (rumored to be Raymond Federman) at the exact same moment as the writer (as noted on the title page of the "novel" (such quotes become necessary when writing on or about Federman (Federman always wanted critics to write about him, but he tended to become uncomfortable when critics wrote on him, since his skin was so sensitive) Raymond Federman (you may need to reread this sentence to understand why Federman's name suddenly appears) (but it remains unclear whether the name Raymond Federman refers to the man who sat at the breakfast table with his astonishing wife, Erica Hubscher, or if the name Raymond Federman is simply part of *Double or Nothing*'s subtitle: "a real fictitious discourse by Raymond Federman") became the narrator and as the fictional narrative became a truth that unsettled the narrator in ways that frightened the narrator into turning away from the story and looking back over his shoulder and out of the book to the writer, hoping the writer would do what writers do and make sense of it all by putting a period somewhere and bringing whatever this was to an end, ideally a happy ending, an ending that someone could adapt into a Hollywood movie. But, truth be told, the sentence was what it was and could only be what it was and nothing more, nothing less, than a failure of Beckettian proportions. And to this day, here in 2016, I am still reading that same sentence and trying to make sense of a Federman, a writer whom I may have invented years ago in the library of Slippery Rock State College as a way to entertain myself while I wrote an essay for a class. (Once I told Federman that I thought he was perhaps not as real as he thought he was, that perhaps I had invented him. And I told him I did not "mean" this in some sort of Post-Structuralist way, because I did not, then, nor do I now, believe in Post-Structuralism. When you live in Pittsburgh as long as I have or when you lived in Buffalo as long as Raymond had, you cannot possibly believe in Post-Structuralism as anything but a rumor shared by cacademics (as Federman called academics). February in Pittsburgh or in Buffalo directly refutes all that Post-Structuralism would have us believe. "To write," Federman once whispered, "should be first of all to quote." But too often the quotes come too late or never arrive or are forgotten before one begins to write. And this story of me inventing Federman must remain definitively unfinished; otherwise, what would become of Federman?)

But that one sentence that appeared to be the beginning of *Double or Nothing* changed something in me as a young writer who had not yet trusted himself to discover his own voice. (Yes, in the simplest sense, the writing of Raymond Federman gave me a license to fail my creative writing classes and write writing in ways that frustrated and disappointed my teachers and parents.) But that sentence was more than that. And I had more than a subtle feeling that James Joyce's Shem the Penman was back among us. In reading that first sentence of *Double or Nothing*, I realized I was not simply reading Federman's sentence. My eyes were, of course, moving over the words of page 0 (Federman's original desire was for *Double or Nothing* to be unpaginated, but the publisher told him then the critics would have no way of citing a page number when they quoted from his novel. This dilemma delighted Federman, but in the end, he gave in and numbered the pages and included an index to make the critic's job even easier. The initial pages are numbered by accumulating zeros, or noodles, before becoming numbers), so as my eyes wandered over the letters of the words on this opening page, entitled "THIS IS NOT THE BEGINNING", I was not merely *seeing* the words; I was *hearing* Federman typing each letter of each word. That is, I was also not hearing some disembodied voice *reciting* the words; rather, I was experiencing the machinery of Federman *making* the words, *forcing* the words into existence. As I looked at those letters on that page, I could hear the sound of Federman pounding the keys of his IBM Selectric typewriter. I remember thinking that this man, Federman, must have blisters on his fingers, and I remember becoming slightly afraid of what would drive a man to type with such a ferocious desire to tell these stories, to scar the page with his fears, his joy, his anger. When Fiction Collective 2 reissued the novel in 1999, the sound of Federman's IBM Selectric typewriter was silenced. While Federman praised the ways that the computer programming allowed for a more accurate and experimental formatting of his text, I mourned the loss of this cacophony of sounds. The new edition is perfectly designed, tight and neat. Everything in place. The typographical soundscape is muted if not completely absent. This edition felt more like a coffin holding the remains of a sound and a fury that formerly signified in the Derridean *presence* of the clacking of Federman's typewriter more than words could appear to represent in their silent stillness on the page. The 1971 Swallow Press edition, itself, as a book, creates the experience of this noodle-loving-writer narrating the story, as much as the words resting quietly on the page.

Because of this view, I have been accused of being nostalgic, of being a luddite. But Federman wrote and typed each page of the Swallow Press edition of *Double or Nothing*. His fingerprints mark each page. When Federman spoke to me about the Fiction Collective 2 reissue of *Double or Nothing*, he spoke of the ease of designing the book. When he recalled the design of the original edition, he spoke of the painful tactile nature of each page. As a reader, this matters to me. Being with each page. Being near-to the breath and sound of each Federmaniacal letter as it is placed on the page. The 1971 edition is noisy, but it also invites a being present with each page that creates moments of deep reflection and insight that have been disappeared from the 1999 edition.

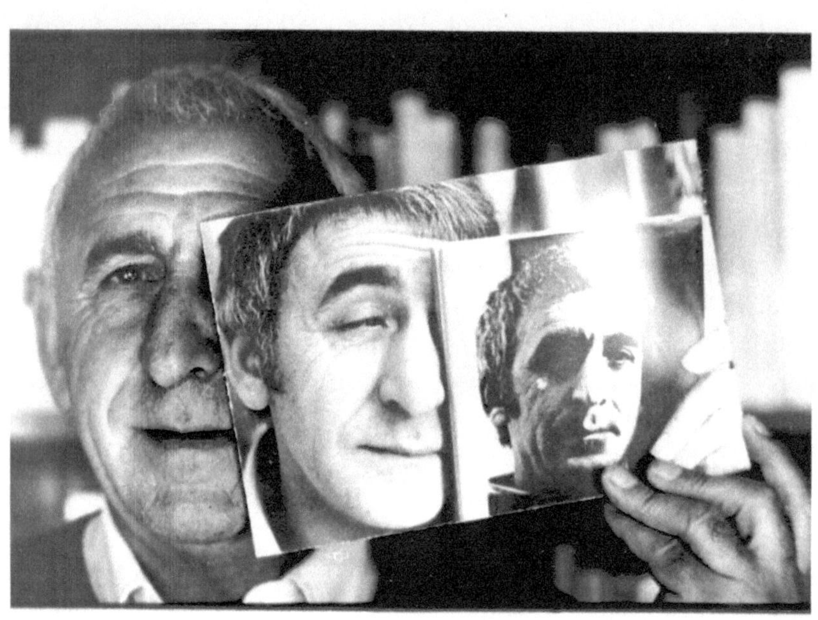

Time Again

RAYMOND FEDERMAN

TIME AND TIME AGAIN

Time rolls on

in due Time

Time flies

keeping Time

once upon a Time

Time goes fast

killing Time

Time to go

every Time

Time is slow

bed-Time

at Time

appointed Time

all the Time

takes Time

every Time

the arrow of Time

Time is up

Time to stop

Time to start again

no Time for trifling

war Time

Time out

lost Time

half-Time

Time piece

plenty of Time

Time-worn

a long Time

in the course of Time

from Time to Time

at the same Time

harvest-Time

hard Time

happier Time

Time zone

as Time goes by

Timelessness

a good Time

Time is money

play for Time

past Time

Time immemorial

Time-keeper

sign of the Time

serving Time

Time exposure

no Time left

*BIBLIOGRAPHY**

Novels

Double or Nothing (1971)
Hardcover, Swallow Press, Chicago, 1971.
Paperback, Ohio University Press, 1976.
Hardcover, Greno Verlag / Eichborn Verlag, Frankfurt, 1986. (tr. Peter Torberg).
Paperback, FC2, Illinois, 1991. Reprinted 1999, 2005.
Paperback, Éditions Al Dante, Romainville, 2004. (tr. Éric Giraud).
Paperback, Two Ravens Press, Ullapool, 2008.
Paperback, Korporacja Ha!art, Kraków, 2010. (tr. Jerzy Kutnik).

Amer Elderado (1974)
Hardcover, Stock 2, Paris, 1974.
Paperback, Weidler Buchverlag, Berlin, 2001. (Revised edition).
Paperback, Éditions Al Dante, Romainville, 2003.

---

*   All attempts have been made, within time, and reason, to list all the translations of Federman's works. However, many more translations into many more languages no doubt exist and will be left to a more intrepid bibliographer. (And one more thing. Several Federman books were first rendered into German or published in Germany. In all cases the first publication date of a title will take precedence over the English publication date, which will be listed below). (Actually, one more note: the stage play, modern ballet, musical, video, audio book, and unfilmed script editions of Federman, which all exist, are not listed here, as some things must be left for the reader to discover).

Take It or Leave It (1976)
Hardcover, Fiction Collective, New York, 1976. Reprinted 1987.
Paperback, FC2, Illinois, 1997.
Paperback, Rogner & Bernhard bei Zweitausendeins, Hamburg, 1998. (tr. Peter Torberg).
Hardcover, Suiseisha, Tokyo, 1999, (tr. Tateo Imamura).
Paperback, Yi lin chu ban she, Nan jing, 2003. (tr. Gong Zhao Li).

The Voice in the Closet / La Voix Dans le Cabinet de Débarras (1979)
Paperback, Coda Press, Wisconsin, 1979.
Paperback, Station Hill Press, New York, 1985.
Paperback, Kellner Verlag, Hamburg, 1989, (tr. Peter Torberg).
Paperback, Tichting Perdu, Amsterdam, 1993.
Paperback, Stacherone Press, New York, 2001.
Paperback, Les impressions nouvelles, Paris, 2002. Reprinted 2008.

The Twofold Vibration (1982)
Hardcover, Indiana University Press, Bloomington / Harvester Press, Sussex, 1982.
Hardcover, Greno Verlag, Nördlingen, 1988. (tr. Gerhard Effertz).
Paperback, Pomorze, Bydgoszcz, 1988 (tr. Jerzy Kutnik)
Paperback, Éditions Circé, Strasbourg, 1991. (tr. Françoise Brodsky).
Paperback, Green Integer, Los Angeles, 2000.
Paperback, Paralela 45, Piteşti, 2005. (tr. Antoaneta Ralian).

Smiles on Washington Square (1985)
Hardcover, Thunder's Mouth Press, New York, 1985.
Hardcover, Greno Verlag, Nördlingen, 1987. (tr. Peter Torberg). Reprinted: Paperback, Suhrkamp, Frankfurt am Main, 1990, 1995. Reprinted: Matthes & Seitz, Berlin (2010).
Paperback, SugarCo, Milano, 1990. (tr. Fabio Vasarri).
Paperback, Európa, Budapest, 1990. (tr. Pásztor Péter).
Paperback, Sun & Moon, Los Angeles, 1995.

Paperback, Ekdoseis Delfini, Athēna, 1996. (tr. Vanēssa Lāppa).

Paperback, Shanghai yi wen chu ban she, Shanghai, 1999. (tr. Jian Lin).

Paperback, Wydawnictwo Arteria, Lublin, 2002, (tr. Konrad Walewski).

Paperback, Paralela 45, Piteşti, 2003. (tr. Antoaneta Ralian).

Paperback, Éditions Al Dante, Romainville/ Éditions Point de fuite, Montréal (2004). (tr. Nicole Mallet).

To Whom It May Concern (1990)

Paperback, FC2, Colorado, 1990.

Paperback, Suhrkamp Verlag, Frankfurt am Main, 1991. (tr. Peter Torberg).

Paperback, Svetovi, Novi Sad, 1993. (tr. Đorđe Jakov).

Paperback, Marsilio, Venezia, 1995. (tr. Stefano Tettamanti & Patrizia Traverso).

Paperback, Guang ming ri bao chu ban she, Beijing, 2000. (tr. Weiqun Tu).

Paperback, Éditions des Écrivains, Paris, 2003. (tr. Nicole Mallet).

La fourrure de ma tante Rachel (1996)

Paperback, Éditions Circé, Strasbourg, 1996.

Hardcover, Faber & Faber, Leipzig, 1997. (tr. Thomas Hartl). Reprinted: DTV, Munich, 2000.

(*Aunt Rachel's Fur*), Paperback, FC2, Illinois, 2001.

Return to Manure (2005/6)

Paperback, Éditions Al Dante, Romainville, 2005. (tr. Eric Giraud).

Paperback, FC2, Alabama, 2006.

Chut (2008)

Paperback, Scheer, Paris, 2008.

Hardcover, Weidle, Bonn, 2008. (tr. Andrea Spingler).

(*Shhh: The Story of a Childhood*) Paperback, Stacherone Books, Buffalo, 2010.

Paperback, Ediciones Turpial, Madrid, 2011. (tr. María Teresa de los Ríos).

Poetry

Among the Beasts / Parmi Les Monstres (1967)
Paperback, Jose Millas-Martin, Paris, 1967.

Me Too (1975)
Paperback, West Coast Poetry Review, Reno, 1975.

Playtexts/Spieltexte (1990)
Hardcover, Literarisches Colloquium, Berlin, 1990. (tr. Peter Torberg)

Duel/Duell (1991)
Paperback, Stop Over Press, Berlin, 1991. (tr. Dana Ranga).

Now Then/Nun Denn (1992)
Paperback, Edition Isele, Freiberg, 1992. (tr. Karin Graf).

99 Handwritten Poems/99 poèmes faits-à-la-main (2001)
Paperback, Weidler Buchverlag, Berlin, 2001.

Two Jazz Poems (2001)
Paperback, Print Matters! Books, Dansville, 2001.

L'extatique de Jule & Juliette (2002)
Paperback, Weidler, Berlin, 2002.
Paperback, Le mot et le reste, Marseille, 2005.

Here and Elsewhere: A Poetic Cul-de-Sac (2003)
Paperback, Six Gallery Press, Macon, 2003.
Paperback, Le mot et le reste, Marseille, 2003.

Future Concentration (2003)
Paperback, Le mot et le reste, Marseille, 2003.

Surcomixxxx (2003)
Paperback, Edition Isele, Eggingen, 2003.

Chair June (2007)
Paperback, le Bleu du Ciel éditions, Coutras, 2007.

Short Prose

Rumor transmissable ad infinitum in either direction (1976)
Poster, Assembling Press, Brooklyn, 1976.

The Rigmarole of Contrariety (1982)
Paperback, The Bolt Court Press, Buffalo, 1982.

The Line (1996)
Paperback, The Club of Odd Volumes, Amherst, 1996.
Paperback, Cadex éd., Sainte-Anastasie, 2008. (tr. Stéphane Rouzé).

Penner-Rap (1998) (with George Chambers)
Paperback, Suhrkamp Verlag , Frankfurt am Main, 1998.
(*The Twilight of the Bums*) Paperback, Alt-X Press, Boulder, 2002.
Paperback, Le mot et le reste, Marseille, 2004. (tr. Nicole Mallet).
Paperback, Stacherone Books, Buffalo, 2007.
E-Book, Dzanc Books, Westland, 2007.
E-Book, Stacherone Books, Buffalo, 2013.

Loose Shoes: A Life Story of Sorts (2001)
Paperback, Weidler Buchverlag, Berlin, 2001.
Paperback, Weidler Buchverlag, Berlin, 2002. (tr. Martin Arndorfer).

The Story of the Sparrow (2002)
Paperback, Spineless Books, Illinois, 2002.

Mon corps en neuf parties (2002)
Paperback, Weidler Buchverlag, Berlin, 2002.
(*My Body in Nine Parts*) Paperback, Stacherone Books, Buffalo, 2005.
Paperback, La Lepre Edizion, Roma, 2008. (tr. Francesca Milaneschi).

More Loose Shoes & Smelly Socks (2005)
Paperback, Six Gallery Press, Los Angeles, 2005.
Paperback, Replenishment Books, New York, 2008.

Elle est là (2005)
Paperback, Carte blanche, Auvers-sur-Oise, 2005.

Coup de Pompes (2007)
Paperback, Le mot et le reste, Marseille, 2007.

The Carcasses: A Fable (2009)
Paperback, BlazeVox Books, Buffalo, 2009.
Paperback, L. Scheer, Paris, 2009. (tr. Stéphane Rouzé). (Earlier version:
Paperback, Librairie Olympique, Bordeaux: 2007).

Criticism

Journey into Chaos: Samuel Beckett's Early Fiction (1965)
Hardcover, University of California Press, Berkeley, 1965.

Samuel Beckett: His Works & His Critics (1970) (with John Fletcher)
Hardcover, University of California Press, Berkeley, 1970.

Surfiction: der Weg der Literatur (1992)
Paperback, Suhrkamp Verlag, Frankfurt am Main, 1992. (tr. Peter
Torberg).
(*Critifiction: Postmodern Essays*) Paperback, State University of New York

Press, Albany, 1993.
Paperback, Le mot et le reste, Marseille, 2006. (tr. Nicole Mallet).

The Supreme Indecision of the Writer: The 1994 Lectures in Turkey (1995)
Paperback, The Bolt Court Press, Buffalo, 1995 / Department of American Culture and Literature, Ankara, 1995.

Memoir

Eine Version meines Lebens (1993)
Paperback, Maro Verlag, Augsburg, 1993.

La Livre du Sam (2006)
Paperback, Al Dante, Paris, 2006.
(*The Sam Book*) Paperback, Two Ravens Press, Ullapool, 2008. (tr. Sharon Blackie).

Plays

The Precipice and Other Catastrophes / Der Abgrund und andere Katastrophen (1999)
Paperback, Poetry Salzburg at the University of Salzburg, Salzburg, 1999. (tr. Thomas Hartl & Gaby Hartl).
Paperback, Make Now Press, Los Angeles, 2003.

Editor

Cinq nouvelles nouvelles (1970)
Paperback, Appleton-Century-Crofts, New York, 1970.

Surfiction: Fiction Now & Tomorrow (1975)
Hardcover, Swallow Press, Chicago, 1975.
Paperback, Ohio University Press, Athens, 1981.

Samuel Beckett (1976) (with Tom Bishop)
Paperback, Éditions de l'Herne, Paris, 1976. Reissued 1985, 1999.

Samuel Beckett: The Critical Heritage (1979)
Hardcover, Routledge & Kegan Paul, London/Boston, 1979. Reissued 1997, 1999, 2004 (e-book).

Sam Changed Tense (1995)
Paperback, The Tailspin Press, Buffalo, 1995.

Translator

Postal Cards — Jacques Temple (1964)
Paperback, Noel Young Editions, Santa Barbara, 1964.

Temporary Landscapes — Yvonne Caroutch (1965)
Paperback, Mica Editions, Venice, 1965.

German Radio Adaptations

The Twofold Vibration, Bayerischer Rundfunk, Munich, 1990.
Double or Nothing, Bayerischer Rundfunk, Munich, 1992.
Smiles on Washington Square, Bayerischer Rundfunk, Munich, 1992.
Playtexts/Spieltexte, Bayerischer Rundfunk, Munich, 1992.
To Whom It May Concern, Bayerischer Rundfunk, Munich, 1992.
The Dialogues of the Bums, Bayerischer Rundfunk, 1997
Aunt Rachel's Fur, Bayerischer Rundfunk, Munich, 1998.
The Precipice and Other Catastrophes, Deutscher Radio, Berlin, 1998.
Take It or Leave It, Bayerischer Rundfunk, Munich, 1999.

Selected Books on Federman

Federman A to X-X-X-X: A Recyclopedic Narrative. Larry McCaffery, Thomas Hartl, Doug Rice, Raymond Federman (eds.), San Diego State University Press, San Diego, 1998.

Keeping Literary Company: Working with Writers Since the Sixties. Jerome Klinkowitz. State University of New York Press, Albany, 1998.

In the Slipstream: An FC2 Reader. Ronald Sukenick, Curtis White (eds.). FC2, 1999, Illinois.

The Laugh that Laughs at the Laugh: Writing from and About the Penman Raymond Federman. Eckhard Gerdes (ed.), Writers Club Press, San Jose, 2002.

Federman's Fictions: Innovation, Theory & the Holocaust. Jeffrey R. Di Leo (ed.), State University of New York Press, Albany, 2010.

Web

http://www.federman.com/ (Federman's old website, last updated in 2002, contains poetry and prose and useful links).

http://raymondfederman.blogspot.co.uk/ (Federman's blog from 2005-2009. Contains archived posts and a deluge of wonderful links to fictions, poems, rare material, and every other important star in the Federman firmament).

http://wings.buffalo.edu/epc/authors/federman/ (Archived poetry)

ABOUT THE CONTRIBUTORS

Jeffrey R. Di Leo is Dean of Arts and Sciences and Professor of English and Philosophy at the University of Houston, Victoria. He is founder and editor of the critical theory journal, *symplokē*, and publisher and editor of the *American Book Review*.

Raymond Federman needs no further biographical elucidation. He died in 2009.

Simone Federman is the daughter of Raymond Federman.

G.N. Forester is something of a nomad and may be based at any one time in Asia, Europe, or the Pacific. Forester currently works as an academic researcher when not writing or editing, and has been known to adopt multiple monikas as a means to obfuscate identification, typical of a paranoid personality.

Julia Frey is the widow of novelist Ronald Sukenick. Most of Federman's correspondence with Sukenick is available to scholars via the University of Texas Harry Ransom Humanities Research Center (www.hrc.utexas.edu search 'Ronald Sukenick').

Geoffrey Gatza is an award winning editor, publisher and poet. He was named by the *Huffington Post* as one of the Top 200 Advocates for

American Poetry. He is the author many books of poetry, including *Apollo* (BlazeVOX 2014), *Secrets of my Prison House* (BlazeVOX 2010), *Kenmore: Poem Unlimited* (Casa Menendez 2009) and *HouseCat Kung Fu: Strange Poems for Wild Children* (Meritage Press 2008). He is also the author of the yearly *Thanksgiving Menu-Poem Series*, a book length poetic tribute for prominent poets, now in its fourteenth year. Most recently his work has appeared in FENCE and Tarpaulin Sky. His play on Marcel Duchamp will be staged in an art installation in Philadelphia this year. His work appears in recent or forthcoming anthologies, including *Litscapes: Collected US Writings* (Steerage Press, 2015), and *Poets for Living Waters: An International Response to the BP Oil Disaster in the Gulf of Mexico* (forthcoming from BlazeVOX). He lives in Kenmore, NY with his girlfriend and two beloved cats.

Eckhard Gerdes has published books of poetry, drama, and fourteen books of fiction, including the novels *Hugh Moore* (for which he was awarded an &Now Award) and *My Landlady the Lobotomist* (a top five finisher in the 2009 Preditors and Editors Readers Poll and nominated for the 2009 Wonderland Book Award for Best Novel of the Year). He has also won the Bissell Award, been a finalist for the Starcherone and the Blatt awards, and was nominated for Georgia Author of the Year. His most recent books are a tongue-in-cheek work of creative nonfiction, *How to Read*, published in October 2014 by Guide Dog Books, a novel, *White Bungalows*, published in August 2015 by Dirt Heart Pharmacy Press, and *Three Plays*, published in June 2016 by Black Scat Books. He lives near Chicago and has three sons and two grandsons.

Steve Katz is a novelist, short story writer, and one of the founders of the Fiction Collective along with Raymond Federman. His works include the novels *The Exagggerations of Peter Prince* (1968), *Saw* (1972), and *Antonello's Lion* (2005). His most recent book, *The Compleat Memoirrhoids*, was published by Stacherone Books in 2013.

Jerome Klinkowitz is one of the foremost scholarly writers on postmodern American literature, first writing on Federman in his book *Literary Disruptions* (1975). He teaches at the University of Northern Iowa and has edited the last four editions of *The Norton Anthology of American Literature*. He has written many books on Kurt Vonnegut, and has written at length on his relationship with Federman in *Keeping Literary Company* (1998).

Douglas Messerli, publisher of Sun & Moon Press and Green Integer, is also a poet, fiction writer, dramatist (writing under the name Kier Peters) and memoirist, whose series of annual *My Year* books extend from 2000 to the present. He was the editor of the noted *From the Other Side of the Century: A New American Poetry 1960-1990*. Messerli was named Officier de l'ordre des Arts et des Lettres by the French government for his publication in English of French literature, and he was awarded The American Book Award and the ALTA Award for his publishing.

Larry McCaffery is one of the foremost critics of American postmodern literature and retired professor of English and Comparative Literature at San Diego State University. He has compiled various seminals books of interviews and anthologies, and is the author of *The Metafictional Muse* (1982).

Serpil Oppermann is Professor of English at Hacettepe University, Ankara, and currently Vice President of EASLCE (European Association for the Study of Literature, Culture and Environment). Her recent publications include *International Perspectives in Feminist Ecocriticism* (with Greta Gaard and Simon Estok, 2013), *Material Ecocriticism* (with Serenella Iovino, 2014), *New Voices in International Ecocriticism* (2015), and *Envriomental Humanities* (with Serenella Iovino, in press). Her recent work is focused on material ecocriticism, posthuman models, and the anthropocene debates in the environmental humanities. She serves in the editorial boards of several international journals and publication series on environmental topics, including *ISLE, Ecozon@, Relations: Beyond*

Anthropocentrism, and *PAN: Philosophy Activism Nature*, and *Ecocritical Theory and Practice* series of Lexington Books.

Jacob Paul is the author of the novels, *A Song of Ilan* (Jaded Ibis, 2015) and *Sarah/Sara* (Ig, 2010), which was named one of 2010's 5 best first fictions by *Poets & Writers*. His collaborations have led to the fine art books, *Home for an Hour* (Otherwise, 2014) and *Feed Mayonnaise to Tuna* (Otherwise, 2016), and the installation "Letters to the New Year" (2016). His work has appeared in *Hunger Mountain, Western Humanities Review, Green Mountains Review, Massachusetts Review, Seneca Review, Mountain Gazette* and *USA Today's Weekend Magazine* as well as on therumpus.net, fictionwritersreview.com and numerocinqmagazine.com. He holds an MFA from the Vermont College of Fine Arts and a PhD from the University of Utah. He also took two fiction writing classes with Raymond Federman at SUNY Buffalo as an undergraduate. He currently teaches creative writing at High Point University in North Carolina.

Ted Pelton is Professor and Chair of the English department at Tennessee Tech University and the author of four fiction titles, including the novel *Malcolm & Jack (and Other Famous American Criminals)*. His stories have appeared in numerous periodicals and anthologies, including *BOMB, Brooklyn Rail, Fiction International, Gargoyle, WebdelSol, The &Now Awards*, volumes 1 and 3, and *The Art of Friction*, and he is the recipient of a National Endowment for the Arts Fellowship in Fiction (1994) and an Isherwood Foundation fellowship (2008), among other honors. He first met Raymond Federman as an undergraduate in 1983, and studied with him as both an undergraduate and graduate student, ultimately earning a PhD in 19th century American literature. In 2000, he founded Starcherone Books, a nonprofit publisher of innovative fiction, and served as Publisher and Executive Director until 2014, during which time the press released over 30 titles, including debut works by Zachary Mason and Alissa Nutting, the anthologies *30 Under 30: Innovative Fiction by Younger Writers*, and *PP/FF: ProsePoetry/FlashFiction*, and four books by Raymond Federman.

Doug Rice is the author of *Here Lies Memory, An Erotics of Seeing, Dream Memoirs of a Fabulist, Blood of Mugwump,* and other works. He is a co-editor of *Federman: A to X-X-X-X.* He was awarded an Akademie Schloss Solitude Literature Fellowship 2012-2014 and has taught at numerous universities.

ABOUT THE PHOTOGRAPHS[*]

p.viii Federman in his office, circa 1980.

p.2 Erica and Ray skiing at Mammoth Mountain, California, circa 1961.

p.8 Reading at Hallwalls, circa 1980. (c) Bruce Jackson.

p.12 Being on the Army swim team allowed Federman to avoid jumping in combat rather he competed for the Army as a back stroker his entire tour. 1952, Japan.

p.18 82nd Airborne Division Fort Bragg, North Carolina, 1952. When at the recruiting meeting asked what division he wanted to be in he said he wanted to be a "Frogman" because the kids in Detroit used to call him a frog. When informed there were no frogmen in the army somebody suggested becoming a paratrooper. He signed up enthusiastically in Federman fashion, having no idea what that meant.

p.30 No info.

p.40 Ray with Michel Foucault & Olga Bernal. SUNY Buffalo, 1970. (c) Bruce Jackson.

p.45 Federman with photo of Federman on backcover of *Double or Nothing*. (c) Bruce Jackson.

p.53 Erica and Ray, Buffalo NY , 1975.

p.65 Raymond and his older and younger sisters Jacqueline and Sarah Montrouge, France, circa 1937. This photo was in a box he found hidden in the apartment on Rue Louis Roland when he went back after the war.

p.73 Federman with Harold Pinter in the 1970s.

---

[*]   All photos (c) Simone Federman unless credited otherwise.

p.77 Federman, Simone, and Erica at the US Open, 1986. (c) Zoe Leonard.

p.91 Photo used for Federman memorial invitation, circa 1980s.

p.95 Tokyo, Japan, circa 1953 Sgt. Federman US Army.

p.116 No info.

p.133 Simone and Federman dancing LA California, 1986. (c) Zoe Leonard

p.136 Simone and Federman the coliseum, Rome, Italy, 1967.

p.138 Federman playing ping pong before coming to America Paris France circa 1947.

p.145 Family ski trip Mammoth Mountain California w/ step children Robin, Steve and Jim Murez, California circa 1963.

p.151 Federman plays his King Sax Special in the kitchen Buffalo NY, 1978

p.162 Federman Buffalo NY circa, 1986 (c) Zoe Leonard

p.180 Marguerite (née Epstein) and Simon Federman, Raymond's parents, 1925 Paris, France.

p.191 Leslie Fiedler and Federman circa 1975 Buffalo, NY (c) Bruce Jackson

p.205 The moment Federman becomes a US citizen Tokyo, Japan 1952.

p.214 Federman and his dog Sam, 1987 Buffalo NY. (c) Zoe Leonard.

p.222 Airmen's mess, Federman with his girlfriend. 1952, Tokyo, Japan.

p.251 Ray and Erica, Santa Barbara, California 1962.

p.258 Federman with photo of Federman and back cover of *Double or Nothing* (c) Bruce Jackson

p.262 Federman always stuck out his tongue a tiny bit when he was thinking, circa 1970s.

p.272 Federman reading in the 1980s.

p.278 Federman reading in the 1970s.

p.281 Federman inscription on the steps, 1970s.

p.282 Simone and her Pop Paris France, 1963.

—Simone Federman